TOXIC INTENT:
ENVIRONMENTAL HARM, CORPORATE CRIME, AND THE CRIMINAL ENFORCEMENT OF FEDERAL ENVIRONMENTAL LAWS IN THE UNITED STATES

Joshua Ozymy & Melissa Jarrell Ozymy

ENVIRONMENTAL LAW INSTITUTE
Washington, D.C.

1730 M Street NW, Washington, DC 20036

Published January 2023.

Printed in the United States of America
ISBN 978-1-58576-242-2

Cover design by Evan Odoms.

Table of Contents

About the Authors

Joshua Ozymy is an Associate Professor of Political Science in the Department of Political Science and Public Service at the University of Tennessee at Chattanooga. His research centers on environmental law and social policy, particularly how we enforce environmental laws and how they might be improved to better protect the most vulnerable members of society. He was previously a Professor of Political Science and Director of the Honors Program and Strategic Initiatives at Texas A&M University-Corpus Christi.

Melissa Jarrell Ozymy is a Professor of Criminology and Department Head of Social, Cultural and Justice Studies at the University of Tennessee at Chattanooga. Her research focuses on environmental crime and victimization, environmental justice, and how environmental crimes are portrayed in the media. She was previously a Professor of Criminal Justice and Dean of University College at Texas A&M University-Corpus Christi.

List of Acronyms

AHERA	Asbestos Hazard Emergency Response Act
AOCs	administrative orders of consent
API	American Petroleum Institute
APPS	Act to Prevent Pollution From Ships
ARP	Acid Rain Program
BACT	best available control technology
BCF	bromochlorodifluoromethane
BJS	Bureau of Justice Statistics
BP	British Petroleum
CAA	Clean Air Act
CAFÉ	Corporate average fuel economy
CAFOs	concentrated animal feeding operations
CERCLA	Comprehensive Environmental Resource, Compensation, and Liability Act
CFCs	chlorofluorocarbons
CID	Criminal Investigation Division
CO	carbon monoxide
COPD	chronic obstructive pulmonary disease
CWA	Clean Water Act
CWSRF	Clean Water State Revolving Funds
DMRs	discharge monitoring reports
DOJ	U.S. Department of Justice
ECS	Environmental Crimes Section
EPA	U.S. Environmental Protection Agency
ENRD	Environment and Natural Resources Division
EPCRA	Emergency Planning and Community Right-To-Know Act
FBI	Federal Bureau of Investigation
FIFRA	Federal Insecticide, Fungicide, and Rodenticide Act
FWS	U.S. Fish and Wildlife Service
FY	fiscal year
HAPs	hazardous air pollutants
HCFCs	hydrochlorofluorocarbons
LAER	lowest achievable emission rate
LEVs	low emission vehicles

MACT	maximum achievable control technology
MBTA	Migratory Bird Treaty Act
NAAQS	national ambient air quality standards
NESHAPs	national emission standards for hazardous air pollutants
NHTSA	National Highway Transportation Safety Administration
NO_x	nitrogen oxide
NOAA	National Oceanic and Atmospheric Administration
NPDES	national pollutant discharge elimination system
NPL	national priorities list
NSPS	new source performance standards
NSR	new source review
O_3	ozone
OCEFT	Office of Criminal Enforcement, Forensics, and Training
OECA	Office of Enforcement and Compliance Assurance
OEE	Office of Environmental Enforcement
OPPT	Office of Pollution and Prevention
PBBs	polybrominated biphenyls
PCBs	polychlorinated biphenyls
PEER	Public Employees for Environmental Responsibility (PEER)
PM	particulate matter
POTWs	publicly owned treatment works
PRASA	Puerto Rico Aqueducts and Sewer Authority
PRPs	potentially responsible parties
PSD	prevention of significant deterioration
RCRA	Resource Conservation and Recovery Act
RGGI	Regional Greenhouse Gas Initiative
RIBITS	Regulatory In-Lieu Fee and Bank Tracking System
RICO	Racketeer Influenced and Corrupt Organizations Act
ROVs	remotely operated underwater vehicles
SARA	Superfund Authorization and Reorganization Act
SEPs	supplemental environmental projects
SIPs	state implementation plans
SO_2	sulfur dioxide
SO_x	sulfur oxide
TCEQ	Texas Commission on Environmental Quality
TSCA	Toxic Substances Control Act
VOCs	volatile organic compounds

Introduction

This book is intended to help readers better understand how the U.S. Environmental Protection Agency (EPA) and the U.S. Department of Justice (DOJ) have historically investigated and prosecuted serious violations of federal environmental law in the United States. When thinking about the relationship between environmental law, crime, policing, and prosecution, the *Deepwater Horizon* case may come to mind, where a major multinational corporation saved billions of dollars through a pattern of criminal malfeasance that killed and injured numerous individuals, brought untold suffering to their families, caused people to lose their livelihoods, wrought economic damages to state and local governments, and permanently polluted many of the environments in the country in which they operated.[1] Whether it is a corporation knowingly engaging in patterned criminal behaviors that kill people or cases of midnight dumping, protecting the environment requires acknowledging that numerous companies and individuals may be committed to willfully breaking the law.[2] Environmental crimes cause more damage than street crime in the United States but are often not conceptualized in such a way by the mass public and most of these stories go untold.[3] Enhancing statutory penalties, developing environmental law enforcement, and professionalizing prosecutorial resources over the past four decades has been undertaken to deter and punish actions that negatively impact humans, animals, and the natural environmental in the United States, but the scope of these efforts remains unclear.[4]

---

1. Elizabeth A. Bradshaw, Deepwater, Deep Ties, Deep Trouble: A State-Corporate Environmental Crime Analysis of the 2010 Gulf of Mexico Oil Spill (2012) (unpublished Ph.D. dissertation, Western Michigan Univ.), https://scholarworks.wmich.edu/cgi/viewcontent.cgi?article=1078&context=dissertations; BP Expl. & Prod. Inc. v. United States, No. 2:12-cr-00292-SSV-DEK (E.D. La. filed Jan. 16, 2013).
2. Michael J. Lynch, *The Sentencing/Punishment of Federal Environmental/Green Offenders, 2000-2013*, 38 Deviant Behav. 991-95 (2017).
3. Melissa L. Jarrell, *Environmental Crime and Injustice: Media Coverage of a Landmark Environmental Crime Case*, 6 Sw. J. Crim. Just. 25-44 (2009); Michael J. Lynch et al., *Media Coverage of Chemical Crimes: Hillsborough County, Florida, 1987-1997*, 40 British J. Criminology 112-14 (2000).
4. David M. Uhlmann, *Prosecutorial Discretion and Environmental Crime*, 38 Harv. Envtl. L. Rev. 159 (2014); Michael J. Lynch et al., *Weak Probability of Punishment for Environmental Offenses and Deterrence of Environmental Offenders: A Discussion Based on USEPA Criminal Cases, 1983-2013*, 37 Deviant Behav. 1095 (2016).

The value of this book lies in developing a broader empirical and conceptual understanding of how federal environmental laws are enforced in the United States through a criminal process. We provide the broadest empirical study to date of the investigation and prosecution of federal environmental crimes in the United States. We systematically collect data on all environmental crimes investigated by EPA that were successfully prosecuted from 1983 to 2019. This approach gives us 2,588 cases to analyze in order to draw out the larger picture of how the criminal enforcement apparatus has evolved over its lifecycle, including what types of crimes are investigated and prosecuted, who commits such crimes, how federal prosecutors use criminal provisions in major environmental statutes to prosecute offenders, and ultimately the patterns in how guilty parties are punished. Through such an analysis we can glean the evolution of the use of criminal enforcement tools for the environment, as well as how environmental law has evolved alongside of and because of these efforts and develop a broader framework for understanding criminal enforcement.

We draw on our own experience for context, as we acted for years as participant observers in a lengthy federal environmental crime prosecution.[5] That case and experience taught us how environmental investigations begin, how task forces are assembled, how agencies work with one another, how prosecutors bring charges and try complex cases, the process of legal defense, the role of the greater community in prosecutions, and the politics of sentencing and appeals. Through our own experiences, but primarily through building a systematic database of criminal investigations and prosecutions, we are able to provide the broadest overview of the evolution of this process to date.

This project locates itself between the legal, public policy, and environmental/green criminology literatures. To be more exacting, we find the

5. The case was *United States v. CITGO Petroleum Corp.*, 908 F. Supp. 2d 812 (S.D. Tex. 2012). The case was unique in that prosecutors worked to include community members near CITGO's refinery as victims under the federal Crime Victims' Rights Act. (18 U.S.C. §3771). We played a role in the initial investigation, prosecution, and orchestrating an appeal to the U.S. Court of Appeals for the Fifth Circuit to have victims recognized under the Act. This became the first federal prosecution that recognized an environmental justice community as victims of a corporate environmental crime in the United States, but was eventually overturned on appeal. For background, see Suzie Canales et al., *Risk Assessment or Risk Acceptance: An Activist's Perspective on Why the EPA's Attempts to Achieve Environmental Justice Have Failed and What They Can Do About It*, 5 Envtl. Just. 59-62 (2012); Melissa L. Jarrell et al., *How to Encourage Conflict in the Environmental Decision-Making Process: Imparting Lessons From Civic Environmentalism to Local Policymakers*, 18 Local Env't 184-200 (2013); Joshua Ozymy & Melissa L. Jarrell, *Implementing a Partial Buyout of an Environmental Justice Community*, 10 Envtl. Just. 43-50 (2017); Joshua Ozymy & Melissa Jarrell, *Righting and "Writing" Wrongs: A Postmortem on a Decade of Environmental Justice Activism in Corpus Christi, Texas*, 11 Envtl. Just. 23-31 (2019).

book's intellectual legacy and fit between Kathleen Brickey's work that was one of the first to bridge criminal law and environmental law, particularly her book *Environmental Crime: Law, Policy, Prosecution* and Joel Mintz's *Enforcement at the EPA: High Stakes and Hard Choices* and related work, which provides a detailed historical and organizational analysis of the founding, work, and struggles of EPA's Criminal Investigation Division (EPA-CID) to build a cohesive and valuable organization with inconsistent budgetary support and consistent political opposition.[6] We are also responding to the green criminology literature that has studied the deterrent effect of criminal sanctioning on environmental offenders, particularly corporate and white collar offenders.[7] With these three literatures, we have a solid understanding of how criminal law developed alongside environmental law, how environmental crimes are policed, how they are prosecuted, and the effects of these efforts on deterring crime.[8] What we lack from all three literatures is a systematic empirical accounting of what EPA-CID and DOJ's Environmental Crimes Section (ECS) have more or less accomplished in the roughly 37 years since the criminal enforcement apparatus was institutionalized. It is the task of arduously collecting, analyzing, and understanding this phenomenon that we have dedicated ourselves.

Chapter 1 lays the foundations for the following chapters, where we delve into major environmental statues to show charging and sentencing patterns

6. Kathleen F. Brickey, Environmental Crime: Law, Policy, Prosecution (Aspen Publishers 2008); Joel A. Mintz, Enforcement at the EPA: High Stakes and Hard Choices (Univ. of Texas Press 2012).

7. Michael J. Lynch & Paul B. Stretesky. Exploring Green Criminology: Towards a Green Revolution in Criminology (Ashgate 2014). *See Weak Probability of Punishment*, *supra* note 4. *See also* Michael J. Lynch, *The Sentencing/Punishment of Federal Environmental/Green Offenders, 2000-2013*, 38 Deviant Behav. 991-95 (2017).

8. Exploring the deterrent value of criminal sanctioning of environmental offenders is still an open question and the nature of criminal law and environmental law, policing, and prosecution are also evolving topics. On all these topics and in line with the work of Lynch, Brickey, and Mintz we have also contributed a series of articles over the years and will shamelessly cite them here: Joshua Ozymy & Melissa L. Jarrell, *Upset Over Air Pollution: Analyzing Upset Events Emissions at Petroleum Refineries*, 28 Rev. Pol'y Res. 28, 363-79 (2011); Melissa L. Jarrell & Joshua Ozymy, *Real Crime, Real Victims: Environmental Crime Victims and the Crime Victims' Rights Act (CVRA)*, 58 Crim. L. & Soc. Change 373-89 (2012); Joshua Ozymy & Melissa L. Jarrell, *Upset Events, Regulatory Drift, and the Regulation of Air Emissions at Industrial Facilities in the United States*, 21 Envtl. Pol. 451-66 (2012); Joshua Ozymy & Melissa L. Jarrell, *Wielding the Green Stick: An Examination of Criminal Enforcement at the EPA Under the Bush and Obama Administrations*, 24 Envtl. Pol. 38-56 (2015); Joshua Ozymy & Melissa L. Jarrell, *Why Do Regulatory Agencies Punish? The Impact of Political Principals, Agency Culture, and Transaction Costs in Predicting Environmental Criminal Prosecution Outcomes in the United States*, 33 Rev. Pol'y Res. 71-89 (2016); Joshua Ozymy & Melissa L. Jarrell, *Administrative Persistence in the Face of a Hostile Regime: How the EPA Can Survive the Trump Administration*, 10 Envtl. Just. 1-8 (2017); Melissa L. Jarrell, et al., *Where the Wild Things Are: Animal Victimization at the Intersection of Wildlife Law and Environmental Law*, 3 Contemp. Just. Rev. 319-35 (2017); and Mike Lynch et al., *Executive Actors and Environmental Enforcement: Examining the "Rick Scott Effect" in the U.S. State of Florida*, 36 Rev. Pol'y Res. 395-413 (2019).

and extrapolate general themes for how prosecutors have used criminal provisions in these laws for about four decades. We approach these systematically and comprehensively, beginning with the Clean Air Act (CAA) in Chapter 2. This is followed by the Clean Water Act (CWA) in Chapter 3 and both the Resource Conservation and Recovery Act (RCRA) and Comprehensive Environmental Response, Compensation, and Liability Act (CERCLA) also known as Superfund in Chapter 4. Chapter 5 analyzes the criminal enforcement of the Toxic Substances Control Act (TSCA) and the Federal Insecticide, Fungicide, and Rodenticide Act (FIFRA).[9] Exploring the application and enforcement of environmental law through a criminal process using these major acts helps provide the larger picture of how we enforce regulations on air, water, hazardous waste, chemical substances, toxic dumps, chemical spills, and other environmental problems.[10] Chapter 6 creates a general framework from the broader themes that emerge from the prosecu-

9. CAA, 42 U.S.C. §85. An analysis of toxicity in the air begins with the Air Pollution Control Act of 1955 (Pub. L. No. 84-159), which was the first major federal effort to identify and control air pollution. While weak, it acknowledged air pollution as a national problem. The CAA of 1963 (Pub. L. No. 88-206) started the process of research methods to control air pollution. The National Emissions Standards Act of 1965 (Pub. L. No. 89-272) set vehicle emissions standards. The CAA Extension of 1970 (Pub. L. No. 91-604) represents the first time the federal government took the lead on regulating air pollution. CWA, 33 U.S.C. §1251. The Federal Water Pollution Control Act Amendments of 1972 (Pub. L. No. 92-500), formed the basis for the CWA, which gives EPA the authority to regulate discharges into the waterways of the United States including rivers, estuaries, and wetlands. Amended in 1977 and 1987, with the Water Quality Act, EPA was given authority to develop a regulatory framework for such discharges. CERCLA, 2 U.S.C. §11001. CERCLA empowers EPA to create a fund to clean up hazardous waste that has no responsible parties or to find responsible parties to fund the cleanup and remediation of hazardous waste sites. CERCLA can act as a companion to the Agency's authority under RCRA and other statutes. RCRA, 42 U.S.C. §82. RCRA establishes a national framework for hazardous waste control. It gives EPA authority over hazardous and solid waste from cradle-to-grave. This authority allows EPA to develop standards for landfills, remediation in ground or surface water, and the operation of disposal facilities for solid and hazardous waste. TSCA, 15 U.S.C. §1261. TSCA authorizes EPA to regulate and manage chemical substances. This provides authority over manufacturing, use, distribution, importation, and exportation of a range of substances. FIFRA, 7 U.S.C. §136. FIFRA is the culmination of a series of laws meant to establish the quality and integrity of pesticides in the United States. This effort began as a truth-in-labeling mandate and evolved to consider risks to public health. EPA is allowed to set tolerances for pesticides so there is "reasonable certainty of no harm" and maximum residue limits for pesticides in food.

10. There are other major federal environmental laws passed in this era of rapid innovation in environmental protection that are germane to the content herein but, based on the low number of prosecutions, do not merit their own chapters; however, they are discussed in each chapter as appropriate. Some that bear mention include: Safe Water Drinking Act (SWDA), 42 U.S.C. §300f, which authorizes EPA to set water quality standards for public water systems and injection wells, but not bottled water or smaller private wells, and allows for the development of maximum containment levels to determine the threshold for some substances in drinking water; Endangered Species Act (ESA), 16 U.S.C. §1531, which creates a framework for conservation of threatened plants, animals, and their habitats and requires federal agencies to consider the impacts of their actions on listed species; and the National Environmental Policy Act (NEPA), 42 U.S.C. §4321, which requires environmental impact assessments for actions of federal agencies (a companion statute, the Environmental Quality Improvement Act (42 U.S.C. §4371), creates the President's Council on Environmental Quality connecting the executive branch to environmental issues).

tions analyzed in the previous chapters. Chapter 7 examines the possibilities for expanding the scope of the criminal enforcement of these laws and explores the challenges to advancing that cause now and in the future.

The United States lies at a critical juncture where the public has slowly developed a greater conscious awareness that we have and continue to orchestrate the rapid onslaught of climate change.[11] This realization and the subsequent effects that are already upon us and are likely irreversible or worse than our imaginations can bear, will cause the greatest shift in the way we view and interact with the natural environment since industrialization. Like the 1970s, where the modern Prometheus was revealed as a sickened and pitiful creature of a poisoned environment, the rapid onslaught of major environmental change that will seem incremental but will in the end become totalizing and will force us to reorient our society in ways we can yet conceive.

Managing this shift will exact a terrible environmental and financial cost and require a collective will that goes beyond our historical-cultural picture of progress through individual will, determination, and mastery, to achieve ascendant consumption. Companies and individuals will not go willingly, and the federal and state governments are ill-equipped to manage this shift in cooperative federalism, particularly as rapidly escalating debt and demographic shifts will prevent us from prioritizing environmental concerns and will lessen the federal government's hold on the states. Managing climate change will require not only a change in focus and laws and regulations, but enforcement. For this shift to work, we must better understand how we manage serious environmental crimes and learn to better prevent them or if not, to punish effectively.

11. Rob Swat & Frank Raes, *Making Integration of Adaption and Mitigation Work: Mainstreaming Into Sustainable Development Policies?*, 7 CLIMATE POL'Y 289-303 (2007).

Chapter 1. Between Us and a Toxic World

I. Profit Over Public Health: Serious Environmental Crimes and Chronic Offenders

On April 20, 2010, a giant fireball erupted into the sky in the Gulf of Mexico (the Gulf) with the glow of the flames rising over 300 feet into the air and visible up to 35 miles away.[1] Beneath the water lay the true problem that roughly 5,000 gallons of oil were spewing into the Gulf and efforts to contain the spill had failed. Eleven people were dead and many more injured on the Deepwater Horizon, one of the world's most sophisticated oil drilling rigs owned by Transocean, one of the world's largest offshore drilling companies.[2] Drilling into the Macondo Prospect, British Petroleum (BP), who had contracted the well through 2013, watched as gas, methane, drilling fluid, and water spewed into the air.[3] The blowout caused the oil well fire and resulted in the world's largest "accidental" release of oil into maritime waters at roughly 4.9 million barrels. This was one of the worst environmental disasters in the country's history.[4]

The aftermath captivated the public's attention until the well was capped on September 19, 2010. Damage to humans and the natural environment from this tragedy are still occurring to this day. Environmental watchdogs and regulators have asked the question of how such a tragedy was allowed to happen and why the responsible companies (BP, Transocean, and Halliburton) seem so incompetent to manage the problem. Deepwater Horizon cost over $350 million to build in 2001 and around $1 million a day to contract

1. Edward Helmore, *The Deepwater Horizon Environmental Disaster Was Even Worse Than Previously Believed*, Mother Jones, Feb. 2020, https://www.motherjones.com/environment/2020/02/the-deepwater-horizon-environmental-disaster-was-even-worse-than-previously-believed/.
2. Antonia Juhasz, *Investigation: Two Years After the BP Spill, A Hidden Health Crisis Festers*, Nation, Apr. 18, 2012, https://www.thenation.com/article/archive/investigation-two-years-after-bp-spill-hidden-health-crisis-festers.
3. John K. Borchardt, *Deconstructing the Deepwater Horizon Blowout*, ASME.org, Sept. 26, 2011, https://www.asme.org/topics-resources/content/deconstructing-the-deepwater-horizon-blowout.
4. Campbell Robertson & Clifford Krauss, *Gulf Spill Is the Largest of Its Kind Scientists Say*, N.Y. Times, Aug. 3, 2010, https://www.nytimes.com/2010/08/03/us/03spill.html.

and operate.[5] The stakes were high and the potential profits outstanding, but the public watched in horror as all the money and technology in the world were unable to essentially plug a hole (albeit a very deep one).[6] Estuaries and marine life were continuously polluted and killed throughout the summer while skimmers, booms, millions of gallons of oil dispersant, blowout preventers, and high-tech remotely operated underwater vehicles (ROVs) were all deployed and nothing seemed to help.[7]

Investigations by the U.S. Environmental Protection Agency (EPA) and other entities led federal prosecutors to file criminal charges against Transocean, Halliburton, and BP.[8] Prosecutors filed a complaint with the U.S. District Court for the Eastern District of Louisiana on December 15, 2010, arguing that the company's discharges into the waters of the United States violated the CWA.[9] Transocean admitted in federal court that their employees aboard the rig acted in a negligent manner when they failed to investigate oil and gas flowing from the well that caused the blowout and ultimately led to the oil spill.[10] The company pled guilty to criminal charges and was sentenced to pay $400 million in criminal penalties on February 14, 2013, as well as serve five years of probation.[11] In a separate civil settlement with the U.S. Department of Justice (DOJ), the company agreed to pay a $1 billion penalty, with 80% of the total penalty spent on efforts to restore the Gulf.[12] Halliburton provided the cement used in the drilling operation at the well.[13] For its role in the disaster, Halliburton pled guilty on September 19, 2013, for destroying evidence during the investigation. They paid a $200,000 fine

5. Igal Berenshtein et al., *Invisible Oil Beyond the Deepwater Horizon Satellite Footprint*, 6 Sci. Advances 1 (2020), https://advances.sciencemag.org/content/6/7/eaaw8863.
6. Guy Crittenden, *Understanding the Initial Deepwater Horizon Fire*, HazMatMag.com, May 10, 2010, https://web.archive.org/web/20100620121041/http://www.hazmatmag.com/issues/story.aspx?aid=1000370689.
7. National Comm'n on the BP Deepwater Horizon Oil Spill and Offshore Drilling, Report to the President (2011), https://www.govinfo.gov/content/pkg/GPO-OILCOMMISSION/pdf/GPO-OILCOMMISSION.pdf.
8. U.S. EPA, *Deepwater Horizon-BP Gulf of Mexico Oil Spill*, https://www.epa.gov/enforcement/deepwater-horizon-bp-gulf-mexico-oil-spill (last visited Mar. 13, 2022).
9. U.S. Department of Justice (DOJ), United States v. BP Exploration and Production Inc., Criminal Information (Nov. 15, 2012), https://www.justice.gov/sites/default/files/criminal-vns/legacy/2012/12/17/2012-11-15-BP-Exploration-Information.pdf.
10. U.S. DOJ, United States v. Transocean Deepwater Inc., Plea Agreement (Jan. 3, 2013), https://www.justice.gov/sites/default/files/criminal-vns/legacy/2013/01/18/2013-01-03-transocean-plea-agreement.pdf.
11. United States v. Transocean Deepwater Inc., No. 13-cr-001-JTM-SS (Feb. 14, 2013).
12. U.S. EPA, *Transocean Settlement*, https://www.epa.gov/enforcement/transocean-settlement (last visited Mar. 13, 2022). John J. Costonis, *The BP MDL and Its Aftermath: Whither OPA's Displacement Jurisprudence?*, 93 Tul. L. Rev. 511-56 (2019).
13. David M. Uhlmann, *After the Spill Is Gone: The Gulf of Mexico, Environmental Crime, and the Criminal Law*, 109 Mich. L. Rev. 1413-61 (2011).

and served three years of probation.[14] Halliburton later agreed to pay over $1 billion in damages to avoid extensive future punitive damages had the court later found it was grossly negligent in its role that caused the blowout.[15]

On December 15, 2010, DOJ filed both civil and criminal cases against BP. On September 2, 2014, the judge determined that BP had been grossly negligent and reckless in its actions, assigning 67% of the blame for the disaster to BP, 30% to Transocean, and 3% to Halliburton.[16] BP pled guilty to 11 counts of felony manslaughter for the workers killed in the explosion, 1 count of felony obstruction, and Clean Water Act (CWA) and Migratory Bird Treaty Act (MBTA) violations.[17] The company admitted in court that the negligence actions exhibited by its two highest ranking supervisors on the rig caused the death of the workers and the company admitted it engaged in obstruction of Congress by withholding records during the investigation.[18] The company was sentenced to pay the largest criminal penalty for an environmental crime in U.S. history of $4 billion plus serve five years of probation.[19] After receiving thousands of lawsuits from individuals and businesses affected by the disaster and lawsuits by various affected states, local governments, and the federal government, BP agreed to a $18.7 billion settlement to resolve most of the government's legal claims and agreed to set up an uncapped fund to compensate for economic harm resulting from the

14. U.S. DOJ, Halliburton Agrees to Plead Guilty to Destruction of Evidence in Connection With Deepwater Horizon Tragedy (2014).

15. Dominic Rushe, *Halliburton Reaches $1.1bn Settlement Over Deepwater Horizon Oil Spill*, Guardian, Sept. 2, 2014, https://www.theguardian.com/environment/2014/sep/02/halliburton-11bn-settlement-deepwater-horizon-spill. Under the Oil Pollution Control Act (Pub. L. No. 101-380), the company would be limited to liability for their actions of $75 million unless they were found grossly negligent. This distinction was extremely important to all three companies, particularly BP, since it was found grossly negligent and thus open to pay substantial damages. BP lobbied extensively during this time period. Some legislators proposed the Big Oil Bailout Prevention Unlimited Liability Act to raise their liability and potential damages. The Act was passed in response to *Exxon Valdez* in order to empower EPA and strengthen regulations in this area. Lauren E. Hume, *Are We Sailing Into Occupied Waters? Rethinking the Availability of Punitive Damages Under the Oil Pollution Act of 1990*, 86 N.Y.U. L. Rev. 1444-81 (2011). Sam Stein, *BP's Influence Peddling in Congress Bears Fruit Two Years After Gulf Spill*, Huff. Post, Mar. 12, 2012, https://www.huffpost.com/entry/bp-oil-spill-gulf-of-mexico-oil-lobbyists_n_1335556.

16. *BP Found "Grossly Negligent" in Gulf of Mexico Oil Spill*, New Orleans Sun, Sept. 5, 2014, https://www.neworleanssun.com/news/225407625/bp-found-grossly-negligent-in-gulf-of-mexico-oil-spill.

17. 16 U.S.C. §703-712. The MBTA prevents the taking of protected migratory birds without the prior authorization of the U.S. Fish and Wildlife Service (FWS). For a discussion of the Act and criminal provisions, see Patrick G. Maroun, *More Than Birds: Developing a New Environmental Jurisprudence Through the Migratory Bird Treaty Act*, 117 Mich. L. Rev. 789-814 (2019), and Emma Hamilton, *A Relic of the Past or the Future of Environmental Criminal Law? An Argument for a Broad Interpretation of Liability Under the Migratory Bird Treaty Act*, 44 Ecol. L.Q. 237-67 (2017).

18. United States v. BP Expl. & Prod. Inc., No. 2:12-cr-00292-SSV-DEK (Jan. 29, 2013).

19. U.S. DOJ, United States v. BP Exploration and Production Inc., Guilty Plea Agreement (2012), https://www.justice.gov/sites/default/files/criminal-vns/legacy/2012/12/17/2012-11-15-BP-Guilty-Plea-Agreement.pdf.

disaster.[20] As of 2020, the total cost to BP for litigation, cleanup, and other related outlays approached $70 billion.[21]

Deepwater Horizon was a rare event for many reasons.[22] It was a salient environmental crime that held sway in the public's mind for five months and continues to receive coverage.[23] During that time, millions of Americans and the world watched as wealthy companies failed to contain the spill that wreaked havoc on the Gulf Coast.[24] For many, it was an exaggerated version of the *Exxon Valdez* oil spill in 1989. The *Exxon Valdez* oil spill had been the largest U.S. spill at the time with about 11 million gallons that leaked from the company's tanker, but the spill lasted only a few days in a remote area of the country.[25] In the Exxon case, which was a bonafide environmental disaster, the company spent about $2 billion on cleanup and was able to reach a civil settlement with the federal government and state of Alaska for $1 billion in payments and restitution and a $25 million criminal fine.[26]

20. Terry Wade & Kristen Hays, *BP Reaches $18.7 Billion Settlement Over Deadly 2010 Spill*, Reuters (July 2, 2015, 8:41 AM), https://www.reuters.com/article/us-bp-gulfmexico-settlement/bp-reaches-18-7-billion-settlement-over-deadly-2010-spill-idUSKCN0PC1BW20150702.
21. Joe Nocera, *BP Is Still Paying for the Deepwater Horizon Spill*, Bloomberg (Feb. 4, 2020, 11:00 AM), https://www.bloomberg.com/news/articles/2020-02-04/bp-is-still-paying-for-the-deepwater-horizon-spill; U.S. EPA, MOEX Offshore 2007 LLC Settlement (2012), https://www.epa.gov/enforcement/moex-offshore-2007-llc-settlement.
22. BP entered into a consent decree with the DOJ and Gulf Coast States for the largest environmental damage settlement in U.S. history exceeding $20 billion. *See* Consent Decree Among Defendant BP Exploration & Production Inc., the United States of America, and the States of Alabama, Florida, Louisiana, Mississippi, and Texas (No. 2:10-md-02179-CJB-SS, E.D. La., Oct. 5, 2015), https://www.epa.gov/sites/production/files/2016-02/documents/deepwaterhorizon-cd.pdf.
23. Lisa Friedman, *Ten Years After Deepwater Horizon, U.S. Is Still Vulnerable to Catastrophic Spills*, N.Y. Times, Apr. 19, 2020, https://www.nytimes.com/2020/04/19/climate/deepwater-horizon-anniversary.html.
24. There were other individuals criminally charged during the Deepwater prosecutions, as well as separate civil settlements negotiated by the DOJ. For example, Connie Marlene Knight defrauded individuals seeking to work on the spill cleanup by impersonating a high-ranking Occupational Safety and Health Officer (OSHA) hazardous waste safety inspector. Knight offered courses ranging from $150-$400 for fake trainings that would ensure individuals would receive lucrative cleanup work. Some of the attendees actually gained work at the site with their fake credentials. On May 16, 2013, Knight was sentenced to 57 months' incarceration and ordered to pay $25,300 in restitution to her victims. *See* United States v. Knight, No. 2:12-cr-261 (E.D. La. May 16, 2013). Anthony Michael Badalamenti, a former cementing technology director at Halliburton, was prosecuted for destroying evidence. He pled guilty and was sentenced to 12 months of probation and a $1,000 fine. *See* United States v. Badalamenti, No. 2:13-cr-00204 (E.D. La. Sept. 19, 2013). Kurt Mix was a drilling engineer for BP. He violated a litigation hold notice by employing a program to delete text messages from his company-owned phone. *See* United States v. Mix, No. 2:12-cr-00171 (E.D. La. May 2, 2012). Mix was sentenced to six months of probation on Nov. 6, 2015. MOEX Offshore settled a civil suit filed by DOJ for $90 million to resolve alleged violations of the CWA. This included $70 million in civil penalties and $20 million in supplemental environmental projects to clean up the Gulf. The company was a 10% owner of the Macondo Well lease.
25. NOAA, *Exxon Valdez* (1989), https://darrp.noaa.gov/oil-spills/exxon-valdez.
26. Kiley Kroh, *25 Years After* Exxon Valdez *Oil Spill, Company Still Hasn't Paid for Long-Term Environmental Damages* (2013), https://archive.thinkprogress.org/25-years-after-exxon-valdez-oil-spill-company-still-hasnt-paid-for-long-term-environmental-damages-b5a325b28ee1/. Exxon was assessed

The federal government chose to prosecute BP, Transocean, and Halliburton criminally for their environmental crimes, which made these efforts unique in that prosecutors chose to expend significant resources to show these crimes were willful or knowing actions and to both punish the companies and deter them and others from similar actions in the future.[27]

Looking to the past shows how BP's actions as a company lead up to this moment. BP was charged on September 23, 1999, on three counts of violating Comprehensive Environmental, Response, Compensation, and Liability Act (CERCLA) reporting requirements and pled guilty to those crimes. The company's unit, BP Exploration Alaska, was prosecuted alongside its drilling contractor, Doyon Drilling, who for years illegally disposed of hazardous wastes by mixing them into drilling muds. BP pled guilty. The court mandated a $500,000 fine, 60 months' probation, and ordered the company to create a nationwide environmental management system at the cost of $15 million. Doyon was sentenced to pay $3 million in fines and six months of probation.[28] BP agreed to a settlement with federal prosecutors to pay $22 million to resolve both criminal and civil claims.[29]

Inspections revealed a leak in one of BP's crude oil pipelines on the Alaska North Slope of Alaska in March 2006. Roughly 200,000-270,000 gallons of oil were released into a nearby lake and spread throughout the adjoining tundra. Prosecutors charged the company with negligent violations for the discharge under the CWA in October 2007. The company pled guilty. The Prudhoe Bay oil spill, caused by the company's knowing neglect of pipeline corrosion, resulted in $20 million in fines and restitution, a $125 special assessment fee, and the company was ordered to serve 36 months of probation.[30] BP later paid a $25 million civil penalty to settle government claims

---

$5 billion for punitive damages in court in Alaska. They entered a legal sojourn lasting until 2008, when in *Exxon v. Baker*, the U.S. Supreme Court reduced the damages to about $500 million. *See* Adam Liptak, *Damages Cut Against Exxon in* Valdez *Case*, N.Y. Times, June 26, 2008, https://www.nytimes.com/2008/06/26/washington/26punitive.html.

27. Robert W. Adler, *Introduction: Environmental Criminal Prosecution: Essential Tool or Government Overreaching?*, 4 Utah L. Rev. 1097-102 (2009).

28. *See* United States v. BP Expl. & Prod. Inc. (Alaska) Inc., No. A99-0141 CR (D. Alaska Sept.23, 1999). Earlier in 1991, the state of Alaska reached a settlement with BP for lost royalties owed to the state in the sum of $185 million for its North Slope activities. Associated Press, *Company News: B.P. Agrees to Pay $185 Million to Alaska*, N.Y. Times, Dec. 28, 1991, https://www.nytimes.com/1991/12/28/business/company-news-bp-agrees-to-pay-185-million-to-alaska.html. PBS Frontline's investigation into BP with ProPublica that focused on a culture of saving money on repairs and maintenance as a likely cause for the disaster. *See* Frontline, *The Spill*, PBS.org (2010), https://www.pbs.org/wgbh/pages/frontline/the-spill/.

29. U.S. EPA, BP Exploration Inc. Multimedia Settlement (1999), https://www.epa.gov/enforcement/bp-exploration-inc-multimedia-settlement.

30. United States v. BP Expl. & Prod. (Alaska) Inc., No. 3:07-CR-00125-TMB (D. Alaska Oct. 24, 2007).

in the case and injunctive relief that allowed for an independent monitor and pipeline integrity management system. BP agreed to settle the state of Alaska's civil claims in the amount of $255 million. The site, however, experienced another spill in March 2009.[31]

On March 23, 2005, a massive explosion rocked BP's Texas City Refinery. The explosion and fire killed 15 workers, injured 180 others, and spurred a series of lawsuits over BP's lack of maintenance, oversight, and negligence that caused the disaster.[32] On October 24, 2007, BP was charged with a knowing violation of the Clean Air Act (CAA) and the company pled guilty on March 12, 2009. The sentence handed down of 36 months of probation and a $50 million fine was the largest fine in a CAA criminal prosecution to date.[33] In addition to the criminal prosecution, BP settled a civil suit with prosecutors to provide injunctive relief to primarily control benzene-containing wastes, monitoring, and internal management practices at a cost of $161 million. The company also paid a $12 million fine and spent $6 million on a supplemental air control project.[34]

There were many other state and federal civil penalties against BP over the years at their refineries, which is not uncommon for a large corporation. The issue at hand is whether the company established a pattern of negligent behavior and took actions at its drilling, pipeline, and refining facilities over the years that represents gross negligence stemming from a pattern of behaviors over the years to save money by reducing investment in maintenance, safety, or simply polluting the environment for financial gain. What if the

31. Patti Epler, *Oil Spill: BP to Pay $25 Million Fine for 2006 Pipeline Leak*, Alaska Daily News, May 3, 2011, https://www.adn.com/energy/article/oil-spill-bp-pay-25-million-fine-2006-pipeline-leak/2011/05/04/; U.S. EPA, BP North Slope Clean Water Act Settlement (2011), https://www.epa.gov/enforcement/bp-north-slope-clean-water-act-settlement; Yereth Rosen, *Alaska to Collect $255 Million for 2006 BP Pipeline Leaks*, Chi. Trib., Nov. 8, 2012, https://www.chicagotribune.com/nation-world/ct-xpm-2012-11-08-sns-rt-us-bp-alaskaspillbre8a800m-20121108-story.html. In 2019, EPA announced it would end its Alaska operations by selling off its remaining assets. The company operated in the area for six decades with sales of $5.6 billion. This includes its operations at Prudhoe Bay and the Trans Alaska Pipeline. Ron Bousso & Tanishaa Nadkar, *BP to Quit Alaska After 60 Years With $5.6 Billion Sale to Hilcorp*, Reuters, Aug. 27, 2019, https://www.reuters.com/article/us-bp-divestiture-idUSKCN1VH21N. The state of Alaska also sued BP and reached a settlement in 2009 for them to pay $1.709 million in civil assessments. Press Release, State of Alaska Department of Law, State Reaches Settlement With BP Exploration (Alaska) Inc., (2009), http://law.alaska.gov/press/releases/2009/092209-BPsettlement.html.
32. U.S. Chemical Safety Board, *Anatomy of a Disaster*, March 21, 2008, https://www.csb.gov/videos/anatomy-of-a-disaster/.
33. United States v. BP Prods. N. Am., No. 4:07-CR-434 (S.D. Tex. 2009).
34. U.S. EPA, BP Texas City Clean Air Act Settlement (2009), https://www.epa.gov/enforcement/bp-texas-city-clean-air-act-settlement. BP also settled a series of private lawsuits by families of the injured workers, as well as OSHA. U.S. Department of Labor, BP Texas City Violations and Settlement Agreements (Aug. 2010), https://www.osha.gov/dep/bp/bp.html; Katy Byron, *BP Plant Explosion Suit Settled for $32 Million*, CNN.com, Nov. 10, 2006, https://www.cnn.com/2006/LAW/11/09/refinery.suit/index.html.

culture of the company is such that it went so far as to engage in knowing or intentional acts over the years that resulted in human deaths, injuries, and severe damage to animals and the natural environment?[35] Certainly, such behaviors require stiffer penalties to punish and deter such actions in the future for the company and serve as a warning for others. As the judge noted when accepting BP's plea in *Deepwater*: "BP will feel the full brunt of the penalties . . . and the agreement provides significant deterrence."[36] As much as any particular case, BP serves as a warning, a case study in the process of finding accountability for serious crimes and chronic violators, and demonstrates the necessity for the criminal enforcement of environmental laws.[37]

II. The Evolution of the Criminal Enforcement of Environmental Crimes in the United States

EPA was born from modest expectations of President Richard M. Nixon and his administration and much broader ambitions by other members of Congress.[38] Over the years it came to encompass a vast empire of responsibility to protect human health and the natural environment.[39] During its infancy, the Agency had to contend with a series of problems involving the development of regulations for air, water, hazardous waste, and other environmental problems.[40] While the lead up to the CWA, the CAA, and other broad federal environmental statutes formed the foundation, this meant that the much more difficult task of developing priorities, scientifically studying proper exposures, and focusing on what technological and regulatory solutions were feasible to achieve positive results lay ahead.

35. Elizabeth Haas Edersheim, *The BP Culture's Role in the Gulf Oil Crisis*, HARV. BUS. REV., June 8, 2010, https://hbr.org/2010/06/the-bp-cultures-role-in-the-gu.
36. U.S DOJ, *United States v. BP Exploration & Prod. Inc.*, Pending Criminal Division Cases (2015), https://www.justice.gov/criminal-vns/case/bpexploration.
37. Prior to Texas City, a civil agreement was reached in 2001 with BP Amoco to resolve CAA violations at eight of the company's refineries. Penalties in the agreement were about $10 million and injunctive relief to fix the problems and improve systems and monitoring was estimated at $600 million at the time. This was part of what became a broader initiative to reduce air emissions in EPA's Petroleum Refinery Initiative. News Release, U.S. EPA, EPA Finalizes Agreement With Petroleum Refinery (2001), https://www.cnn.com/2006/LAW/11/09/refinery.suit/index.html; U.S. EPA, *Petroleum Refinery National Case Results* (2020), https://www.epa.gov/enforcement/petroleum-refinery-national-case-results (last updated March 23, 2022).
38. Jonathan H. Adler, *The Environmental Protection Agency Turns Fifty*, 70 CASE W. RES. L. REV. 871-72 (2020).
39. U.S. EPA, *Milestones in EPA and Environmental History*, https://www.epa.gov/history/milestones-epa-and-environmental-history (last visited Apr. 5, 2022).
40. U.S. EPA, *50 Years of EPA: Progress for a Stronger Future*, https://www.epa.gov/history (last visited Apr. 5, 2022).

Once EPA started taking the lead and developing permitting systems for stationary sources for such important statutes as the CAA, the CWA, and the Resource Conservation and Recovery Act (RCRA), it had to contend with the fact that many individuals and companies would choose to commit serious and chronic crimes. This meant the development of an apparatus that would focus on compliance (attempts by Agency personnel to bring the regulatory community in line with the law through pressure, negotiation, and other tactics) or deterrence (the application of punitive measures via a legal process to deter bad behavior and set an example for others).[41] Compliance alone cannot manage more serious cases that occur consistently in such a large system. The regulated community is not composed merely of criminals and traditional law enforcement approaches to punishment and deterrence are insufficient and inappropriate to enforce the totality of the regulatory regime. Many larger companies have more or less infinite resources to challenge EPA in court or forestall regulatory actions and many regulations are not as clear cut as we would like to believe.[42] There was no systematic effort by the federal or state governments during this time period to develop criminal sanctions to achieve environmental goals; this evolution was gradual.[43]

In choosing to pursue civil or criminal remedies for environmental violations, the government focuses first on a distinction between civil and criminal liability. Civil liability involves violations of the law. Criminal liability tends to involve intent. Crimes involving significant harm or culpable conduct often fall into the latter category.[44] Committing crimes of significant effect or intent does not guarantee they will move through a criminal process. Civil liability centers on a preponderance of the evidence standard that the evidence prosecutors present of a crime is more likely true than not. This standard of civil guilt is lower than criminal guilt, which establishes beyond a reasonable doubt that the defendant committed the crimes for which they are charged. EPA investigates environmental violations and considers them for the criminal liability path typically when they may be willful or involve

41. U.S. EPA, *Basic Information on Enforcement*, https://www.epa.gov/enforcement/basic-information-enforcement (last visited Apr. 5, 2022).

42. Carole M. Billiet & Sandra Rousseau, *How Real Is the Threat of Imprisonment for Environmental Crime?*, 37 European J. L. & Econ. 183-86 (2014) and Joshua Ozymy & Melissa L. Jarrell, *Why Do Regulatory Agencies Punish? The Impact of Political Principals, Agency Culture, and Transaction Costs in Predicting Environmental Criminal Prosecution Outcomes in the United States*, 33 Rev. Pol'y Research 73 (2016).

43. Richard J. Lazarus, *Assimilating Environmental Protection Into Legal Rules and the Problem With Environmental Crime*, 27 Loy. L. Rev. 867-69 (1994) [hereinafter Lazarus].

44. U.S. EPA, *Basic Information on Enforcement*, https://www.epa.gov/enforcement/basic-information-enforcement.

intent.[45] It is not so easy to make the decision. Doing so involves a complex calculation of costs versus benefits, the propensity of other agencies to cooperate, and the ability of federal prosecutors to invest in such a process. EPA faces significant incentives to resolve violations civilly and to avoid going to court.[46] While a criminal process can result in enhanced punishments, some defendants with resources also present deterrence costs to prosecution to pursue such actions.[47]

Federal law enforcement agencies maintain a deterrence-based culture.[48] The goals of criminal enforcement are to punish offenders and to deter future offenses.[49] Effective deterrence requires the costs of offending to outweigh the benefits of illegal activity.[50] This requires sufficient police resources to monitor and survey the population of potential offenders and resources to enable certain and significant punishment for those that break the law.[51] Empirical studies question whether policing and prosecuting environmental crimes is effective, given limited resources and the research finds mixed results concerning whether criminal sanctioning of environmental offenders ultimately deters crime.[52] This broad question is difficult to answer. Fed-

45. Earl E. Devaney, The Exercise of Investigative Discretion 2 (1994), https://www.epa.gov/sites/production/files/documents/exercise.pdf.
46. Evan J. Ringquist & Craig E. Emmert, *Judicial Policymaking in Published and Unpublished Decisions: The Case of Environmental Civil Litigation*, 52 Pol. Research Q. 12 (1999).
47. *See* Harland Prechel & Alesha Istvan, *Disproportionality of Corporations' Environmental Pollution in the Electrical Energy Industry*, 59 Soc. Persp. 505-07 (2016) and Richard A. Posner, *An Economic Theory of the Criminal Law*, 85 Colum. L. Rev. 1193-200 (1985) [hereinafter Posner, *Economic Theory of Criminal Law*].
48. A management review of the division noted: "To the extent any single pattern dominates, it is the law enforcement orientation of the Immediate Office, CID, and (to a lesser extent) LCRMD (Legal Counsel and Resources Management Division)." *See* John Peter Suarez, Management Review of the Office of Criminal Enforcement, Forensics, and Training ii (2003), https://www.epa.gov/sites/production/files/documents/oceft-review03.pdf.
49. Criminal Enforcement Program, U.S. EPA, America's Environmental Crime Fighters 3 (2020), https://www.epa.gov/sites/production/files/documents/oceftbrochure.pdf.
50. Gary Becker, *Punishment: An Economic Approach*, 169 J. Pol. Econ. 183 (1968).
51. Posner, *Economic Theory of Criminal Law*, *supra* note 47.
52. Key studies in this literature follow: Michael J. Lynch et al., *Environmental Law Violations Against Petroleum Refineries: Race, Ethnicity, Income, and Aggregation Effects*, 17 Soc'y & Nat. Resources 17, 333-47 (2004); Paul B. Stretesky & Jackie Gabriel, *Self-Policing and the Environment: Predicting Self-Disclosure of Clean Air Act Violations Under the U.S. Environmental Protection Agency's Audit Policy*, 18 Soc'y & Nat. Resources 871-87 (2005); Paul B. Stretesky & Michael J. Lynch, *Does Self-Policing Reduce Chemical Emissions?*, 46 Soc. Sci. J. 459-73 (2009); Paul P. Stretesky et al., *Does Environmental Enforcement Slow the Treadmill of Production? The Relationship Between Large Monetary Penalties, Ecological Disorganization, and Toxic Releases Within Offending Corporations*, 36 J. Crime & Just. 36, 233-47 (2013). *See also* David M. Uhlmann, *Prosecutorial Discretion and Environmental Crime*, 38 Harv. Envtl. L. Rev. 159 (2014); Michael J. Lynch et al., *Weak Probability of Punishment for Environmental Offenses and Deterrence of Environmental Offenders: A Discussion Based on USEPA Criminal Cases, 1983-2013*, 10 Deviant Behav. 37, 1095 (2016); Paul B. Stretesky et al., *Does the Modernization of Environmental Enforcement Reduce Toxic Emissions? An Examination of Self-Policing, Criminal Prosecutions, and Toxic Releases in the United States, 1988-2014*, 37 Soc. Spectrum 37, 48-

eral criminal enforcement tools were always meant to be used strategically alongside civil enforcement tools and state enforcement actions. EPA does not devest criminal enforcement activities to the states, although state environmental agencies play large roles in permitting and engaging in civil and criminal enforcement efforts. As the past director of the Office of Enforcement, Earl E. Devaney, noted:

> It is unlikely the Office will ever be large enough in size to fully defeat the ever-expanding universe of environmental crime . . . it must maximize its presence and impact through discerning case selection, and then proceed with investigations that advance EPA's overall goal of regulatory compliance and punishing criminal wrongdoing.[53]

The difficulties of gathering data on environmental criminal sanctioning and the general lack of data on corporate environmental crime leaves the complex question of the broader deterrent value of criminal enforcement open.[54]

The process of developing the tools for criminal enforcement evolved in the 1970s out of a distinct need to manage serious and knowing violations of environmental laws.[55] The federal government and regulators had yet to develop an organized system for pursuing such prosecutions and only 25 criminal cases were prosecuted by the federal government prior to 1982.[56] EPA's first efforts were to focus on bringing industry into compliance with federal law. The process of developing criminal sanctions required the inclusion of misdemeanor and then felony provisions in federal environmental statutes, as well as institutionalized resources for policing and prosecuting environmental crimes.

---

62 (2017); Michael J. Lynch, *The Sentencing/Punishment of Federal Environmental/Green Offenders, 2000-2013*, 38 Deviant Behav., 991-95 (2017); Matthew J. Greife et al., *Corporate Environmental Crime and Environmental Justice*, 28 Crim. Just. Pol'y Rev. 327 (2017); Michael J. Lynch et al., *Environmental Crime Prosecutions in Ireland, 2004-2014*, 43 Int'l J. Comp. & Appl. Crim. Just. 277-93 (2019); Matthew J. Greife & Michael O. Maume, *Do Companies Pay the Price for Environmental Crimes?: Consequences of Criminal Penalties on Corporate Offenders*, 73 Crime, L. & Soc. Change 337-56 (2020).

53. Earl E. Devaney, The Exercise of Investigative Discretion 2-3 (1994), https://www.epa.gov/sites/production/files/documents/exercise.pdf.

54. Lori S. Bennear, *What Do We Really Know?: The Effect of Reporting Thresholds on Inferences Using Environmental Right-To-Know Data*, 2 Reg. & Gov. 293-95 (2008) and Carol Gibbs & Sallie S. Simpson, *Measuring Corporate Environmental Crime Rates: Progress and Problems*, 51 Crime, L. & Soc. Change 87-90 (2009).

55. Washington Legal Fund, Environmental Protection Agency Criminal Enforcement Policies ch. 2, at 2-1 to 2-18 (2007), https://s3.us-east-2.amazonaws.com/washlegal-uploads/upload/Chapter2EPA.pdf [hereinafter Washington Legal Fund].

56. Celia B. Campbell-Mohn, Sustainable Environmental Law (West Publishing Co. 1993).

The first federal environmental statute that allowed for federal prosecution of environmental crimes came with the Rivers and Harbors Act of 1899. This Act made it a misdemeanor to illegally discharge or obstruct waterways in the United States.[57] The following year Congress provided additional environmental crime fighting tools when it prohibited the unregulated interstate trade in wildlife under the Lacey Act.[58] The MBTA was passed in 1918 and prohibited the illegal taking, trading, or transporting of migratory birds without prior approval of the U.S. Fish and Wildlife Service (FWS).[59] As environmental law became more expansive to deal with the ever-growing problems of pollution in an industrialized society, it took some time for various statutes to grow teeth.

While the major environmental laws of the 1970s contained misdemeanor provisions, it was not until the 1980s with the passage of the hazardous and solid waste amendments to RCRA that felony provisions made their way into federal environmental law.[60] The RCRA Amendments introduced the concept of knowing violations into environmental criminal law. Criminal liability requires mens rea but linking corporate officers to knowing violations of hazardous waste laws when they rarely store, transport, or dispose of the waste themselves was exceptionally difficult prior to these changes.[61] The U.S. Sentencing Commission issued new *Sentencing Guidelines* in 1987 for individuals convicted of federal offenses that imposed more severe sentencing that extended to environmental crimes.[62] Congress amended the CWA in 1987 to change knowing violations to felonies instead of misdemeanors and the CAA Amendments of 1990 changed the law to include felony provisions. Felony provisions and penalties in federal environmental statues are now commonplace and represent the legacy of these changes.[63] These changes

---

57. Rivers and Harbors Act of 1899, 33 U.S.C. §403.
58. Lacey Act, 16 U.S.C. §§3371-3378 (1900).
59. MBTA, 16 U.S.C. §§703-712 (1918). U.S. FWS, *Migratory Bird Treaty Act*, https://fws.gov/birds/policies-and-regulations/laws-legislations/migratory-bird-treaty-act.php (last visited Apr. 5, 2022).
60. *See* Environment & Natural Resources Division, U.S. DOJ, *Historical Development of Environmental Criminal Law* https://www.justice.gov/enrd/about-division/historical-development-environmental-criminal-law (last updated May 13, 2015); U.S. EPA, 25 Years of RCRA: Building On Our Past to Protect Our Future (2020), https://nepis.epa.gov/Exe/ZyPDF.cgi/10000MAO.PDF?Dockey=10000MAO.PDF.
61. David T. Barton, *Corporate Officer Liability Under RCRA: Stringent But Not Strict*, 4 Brigham Young U. L. Rev. 1548 (1991).
62. Washington Legal Fund, *supra* note 55, at 2-3.
63. For examples of criminal provisions in federal environmental law, see U.S. EPA, *Criminal Provisions of the Clean Air Act*, https://www.epa.gov/enforcement/criminal-provisions-clean-air-act (last updated March 30, 2022); U.S. EPA, *Criminal Provisions of Water Pollution*, https://www.epa.gov/enforcement/criminal-provisions-water-pollution (last updated Nov. 18, 2021); U.S. EPA, *Criminal Provisions of the Resource Conservation and Recovery Act (RCRA)*, https://www.epa.gov/enforcement/criminal-provisions-resource-conservation-and-recovery-act-rcra (last updated March 30, 2022).

also reflect a broader worldwide trend in environmental law beginning in the mid-1980s to establish more significant sanctions for environmental harm.[64]

By the beginning of the 1980s, the institutionalization of a process for criminal enforcement began to take hold.[65] In 1981, EPA's Office of Environmental Enforcement (OEE) was created and this was later changed to the Office of Enforcement and Compliance Assurance (OECA), which houses EPA's Criminal Investigation Division (CID).[66] In 1982, EPA's General Counsel issued a formal statement noting that criminal enforcement would become an important aspect of their overall enforcement strategy.[67] With the creation of this unit there was now an institutionalized structure formed to develop the needed policing resources for the environment.[68] Special agents, also known as criminal investigators or 1811s, lacked law enforcement authority and were authorized by the U.S. Attorney General in 1984 as Special Deputy U.S. Marshals and this process required annual renewal until 1988 when Congress granted EPA full law enforcement powers.[69] Today about 150 criminal enforcement agents in EPA-CID are stationed in about 40 locations throughout the country.[70] The Office of Criminal Enforcement, Forensics, and Training (OCEFT) was organized in 1995 and charged with investigating violations and providing forensics support in civil and criminal cases.[71] EPA-CID functions as a federal law enforcement agency and special agents carry firearms, and promote their successes with punishment and deterrence in official press releases and advance a public image as "America's Environmental Crime Fighters."[72]

64. Michael R. Pendleton, *Beyond the Threshold: The Criminalization of Logging*, 10 Soc'y & Nat. Resources 191-93 (1997).

65. David Uhlmann, *Environmental Crime Comes of Age: The Evolution of Criminal Enforcement in the Environmental Regulatory Scheme*, 4 Utah L. Rev, 1224 (2009).

66. U.S. EPA, *Criminal Enforcement,* https://www.epa.gov/enforcement/criminal-enforcement (last updated Aug. 23, 2021).

67. Daniel Riesel, *Criminal Prosecution and Defense of Environmental Wrongs*, 15 ELR 10065-69 (Mar. 1985).

68. John F. Cooney, *Multi-Jurisdictional and Successive Prosecution of Environmental Crimes: The Case for a Consistent Approach*, 96 J. Crim. L. & Criminology 435-64 (2006) and David M. Uhlmann, *Environmental Crime Comes of Age: The Evolution of Criminal Enforcement in the Environmental Regulatory Scheme*, 4 Utah L. Rev. 1223-52 (2009).

69. John Peter Suarez, Management Review of the Office of Criminal Enforcement, Forensics and Training 7 (2003), https://www.epa.gov/sites/production/files/documents/oceft-review03.pdf.

70. Public Employees for Environmental Responsibility (PEER), EPA CID Agent Count (2019), https://www.peer.org/wp-content/uploads/2019/11/11_21_19-Federal_Pollution_EPA_CID_Agent_Count.pdf; and U.S. EPA, *Criminal Enforcement: Special Agents*, https://www.epa.gov/enforcement/criminal-enforcement-special-agents (last updated July 14, 2021).

71. For a discussion of the forensics process for investigating environmental crimes, see Jennifer A. Suggs et al., *Guidelines and Resources for Conducting an Environmental Crime Investigation in the United States*, 3 Envtl. Forensics 91-113 (2002).

72. U.S. EPA, Working Together: FY 2018-2022 U.S. EPA Strategic Plan (2020), https://www.epa.gov/sites/production/files/2018-02/documents/fy-2018-2022-epa-strategic-plan.pdf.

Figure 1. Total EPA-CID Special Agents by EPA Fiscal Year, 1997-2019

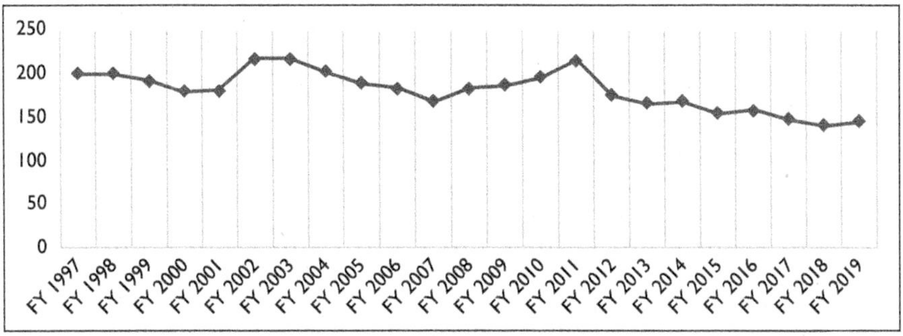

In the 1980s, the number of special agents employed by EPA to undertake criminal investigations was relatively small.[73] The Pollution Prosecution Act of 1990 greatly professionalized criminal investigations by mandating a statutory minimum of 200 staff.[74] In 1982, there were 23 criminal investigators employed by the then-newly created Office of Criminal Enforcement and that number grew to 34 by 1985, and then 55 by 1990. By 1995, EPA-CID employed 220 special agents.[75]

In Figure 1 we show the number of special agents employed by EPA-CID to engage in environmental criminal investigations by EPA fiscal years (FY) 1997-2019. The number of agents declines in the late 1990s under the statutory minimum in FY 1999. By FY 2002 that number increased to 212 and then starts a measured decline to 168 by FY 2007. In FY 2011, we see 215 agents employed by the Agency and then a marked decline comes to a low point of 140 in FY 2018 and 145 in FY 2019. This decline lags the 2009 financial crisis by a few years but has yet to recover to the numbers in the late 1990s.[76]

Institutionalizing the ability to prosecute environmental crimes can be traced to the founding of DOJ's Public Lands Division, formed in 1909 and

73. *See* U.S. EPA, News Release: EPA Announces 2019 Annual Environmental Enforcement Results (Feb. 13, 2020), https://www.epa.gov/newsreleases/epa-announces-2019-annual-environmental-enforcement-results; U.S. EPA, Criminal Enforcement Program: America's Environmental Crime Fighters (2020), https://www.epa.gov/sites/production/files/documents/oceftbrochure.pdf.
74. The Pollution Prosecution Act of 1990, Pub. L. No. 101-593.
75. *See* Washington Legal Fund, *supra* note 55, ch. 2, at 2-2.
76. Measuring the number of special agents or 1811s is not completely straightforward. This can be measured by the number of personnel dedicated to investing crimes (case agents) and/or supervisors. The numbers are consistent but vary a bit from our own data requests and across the following sources we used to gather data for Fig. 1. *See* Personal requests by the authors of OECA staff and Washington Legal Fund, *supra* note 55, ch. 2; PEER, *supra* note 70; U.S. EPA, Criminal Enforcement Program Overview 8-11 (2017), https://19january2017snapshot.epa.gov/sites/production/files/documents/oceft-overview-2011.pdf.

now known as the Environment and Natural Resources Division (ENRD).[77] In 1982, the Environmental Crimes Section (DOJ-ECS) was founded to center resources and professional expertise on prosecuting environmental crimes. In 1987, DOJ-ECS became its own section within ENRD.[78] DOJ-ECS has about 43 prosecutors and a dozen support staff.[79] Typically, environmental crimes are prosecuted by attorneys in DOJ-ECS or specialized attorneys within the U.S. Attorney's Office.

Successful criminal enforcement begins with investigation and cooperation.[80] The devolved nature of enforcement and permitting for major statutes, such as the CAA and The CWA means state environmental agencies are the first line of defense to make sure the regulated community is in compliance with federal law.[81] EPA must work with DOJ or the U.S. Attorney's Office to pursue criminal prosecution. Additional federal and state agencies are often involved in developing investigations and cases against possible defendants, as well as collaborating on prosecutions at various points. Typical sources that alert EPA investigators to a potential compliance issue that might determine the need for an investigation often come from on-site inspections, self-monitoring, recordkeeping, and self-reporting, citizen complaints, or ambient monitoring of conditions near facilities. EPA investigators are alerted to criminal issues via a few typical routes, including former employees, self-reported forms and documents, civil inspectors from outside the Agency that notice violations in the course of their inspections, or civil investigations undertaken by state or federal environmental agencies.[82] Investigators with the CID build evidence and then approach federal prosecutors with known interests in the area or with relevant responsibilities. If evidence is sufficient, prosecutors may seek indictments from a grand jury

77. Environment & Natural Resources Division, U.S. DOJ, *History*, https://www.justice.gov/enrd/history (last updated May 18, 2021).

78. The Environmental Enforcement Section handles civil/judicial cases. *See* Environment & Natural Resources Division, U.S. DOJ, *Historical Development of Environmental Criminal Law* https://www.justice.gov/enrd/about-division/historical-development-environmental-criminal-law (last updated May 13, 2015); and Environment & Natural Resources Division, U.S. DOJ, *An Overview of Our Practice*, https://www.justice.gov/enrd/overview-our-practice (last updated May 14, 2015).

79. Numbers are given as of 2015. *See* Environment & Natural Resources Division, U.S. DOJ, *Environmental Crimes Section*, https://www.justice.gov/enrd/environmental-crimes-section (last updated July 2, 2021).

80. Joel A. Mintz, *Some Thoughts on the Interdisciplinary Aspects of Environmental Enforcement*, 36 ELR 10495-96 (July 2006) [hereinafter *Some Thoughts on the Interdisciplinary Aspects of Environmental Enforcement*].

81. Joel A. Mintz, Enforcement at the EPA: High Stakes and Hard Choices (Univ. of Texas Press 2012).

82. *See Some Thoughts on the Interdisciplinary Aspects of Environmental Enforcement*, *supra* note 80, at 10495.

or file a criminal information document with a U.S. district court to pursue prosecution.[83]

The necessity of cooperation to pursue such cases became evident early on in the evolution of the criminal enforcement apparatus.

> Cooperation and collaboration among prosecutors, law enforcement officials, regulators, laboratories, and legislators are all the more essential because of the growing sophistication of environmental criminals and their defense attorneys. Although there are still numerous cases of "midnight dumping"—that is, simply dumping or abandoning hazardous materials or waste by the roadside or in vacant lots—increasing numbers of businesses systematically and knowingly are violating the environmental laws to save money and increase profit margins.[84]

Pursuing such prosecution represents an investment in agency resources, cooperation between agencies, federal involvement and desire to prosecute, and the appropriate type of violation suitable for criminal sanctions, and whether the government feels it can meet a higher burden of guilt and win in court. It has typically been the case that both DOJ prosecutors and EPA criminal investigators have enjoyed a high degree of autonomy when deciding what cases to prosecute and investigate, although after 9/11 many staff complained that the focus of their efforts shifted toward homeland security and away from environmental concerns.[85]

All of the above factors push most violations toward civil remedies.[86] In FY 2007 there were 3,683 civil enforcement conclusions. This number has declined fairly steadily to 1,964 by FY 2017. EPA filed 1,080 administrative enforcement cases in FY 2017.[87] In contrast, criminal investigations and prosecutions are much fewer in number. Data suggests that EPA received 314 criminal referrals and filed 153 prosecutions in FY 2007. In FY 2017, EPA

83. Joel. A. Mintz, *Neither the Best of Times Nor the Worst of Times: EPA Enforcement During the Clinton Administration*, 35 ELR 10390-93 (June 2005).
84. Theodore M. Hammett & Joel Epstein, Local Prosecution of Environmental Crime XIV (National Inst. of Justice 1993).
85. Joel A. Mintz, *Treading Water: A Preliminary Assessment of EPA Enforcement During the Bush II Administration*, 34 ELR 10912 (Oct. 2004) and PEER, 2003 Survey of EPA Office of Criminal Enforcement, Forensics and Training 2-3 (2003), https://www.peer.org/wp-content/uploads/attachments/EPA-OCEFT_Survey_Sample_Essay_Responses.pdf.
86. Joel. A. Mintz, *EPA Enforcement of CERCLA: Historical Overview and Recent Trends*, 41 Sw. L. Rev. 645-59 (2012) and David M. Uhlmann, *Environmental Crime Comes of Age: The Evolution of Criminal Enforcement in the Environmental Regulatory Scheme*, 4 Utah L. Rev. 1223-52 (2009).
87. PEER, Total Civil Enforcement Case Initiation and Conclusions (2017), https://www.peer.org/wp-content/uploads/attachments/3_29_18_Civil_Enforcement_Case_Initiations_Conclusions_2007-17.pdf; PEER, EPA Administrative Enforcement Cases Filed: 2008-2018 (2018), https://www.peer.org/wp-content/uploads/attachments/3_29_18_Civil_Enforcement_Case_Initiations_Conclusions_2007-17.pdf.

received 206 referrals and filed 94 prosecutions.[88] In comparison, our data, which we will explore in the later chapters, shows that in FY 2007, federal prosecutors closed 51 cases investigated by EPA and only 33 in FY 2017.

Civil administrative or judicial actions can offer a wide range of punishments or solutions to gain compliance among the regulated community. This can include civil fines, penalties, fees assessments, or restitution, settlements, injunctive relief to order an individual or company to perform some set of actions, required mitigation plans, administrative orders of consent (AOCs), or supplemental environmental projects (SEPs). Civil actions can take shape against a particular entity or become part of an industry-wide effort to induce change as part of a broader compliance monitoring strategy.[89]

A good example of a civil settlement campaign to gain compliance and target key sources of emissions across a sector would be the Agency's Petroleum Refinery Initiative. Ambient air emissions are an extremely tricky regulatory problem. While states employ air monitoring stations around petroleum refineries, air monitoring is often insufficient to capture the scope of what is emitted via stacks and other sources. EPA has focused their efforts historically on technology-forcing solutions. EPA worked with American Petroleum Institute (API), a petroleum industry group, to incentivize compliance through a Storage Tank Emission Reduction Partnership Program. Storage tanks containing volatile organic compounds (VOCs) contain devices called slotted guide poles that guide the motion of external floating roofs and sample the contents of the tank. EPA agreed to waive penalties to incentivize the addition of emissions controls, given that each tank is estimated to emit some 20,000 pounds of VOCs annually. The cumulative effect would help companies meet guidelines under the CAA, as well as aid the Agency in meeting its air quality goals.[90]

Petroleum refineries also flare or release material through a device that rapidly incinerates which is a major problem with ambient air emissions; the extent to which emissions are flared and the effects are often not completely

88. PEER, Federal Criminal Enforcement Environmental Protection Agency (2018), https://www.peer.org/wp-content/uploads/attachments/3_29_18_EPA_Crim_cases_Referred_Prosecuted_1986-2018.pdf.

89. Kathleen F. Brickey, *Environmental Crime at the Crossroads: The Intersection of Environmental and Criminal Law Theory*, 487 Tul. L. Rev. 494-95 (1996); Kathleen F. Brickey, *Charging Practices in Hazardous Waste Crime Prosecutions*, 62 Ohio St. L.J. 1077-124 (2001); Michael M. O'Hear, Sentencing the Green-Collar Offender: Punishment, Culpability, and Environmental Crime, 95 J. Crim. L. & Criminology 133-76 (2004); U.S. EPA, Basic Information on Enforcement (2020), https://www.epa.gov/enforcement/basic-information-enforcement.

90. Office of Reg. Enforcement, *EPA Announces Clean Air Act Compliance Incentive Program Developed With API*, Enforcement Alert (EPA May 2000), https://www.epa.gov/sites/production/files/documents/aboveground.pdf.

known to regulators. EPA also had problems with state regulators that would give refineries a pass on penalties for flaring, malfunctions, or other upset events that were reported as unavoidable, which clashed with federal guidelines.[91] Research demonstrates these events collectively can have significant impacts on ambient air emissions.[92]

EPA ultimately worked for years to settle 37 cases with U.S. companies that covered 112 refineries in 32 states with civil penalties totaling $116 million and the agreement to invest $7 billion in control technologies. Expectations for the settlement include significant reduction in sulfur dioxide (SO2), nitrogen oxide (NOX), and VOCs, such as benzene and particulate matter (PM). This was undertaken as a broader compliance monitoring strategy under the CAA to reduce the key sources of emissions at refineries.[93] As opposed to a criminal approach focusing on deterrence, this compliance-based approach centered on cooperation, cajoling, legal maneuvering, and pressure. But would such an approach be sufficient for BP or other companies that do not care to comply with regulations? What is the ultimate reach of EPA and the environmental revolution that spawned its birth to produce and enforce such regulations?[94]

DOJ's criminal enforcement record came under scrutiny of Congress when the U.S. House of Representatives' Subcommittee on Investigations and Oversight held hearings in the early 1990s, challenging their choices not to pursue cases against powerful companies or work with EPA and other agencies when settling cases.[95] The outcome was the perception that DOJ needed to strengthen its prosecutorial efforts. As Congress continued to strengthen criminal provisions in federal environmental statues and increase statutory penalties, as well as the budget for policing and prosecution resources, these

91. Office of Reg. Enforcement, *Frequent, Routine, Flaring May Cause Excessive, Uncontrolled Sulfur Dioxide Releases*, Enforcement Alert (EPA Oct. 2000), https://www.epa.gov/sites/production/files/documents/flaring.pdf.

92. Environmental Integrity Project, Gaming the System: How Off-the Books Industrial Upset Emissions Cheat the Public Out of Clean Air (2004), http://www.environmentalintegrity.org/pdf/publications/Report_Gaming_the_System_EIP.pdf; Environmental Integrity Project, OFF THE BOOKS: Air Pollution Missing From Texas Annual Emission Inventory (2005), http://www.environmentalintegrity.org/pdf/publications/Report_Off_The_Books.pdf; Environmental Integrity Project, Comments on Proposed Amendments to the Current Standards of Performance for Petroleum Refineries (2005), http://www.environmentalintegrity.org/pdf/publications/Refinery_GHG_Comments.pdf.

93. U.S. EPA, 2020, Petroleum Refinery National Case Results, http://www.environmentalintegrity.org/pdf/publications/Refinery_GHG_Comments.pdf.

94. Lynn E. Blais, *The Legitimate Reach of the Environmental Revolution*, 37 Harv. J. L. & Pub. Pol'y 13-22 (2014).

95. Debra Jacobson, 1992-1994 Investigation of the Justice Department's Environmental Crimes Program (2017), https://archive.constitutionproject.org/wp-content/uploads/2017/05/EnvironmentalCrimes.pdf.

actions showed a willingness and desire on their part to enhance criminal enforcement to reduce environmental harms.

Resources for environmental policing and prosecution have always been limited and the notion that investigators and prosecutors should have discretion to pursue significant penalties against individuals and companies that harm humans, animals, or the natural environment has always been a politically contentious issue with Congress.[96] While supporters sent strong signals and enhanced EPA and DOJ's ability to investigate and prosecute environmental crimes through the early 1990s, the longer term picture has been one of treading water between supporters and opponents in the White House and Congress, where efforts to maintain the criminal enforcement apparatus often suffer and have rarely been rewarded with expanded budgets and staff since that time.[97] Central to the fight over what political principals want out of criminal enforcement has been the issue of prosecutorial discretion, the use of criminal law as it is applied to environmental law, and the relationship between civil and criminal law.[98]

As Prof. Kathleen Brickey notes, environmental law has three distinct characteristics: aspirational qualities; evolutionary nature; and a high degree of complexity.[99] The aspirational qualities embodied in environmental law includes its desire to bring about significant change in human behavior to reduce environmental degradation, hazards, and threats to human health through technology-forcing mandates with deadlines that are often impossible or infeasible. Because these standards are based on prevailing technology and scientifically informed value judgments, environmental law is constantly evolving and in flux.[100] This feature makes the application and compliance with environmental law uncertain and unpredictable. Aggregating aspirational and evolutionary characteristics and the high degree of complexity imbued within environmental law often makes statutes obscure and throws up real barriers to compliance.[101]

---

96. Judson W. Starr, *Turbulent Times at Justice and EPA: The Origins of Environmental Criminal Prosecutions and the Work that Remains*, 59 G.W. L. Rev. 900-02 (1991).
97. Joel A. Mintz, *Running on Fumes: The Development of New EPA Regulations in an Era of Scarcity*, 46 ELR 10510-12 (June 2016).
98. Theodora Galactos, *The United States Department of Justice Environmental Crimes Section: A Case Study of Inter- and Intra-Branch Conflict Over Congressional Oversight and the Exercise of Prosecutorial Discretion*, 64 Fordham L. Rev. 590-95 (1995).
99. Kathleen F. Brickey, Environmental Crime: Law, Policy, Prosecution 9 (Aspen Publishers 2008) [hereinafter Brickey, Environmental Crime].
100. A. Dan Tarlock, *The Non-Equilibrium Paradigm in Ecology and the Partial Unraveling of Environmental Law*, 27 Loyola L. Rev. 1121-33 (1994).
101. *See* Brickey, Environmental Crime, *supra* note 99, at 9-13.

These three issues bring into question the fairness of the enforcement process for such laws and have created significant detractors in Congress, the White House, and the legal and regulated community over time. Central to this debate is that in a complex system of evolving mandates, should criminal sanctions be applied as in other areas of federal regulatory law or should they be reserved for very specific circumstances? As Prof. Richard Lazarus notes, Congress made most knowing and negligent violations of environmental law subject to both criminal and civil sanctions without thresholds applied for determining when either set of sanctions would be applied.[102] Traditional notions of culpability do not apply to environmental standards that are based on a more precautionary approach. Pollution is not in and of itself illegal like crimes such as murder or assault, so criminal guilt often comes down to matters of degree. This makes applying traditional ideas of mens rea to environmental crimes difficult. Action standards for compliance are based on predictions for what is possible and are based on uncertain science, instead of long-standing norms or existing conduct as in other areas of criminal law. By these standards, criminal sanctions risk becoming just another enforcement tool, rather than being fundamentally different in character, blurring the lines between civil and criminal law and private and public wrongs.[103]

---

102. This section quotes liberally from the following, *id.* at 20-21. *See* Lazarus *supra* note 43, at 867-83. *See also* Richard J. Lazarus, The Making of Environmental Law 88-90 (Univ. of Chicago Press 2004).

103. Brickey, Environmental Crime, *supra* note 99, at 22-23. Some have argued that the line between civil and criminal law at the federal level has become increasingly blurred across the board. *See* John C. Coffee Jr., *Does Unlawful Mean Criminal?: Reflections on the Disappearing Tort/Crime Distinction in American Law*, 71 Brigham Young U. L. Rev. 193 (1991).

Chapter 2. I Know What You Did With the Asbestos Last Summer: The Criminal Enforcement of the U.S. Clean Air Act

I. Enforcing the U.S. Clean Air Act

The development and exploitation of fossil fuels was arguably one of the most important scientific discoveries of humankind. Coal, oil, and natural gas significantly increased the amount of energy we have available to avail ourselves of the crushing labor required by an agrarian society under which we toiled as a species reliant on manual labor and beasts of burden to secure our existence.1 By replacing wood, biomass, water, and steam, fossil fuels propelled the Industrial Revolution and brought our species into a new era of existence focused on pursuits of leisure and consumption, as well as capital accumulation and scientific innovation. The primary source of energy available to most American families throughout history was burning wood, until it was replaced with coal in the latter half of the 19th century, which was then overtaken by oil and natural gas by the mid-20th century.[2] It took some time for humans to realize the physical and health impacts caused by the use of fossil fuels as industrialization took hold. Polluted rivers, blackened skies, damaged lungs, premature deaths, poisoned forests, and mass extinctions have resulted from our gluttonous extraction of these wondrously compressed plants and animals from millions of years ago that propelled the greatest social, political, and technological changes in the history of our species.[3]

1. Environmental & Energy Study Inst., *Fossil Fuels*, https://www.eesi.org/topics/fossil-fuels/description (last updated July 22, 2021).
2. U.S. Energy Info. Admin., *Fossil Fuels Have Made Up at Least 80% of U.S. Fuel Mix Since 1900* (July 2, 2015), https://www.eia.gov/todayinenergy/detail.php?id=21912.
3. It is often forgotten today that Britain's lust for world power was propelled in great part by a tremendous reliance on wood. That reliance was precarious, as it had long ago exhausted its own sufficient domestic supply of lumber, as had many other European powers. In addition to its bent for empire and the need to get rid of undesirables, America's primeval forests were coveted by the Crown. The British had a particular need for old growth white pine used in mast building for the ships of the British Royal Navy. Among other factors, making vast swaths of valuable forests off-limits incensed the colonists. The insatiable need for energy propels empires ever forward at increasing rates as it did for timber in the case of the British in the 18th century, as was with need for coaling stations to refuel

While we pollute our waterways, drain aquifers for agriculture, dump hazardous waste in landfills and the ocean, and force chemicals deep in the earth's crust, in the era of climate change, however, no political issue today should be more pressing to us than reducing air pollution. Humans have engineered the natural environment for most of history causing untold destruction to each other and animals. Yet we have never faced a danger as severe as climate change and its potential to collectively alter the course of our entire planet. Even ignoring its health benefits, combating climate change by reducing air pollution is the most important and immediate action that we can take.[4] Our continued reliance on fossil fuels and the air emissions generated from power plants, factories, and cars is already causing catastrophic impacts on our natural world and our health.[5]

Sending toxic emissions into the air for less than two centuries has created a situation where we now have to prepare for the immediate and mid-term impacts of climate change faster than we can reduce our behaviors that cause it.[6] There is broad scientific consensus that these effects are already observable and escalating with the rapid pace of industrialization across the world.[7] Current effects include: changes in precipitation patterns; longer growing seasons in some areas; rising temperatures; increased drought and temperatures; stronger hurricanes; sea-level rise; and reduced sea ice in the Arctic Ocean.[8] What is unknown is whether we can overcome our collective action problem as a species to reduce these emissions to save ourselves long term.[9]

In various ways we have known for some time that sending harmful pollution into the air imperils humans, animals, and the future of our existence as a species.[10] Just like our forebears, individuals living in developing countries

its battleships that compelled the United States to acquire overseas territories in the 19th century, and to fight wars in the Middle East to secure oil in the 20th century. *See* R.J.B. Knight, *New England Forests and British Seapower: Albion Revisited*, 46 Am. Neptune 221-29 (1986), http://rogerknight.org/pdf/New%20England%20Forests%20and%20British%20Seapower.pdf. *See also* Naval History & Heritage Command, *The U.S. Navy in Hawaii, 1826-1945: An Administrative History*, https://www.history.navy.mil/research/library/online-reading-room/title-list-alphabetically/u/the-us-navy-and-hawaii-a-historical-summary/development-of-the-naval-establishment-in-hawaii.html (Apr. 23, 2015.

4. U.S. EPA, *Air Pollution: Current and Future Challenges*, https://www.epa.gov/clean-air-act-overview/air-pollution-current-and-future-challenges (last updated March 30, 2022).
5. Centers for Disease Control & Prevention, *Air Pollution*, https://www.cdc.gov/climateandhealth/effects/air_pollution.htm (last reviewed Dec. 21, 2020).
6. U.N. Environment Programme, *Why Does Climate Action Matter?*, https://www.unep.org/explore-topics/climate-action/why-does-climate-action-matter (last visited Feb. 28, 2022).
7. Naomi Oreskes, *Beyond the Ivory Tower: The Scientific Consensus on Climate Change*, 306 Science 1686 (2014).
8. John Cook et al., *Quantifying the Consensus on Anthropogenic Global Warming in the Scientific Literature*, 8 Envtl. Res. Letters 1-7 (2013).
9. NASA, *The Effects of Climate Change*, https://climate.nasa.gov/effects/ (last updated March 23, 2022).
10. Peter T. Doran & Maggie Kendal Zimmerman, *Examining the Scientific Consensus on Climate Change*, 90 Eos Transactions 22-23 (2009).

today can see air pollution when they burn wood or coal and the soot and PM become evident inside their houses, in the air, and later, in their lungs.[11] We see this with ground-level ozone we call smog that is apparent, particularly in urban areas, when combusting fossil fuels react with sunlight.[12] Although we cannot always see it, we can feel the effects of toxic air emissions in greatly increased rates of respiratory diseases, such as bronchitis, asthma, and chronic obstructive pulmonary disease (COPD), skin conditions, and cancer.[13] We should have moved past the point as a society of arguing that living near heavy industry, power plants, large concentration of motor vehicles, and other sources of air pollution significantly lowers our quality of life and often leads to early death.[14] There should be no debate about this.

The year 2020 marks the 50th anniversary of the modern CAA and the turning point when the U.S. federal government took the reins for cataloging, measuring, regulating, and reducing air pollution.[15] Focusing events, such as the Donora smog, inspired the need for federal oversight and leadership in managing air pollution.[16] The CAA is arranged by six titles (Titles I-VI). It empowers EPA to manage air quality throughout the United States and protects the earth's stratospheric ozone layer.[17] We list these titles in Table 1.[18]

Title I establishes the basis for preventing air pollution and creates air quality control regions that develop the dichotomy of attainment/non-attainment areas that meet or do not meet national standards for primary or secondary ambient air quality and establishes grants and technical guidance for these regions.[19] It develops new source review (NSR) permits for areas in attainment with the national ambient air quality standards (NAAQS) or

11. Nigel Bruce et al., *Indoor Air Pollution in Developing Countries: A Major Environmental and Public Health Challenge*, 78 Bull. World Health Org. 1078-92 (2000).
12. U.S. EPA, *Health Effects of Ozone Pollution*, https://www.epa.gov/ground-level-ozone-pollution/health-effects-ozone-pollution, (last updated May 5, 2021).
13. World Health Org., *Ambient Air Pollution: Health Impacts*, https://www.who.int/airpollution/ambient/health-impacts/en/.
14. Jillian Mackenzie & Jeff Turrentine, *Air Pollution: Everything You Need to Know: How Smog, Soot, Greenhouse Gases, and Other Top Air Pollutants Are Affecting the Planet and Your Health*, Nat. Resources Def. Council (June 22, 2021), https://www.nrdc.org/stories/air-pollution-everything-you-need-know.
15. U.S. EPA, *Clean Air Act Requirements and History*, https://www.epa.gov/clean-air-act-overview/clean-air-act-requirements-and-history (last updated Aug. 12, 2021).
16. Elizabeth T. Jacobs & Jeffrey L. Abbott, *The Donora Smog Revisited: 70 Years After the Event That Inspired the Clean Air Act*, 108 Am. J. Pub. Health S85-S88 (2018).
17. Joseph Goffman & Laura Bloomer, *Disempowering the EPA: How Statutory Interpretation of the Clean Air Act Serves the Trump Administration's Deregulatory Agenda*, 70 Case W. Res. L. Rev. 929-70 (2020).
18. For a fuller description of the CAA, see U.S. EPA, *Clean Air Act Table of Contents by Title*, https://www.epa.gov/clean-air-act-overview/clean-air-act-text#toc (last updated March 24, 2021).
19. U.S. EPA, *Nonattainment Areas for All Counties Criteria Pollutants (Green Book)*, https://www.epa.gov/green-book (last updated March 31, 2022) [hereinafter *Criteria Pollutants*].

areas that are unclassifiable, there are the prevention of significant deterioration (PSD) permits.[20] These are permits for any stationary source constructed or significantly modified. For non-attainment areas these permits are called non-attainment area permits.[21] For an NSR permit, EPA requires that best available control technology (BACT) be used to achieve the maximum degree of air pollution control available through equipment or improved processes. Permits require BACT, an air quality analysis, impacts analysis, and public involvement.[22] The goal of the process is to establish that permitting a new source or modifying an existing source will not cause the significant deterioration of current air quality in the area.[23]

Title II establishes EPA authority over mobile sources of air pollution, particularly centered on aircraft, motor vehicles, and motorcycles.[24] EPA rules have traditionally focused on technology-based approaches, such as catalytic converters to reduce exhaust emissions in motor vehicles, low emission vehicles (LEVs), emissions standards for aircraft, and the reformulation of gasoline, including prohibiting the production of engines requiring leaded gasoline.[25]

Title III mandates EPA establish a list of hazardous air pollutants (HAPs) and provisions for citizen lawsuits if EPA fails to come into compliance with

---

20. Environmental & Energy Law Program, *New Source Review*, Harvard Law School, https://eelp.law.harvard.edu/2018/12/new-source-review/ (Dec. 11, 2018).
21. Virginia Dep't of Envtl. Quality, *Types of Air Permits*, https://www.deq.virginia.gov/Programs/Air/PermittingCompliance/Permitting/TypesofAirPermits.aspx (last visited Apr. 20, 2021).
22. U.S. EPA, *Best Available Control Technology (BACT) Procedure*, https://www.epa.gov/nsr/best-available-control-technology-bact-procedure (last updated Feb. 14, 2022).
23. Obtaining an air permit for a new facility or significant modification is the real touchpoint for individual facilities that sparks the ability for regulators to use a "technology-forcing" approach to limit air emissions at a particular facility. The goal is to look at its impact more generally in the region and to see if the permit will greatly deteriorate air quality or cause it to go into non-attainment. In practice this process is heavily negotiated and there may be a range of options to meet compliance. The owner of a new chemical plant would likely provide data that the impact would not be that significant, but such data is often speculative. Whether an existing modification is significant enough to require a permit is also a point of contention and a negotiated process. This is an important touchpoint for environmental groups to force public participation hearings or file lawsuits to challenge the data provided by industry and get the public involved. U.S. EPA, *New Source Review (NSR) Permitting*, https://www.epa.gov/nsr/prevention-significant-deterioration-basic-information#AQA (last updated Feb. 14, 2022).
24. U.S. EPA, *Mobile Source Pollution and Related Health Effects* (2020), https://www.epa.gov/mobile-source-pollution (last updated March 22, 2022).
25. Corporate average fuel economy (CAFE) standards set standards to improve the fuel economy of cars. EPA measures fuel economy, but it is set by the National Highway Traffic Safety Administration (NHTSA). These were first introduced in 1978 for passenger vehicles. While generally effective at increasing fuel efficiency, CAFE standards are criticized because the measurements are often inaccurate, sport utility vehicles and trucks are subjected to a much lower standard, and manufacturers can pay penalties rather than comply with minimum standards. NHTSA, *Corporate Average Fuel Economy*, https://www.nhtsa.gov/laws-regulations/corporate-average-fuel-economy.

congressional intent or deadlines under the CAA.[26] Title IV and IV-A manage acid rain, primarily caused by NOX and SO2 emitted from power plants. It gives greater flexibility to reduce these emissions and mandates emissions reductions by 1995 and 2000, respectively. Title V creates a national permitting program for stationary sources, including mandating they measure and develop plans to control their emissions. Title VI regulates ozone-depleting or ozone-destroying chemicals. These are classified into Class I and Class II, based on the timeline of their phaseout in production. This title focuses primarily on the regulation and phaseout of chlorofluorocarbons (CFCs), also known as freon or R-12 used in refrigeration, packaging, and asthma inhalers, as well as bromochlorodifluoromethane (BCF), such as halon 1211 used in fire suppression.[27]

Table 1. Major Statutory Provisions of the Clean Air Act

Title	Description
I	Stationary Sources, Attainment/Non-Attainment Areas
II	Mobile Sources, Aircraft, Motor Vehicles, and Fuel Standards
III	General Provisions, Citizen Suits, and Standards for Hazardous Air Pollutants (HAPs)
IV	Noise Pollution Control, Acid Rain/Deposition Control (IV-A)
V	National Operating Permit Program
VI	Stratospheric Ozone

The modern CAA represents the evolution of various pieces of congressional legislation going back to the 1950s.[28] The Air Pollution Control Act of 1955 was the first effort by Congress to begin identifying air pollution as a serious public problem.[29] The Act did very little to measure air emissions, regulate air pollution, or punish individuals and companies that polluted

26. *See* U.S. EPA, *Initial List of Hazardous Air Pollutants With Modifications*, https://www.epa.gov/haps/initial-list-hazardous-air-pollutants-modifications (last updated Jan. 5, 2022). *See also* Victor B. Flatt, *Gasping for Breath: The Administrative Flaws of Federal Hazardous Air Pollution Regulation and What We Can Learn From the States*, 34 Ecology L.Q. 107-73 (2007).

27. CFCs were banned by the 1987 Montreal Protocol. The production of CFCs was banned by 1996 in the United States, but is still present in some asthma inhalers. Other countries, particularly China have increasingly ignored the ban even if they are a signatory to the treaty and thus, the deterioration of the ozone layer has increased. Agence France-Presse, *China Releasing Thousands of Tonnes of Illegal CFC Gasses, Study Finds*, Guardian, May 22, 2019, https://www.theguardian.com/world/2019/may/23/china-factories-releasing-thousands-of-tonnes-of-illegal-cfc-gases-study-finds.

28. *See* CAA of 1955, Pub. L. No. 84-159, 69 Stat. 322; CAA of 1963, Pub. L. No. 88-206, 77 Stat. 392; CAA of 1965, Pub. L. No. 89-272, 79 Stat. 992; CAA of 1970, Pub. L. No. 91-604, 84 Stat. 1676; CAA of 1977, Pub. L. No. 95-95, 91 Stat. 685; and CAA of 1990, Pub. L. No. 101-549, 104 Stat. 2399.

29. David M. Driesen et al., *Half a Century of Supreme Court Clean Air Interpretation: Purposivism, Textualism, Dynamism, and Activism*, 75 Wash. & Lee L. Rev. 1781-1857 (2018).

the ambient air. The U.S. Surgeon General provided guidance and Congress relied on states for any potential enforcement. Most importantly, the Act had the federal government acknowledge air pollution as a public health threat. The CAA of 1963 built on the 1955 Act. It authorized the U.S. Public Health Service to begin researching scientific methods to monitor and potentially control air pollution. The 1963 Act was amended by the National Emissions Standards Act of 1965. This Act set standards for new vehicle emissions for the first time at the federal level, beginning with vehicles manufactured for the 1968 model year.

The modern CAA as we know it came into being with the CAA Extension of 1970.[30] This amendment moved much farther than the previous acts toward obligating the federal government to address the problem of air pollution, which had at that time grown into a public health crisis, particularly for those living in urban areas and near major sources of industrial pollution.[31] The second major move forward was that federal regulatory responsibilities for regulating air, as well as water pollution and waste were transferred to one federal agency.[32] Prior to 1970, these responsibilities were spread across various federal agencies. A third important step forward after 1970 is that the federal government now agreed to take the lead on managing these forms of pollution.[33] This move meant the states would now assist the federal government in this effort, but would be required to abide by certain guidelines and meet certain obligations or minimum standards in the process.[34]

One of the primary goals for managing air pollution was to identify the most problematic sources of toxic air emissions in the country and develop standards for those that may impact public welfare for those that are sensitive to air pollution (children, those with asthma, etc.), and negatively impact the environment (crops or vegetation).[35] NAAQS was developed for six criteria pollutants, including: (1) sulfur oxides (SO_X); (2) atmospheric PM (PM_{10} and

30. Paul Rogers, *EPA History: The Clean Air Act of 1970*, EPA Journal (Jan./Feb. 1990), *available at* https://archive.epa.gov/epa/aboutepa/epa-history-clean-air-act-1970.html.
31. Congressional Res. Serv., Clean Air Act: A Summary of the Act and Its Major Requirements (Jan. 19, 2022), https://fas.org/sgp/crs/misc/RL30853.pdf.
32. Phil Wisman, *EPA History: 1970-1985*, EPA (Nov. 1985), https://archive.epa.gov/epa/aboutepa/epa-history-1970-1985.html.
33. American Experience, *The Modern Environmental Movement*, PBS.org, https://www.pbs.org/wgbh/americanexperience/features/earth-days-modern-environmental-movement/ (last visited Apr. 4, 2022).
34. Jonathan H. Adler & Nathaniel Stewart, *Is the Clean Air Act Unconstitutional? Coercion, Cooperative Federalism, and Conditional Spending After* NFIB v. Sebelius, 43 Ecology L.Q. 671-722 (2016).
35. More recently EPA attempted in the Obama Administration to apply the CAA to regulate greenhouse gasses, provoking obvious legal and political fighting. *See Clean Air Act Stationary Source—Greenhouse Gas Regulation—* Utility Air Regulatory Group v. EPA, 128 Harv. L. Rev. 361-70 (2014) and Arnold W. Reitze Jr., *The Intersection of Climate Change and the Clean Air Act Stationary Source Programs*, 43 Ariz. St. L.J. 901-42 (2011).

$PM_{2.5}$); (3) carbon monoxide (CO); (4) ozone (O_3); (5) NO_x; and (6) lead.[36] These standards have subsequently been reevaluated to other areas germane to air pollution, such as carbon emissions contributing to climate change.[37] States were given discretion to develop plans know as state implementation plans (SIPs) to comply with ambient air quality standards.[38] SIPs were meant to be both enforceable by law and manage air quality in each state, as well as considering actions in one state that affected another.[39] A good example would be coal-fired power plants in the Northeast, which were causing acid rain that was damaging buildings and trees downwind.[40]

Congress was reacting to the rapid proliferation of automobiles and industrial sources that were lowering air quality throughout the country.[41] New sources of stationary pollution would be regulated with BACT to determine how stringent facilities would have to be in reducing pollution, while existing facilities would be subjected to lower standards. The same standards applied to vehicles. A good example would be the adoption of two-way catalytic converters to control CO emissions on 1975 model-year cars and later in an effort to come into compliance with EPA rules on exhaust emissions. By the 1980s, three-way converters were adopted that also reduced NO_x emissions.[42] Because coal plants were a large source of SO_2 that caused acid rain, scrubbers—a technology-based solution to reducing air emissions—were adopted.[43]

36. For current and historical standards for the NAAQS, see U.S. EPA, *Reviewing National Ambient Air Quality Standards (NAAQS): Scientific and Technical Information*, https://www.epa.gov/naaqs (last updated Aug. 18, 2021).
37. Kimberly M. Castle & Richard L. Revesz, *Environmental Standards, Thresholds, and the Next Battleground of Climate Change Regulations*, 103 Minn. L. Rev. 1349-437 (2019).
38. U.S. EPA, *Basic Information About Air Quality SIPs*, https://www.epa.gov/sips/basic-information-air-quality-sips (last updated Jan. 25, 2022).
39. K.T. Bowman, *State Implementation of Permit Requirements Under the 1977 Clean Air Act Amendments*, 28 J. Air Pollution Control Ass'n 802 (1978).
40. U.S. EPA, *Cross-State Air Pollution Rules* (2020), https://www.epa.gov/csapr (last updated March 11, 2022).
41. U.S. EPA, *History of Reducing Air Pollution From Transportation in the United States* (2020), https://www.epa.gov/transportation-air-pollution-and-climate-change/accomplishments-and-success-air-pollution-transportation (last updated Apr. 7, 2021).
42. The technology behind catalytic converters had been developed much earlier, but was enhanced to meet EPA standards. While catalytic converters were often criticized for reducing vehicle performance, the technology helped lower passenger vehicle emission levels. *See* Tim Palucka, *Doing the Impossible*, Invention & Tech., Winter 2004, https://www.inventionandtech.com/content/doing-impossible-0.
43. Stack scrubbers work by channeling the gas from the stacks through a tank that sprays limestone and water. Gypsum is produced that can be used in drywall and other applications. Wet scrubbers spray the gas, treat and recycle the water, and dry scrubbers create an electrostatic charge resulting in a dry, rather than wet waste product. While this is a very effective technology, industry is not required to recycle and reuse the waste and often simply dumps it back into coalmines. More emblematic of problems with the CAA in general, EPA data suggests a majority of coal-fired power plants do not have scrubbers. Many never had to install them due to grandfathering or simply did not for lack of sufficient punishment. In the early 2000s, data suggested power plants, particularly coal-fired plants,

The 1970 extension also introduced new source performance standards (NSPS) for pollution controls.[44] NSPS set pollution standards for new stationary sources.[45] Different standards are set for various industries, based on the BACT at the time and the maximum upper limit for criteria pollutants allowed by that technology.[46] National emission standards for hazardous air pollutants (NESHAPs) were introduced to regulate air pollutants at stationary sources not covered by NAAQs.[47] These are any HAPs, which are known to cause cancer or other serious adverse health or environmental effects and include numerous applications, such as petroleum refineries, pharmaceutical manufacturing, plastic coatings, phosphate fertilizer manufacturers, and other facilities that generate toxic emissions.[48]

Major amendments to the 1970 CAA extension came in 1977 and 1990.[49] The 1977 Amendments required PSD standards of areas meeting air quality

---

generated 40% of CO, two-thirds of SO_2, and 22% of NO_x nationally in the United States. In the George W. Bush Administration, there was a race to build more coal-fired power plants. While this advancement was halted by the environmental movement and rules from the Obama Administration, the other reason they are falling out of favor is the vast development of natural gas brought about by hydraulic fracturing that undercuts the cost of coal. The Trump Administration weakened rules put in place during the Obama Administration that would have reduced wastewater from coal-fired powerplants. The Biden Administration has acted to reintroduce the power plant wastewater rule.

See David. B. Ryan, *What Do Scrubbers Do in Smoke Stacks?*, Sciencing, Nov. 22, 2019, https://sciencing.com/do-scrubbers-do-smoke-stacks-5004709.html. *See also* Environmental Integrity Project, Dirty Kilowatts (July 2007), http://environmentalintegrity.org/pdf/publications/Dirty_Kilowatts_2007.pdf; Ellie Kaufman, *EPA Rolls Back Obama-Era Plan Limiting Coal-Fired Power Plant Emissions*, CNN (2019), https://www.cnn.com/2019/06/19/politics/epa-rolls-back-obama-coal-emissions/index.html; Matthew Brown & Travis Loller, *Trump Administration Finalizes Coal Plant Pollution Rollback*, AP News, Aug. 31, 2020, https://apnews.com/article/mt-state-wire-technology-business-science-wy-state-wire-7dff4afe289890f99e783aa26e4234fb; Dino Grandoni, *Biden Administration to Curb Toxic Wastewater from Coal Plants with New Rule*, Wash. Post., July 26, 2021, https://www.washingtonpost.com/climate-environment/2021/07/26/biden-administration-curb-toxic-wastewater-coal-plants-with-new-rule/

44. Casey Roberts, New York v. EPA: *State Response to a Federal Regulatory Rollback*, 33 Ecology L.Q. 613-52 (2006).
45. Brian H. Potts, *The U.S. Supreme Court's New Dukedom: The Hour and Year, or a Proposal Quieter Near*, 33 Ecology L.Q. 517-43 (2006).
46. Emblematic of all EPA regulatory actions, NSPS sounds as though the process is based on objective science, but that is hardly the case. The process is extremely political in determining best technologies that should be imposed on an industry and the upper limits a new stationary source should be allowed to produce. Making such determinations is as political as it is scientific. Hilda A. Akopyan, *The EPA's Threat to New Source Performance Standards*, Def. Litig. Insider, Feb. 19, 2019, https://www.defenselitigationinsider.com/2019/02/19/the-epas-threat-to-the-new-source-performance-standards/.
47. Office of Envtl., Health, Safety & Security, U.S. Dep't of Energy, *National Emissions Standards for Hazardous Air Pollutants (NESHAP) Compliance Monitoring* (Jan. 15, 2020), https://www.energy.gov/ehss/downloads/national-emission-standards-hazardous-air-pollutants-neshap-compliance-monitoring.
48. EPA maintains a list of HAPs or air toxics known to cause cancer or other ill health effects that form the basis for this regulation. U.S. EPA, *National Emissions Standards for Hazardous Air Pollutants*, https://www.epa.gov/stationary-sources-air-pollution/national-emission-standards-hazardous-air-pollutants-neshap-9 (last updated Feb. 22, 2021).
49. Chris Zajchowski et al., *"Now Is Not the Time to Take a Breather": United States Federal Land Management Agency Professionals' Perceptions at the 40th Anniversary of the Clean Air Act Amendments of 1977*,

standards and created new provisions for non-attainment areas that meet or violate ambient air quality standards for the criteria pollutants designated under NAAQS.[50] Some areas can be attainment for one criteria pollutant and a non-attainment area for others. Areas in non-attainment must develop a plan to come into compliance or possibly risk the loss of federal funding. These were put in place as the states had not achieved national goals for reducing auto emissions and put sufficient rules in place to reduce the deterioration of air quality occurring in various sections of the country.[51]

The 1990 Amendments were much broader than any additions to the CAA since the 1970 extension.[52] New measures focused on renewing rules on operating permits for stationary sources, controlling acid rain from coal-fired power plants, creating a cap-and-trade system for SO_2, introducing citizen lawsuits into the realm of air pollution, and phasing out many ozone-depleting chemicals. The production of ozone-destroying chemicals that caused the most immediate harm, such as CFCs, halons, and methyl chloroform were banned by the mid-1990s.[53] Certain diagnostic tools on domestic vehicles were created leading to on-board diagnostics requirements in new cars, such as the dreaded "check engine light."[54]

The SO_2 program, also known as the Acid Rain Program, set total emissions of SO_2 at half the level of the power section in 1980.[55] This program creates a cap-and-trade program in air pollution in the United States.[56] All regulated sources are given allowances to pollute alongside regionwide caps.[57] If stationary sources go over their allowances, they are automatically penal-

32 Soc'y & Nat. Resources 1003-20 (2019).

50. Most metro areas in the United States violate standards for eight-hour ozone. Other offenders tend to be PM and in a few cases SO_2. The reality is that measuring ambient air quality is a guess of how much air pollution is in the area and there are arguably many areas of the country that if subjected to greater scrutiny, would likely be in non-attainment. EPA maintains the Air Quality System (AQS) that contains data collected on air quality from various sources across the country. *See Criteria Pollutants*, *supra* note 19; U.S. EPA, *Air Quality System (AQS)*, https://www.epa.gov/aqs (last updated March 17, 2022).

51. U.S. EPA, *SIP Status Reports*, https://www.epa.gov/air-quality-implementation-plans/sip-status-reports (last updated March 21, 2021).

52. U.S. EPA, THE CLEAN AIR ACT: Highlights of the 1990 Amendments (2015), https://www.epa.gov/sites/production/files/2015-11/documents/the_clean_air_act_-_highlights_of_the_1990_amendments.pdf.

53. U.S. EPA, Ban on Aerosols Containing CFCs and HCFCs Under the Clean Air Act (1993), https://www.epa.gov/sites/production/files/2014-04/documents/pr93-4.pdf.

54. U.S. EPA, Clean Air Act 101 Module 2 Mobile Source Controls/Strategies (2010), https://archive.epa.gov/apti/video/web/pdf/cleanair101module2mobilesourcesfinal_otaq_ogc_8-26-10.pdf.

55. U.S. EPA, *Acid Raid Program Results*, https://www.epa.gov/acidrain/acid-rain-program-results (last updated March 13, 2022).

56. Press Release, U.S. EPA, EPA Expands Open-Market Trading of Acid Rain Credits (March 20, 1995), https://archive.epa.gov/epa/aboutepa/epa-expands-open-market-trading-acid-rain-credits.html.

57. Lauraine G. Chestnut & David M. Mills, *A Fresh Look at the Benefits and Costs of the U.S. Acid Rain Program*, 77 J. Envtl. Mgmt. 252-66 (2005).

ized. Companies are given regulatory flexibility to decide how to lower their emissions below their allowances (cap) and then they can sell the excess on the market to other companies that need to purchase them to avoid penalties or bank them for the future.[58] This change created a marketplace for buying and selling pollution credits.[59]

Citizens can bring suit against an individual, company, or the government for violating a statute, sue a governmental body for failing to perform a non-discretionary duty, such as bringing suit against EPA for failing to implement provisions of the CAA, and it allows plaintiff's attorneys to recover fees and litigation costs.[60] This provision allowed the proliferation of citizen suits by nongovernmental organizations, environmental law clinics, and plaintiff's attorneys.[61] These suits often require them to find individuals with standing, which can be difficult as three conditions must be met: (1) the plaintiff must have suffered an injury-in-fact; (2) the injury and the action must be reasonably traceable to the defendant; and (3) it must be likely that the injury will be redressed by a favorable court decision.[62]

EPA maintains a compliance monitoring strategy for the CAA to focus enforcement resources.[63] The first is the Acid Rain Inspection and Trading

58. Denny A. Ellerman & Juan-Pablo Montero, *The Efficiency and Robustness of Allowing Banking in the U.S. Acid Rain Program*, 28 ENERGY J. 47-71 (2007).
59. U.S. EPA, *Market-Based Mechanisms*, https://www.epa.gov/airmarkets/market-based-mechanisms (updated June 1, 2021). Other cap-and-trade programs exist in the United States to reduce other sources of pollution, primarily from the power sector. For example, the Regional Greenhouse Gas Initiative (RGGI) is a compact between northern states to create a cap-and-trade system for CO_2 in the power sector. *See* RGGI, *The Regional Greenhouse Gas Initiative*, https://www.rggi.org/program-overview-and-design/elements (last visited Apr. 6, 2022). Another example was the NO_x cap-and-trade program in existence from 2003-2008 and replaced in 2009 with the Clean Air Interstate Rule to reduce PM and ozone in 28 eastern states. *See* U.S. EPA, *Clean Air Interstate Rule*, https://archive.epa.gov/airmarkets/programs/cair/web/html/index.html (Feb. 21, 2016).
60. Joshua Frank et al., *Clean Air Act Citizen Suits: Defense and Litigation Strategies*, STRAFFORD CLE WEBINAR (July 18, 2017), http://media.straffordpub.com/products/clean-air-act-citizen-suits-defense-and-litigation-strategies-2017-07-18/presentation.pdf.
61. Anuradha Sivaram, *Why Citizen Suits Against States Would Ensure the Legitimacy of Cooperative Federalism Under the Clean Air Act*, 40 ECOLOGY L.Q. 443-82 (2013).
62. In the authors' personal experience living near one of the country's largest petrochemical ports, a petroleum coke power plant was proposed in 2008. The state environmental regulator, Texas Commission on Environmental Quality (TCEQ), approved the air permit—state agencies are often functionally in control of this process. We participated in a grass-roots movement that started with lawsuits by the Environmental Defense Fund, Environmental Integrity Project, and the Sierra Club, in conjunction with local groups organized as the Clean Economy Coalition to challenge the air permit in court. This corresponded with the Obama-era movement to begin greatly restricting emissions at coal-fired power plants and part of Public Citizen's campaign to end coal-fired power plants. In a rare step, the permit was held up for years and the company decided not to build the plant. The air permit was reversed because the judge determined the TCEQ did not show that Las Brisas would meet MACT standards for certain air toxins prior to issuing the permit. Arguably, many states issue such permits in a proforma manner or without seriously questioning the data presented by the applicant.
63. Robert J. Jackson Jr. & David Rosenberg, *A New Model of Administrative Enforcement*, 93 VA. L. REV. 1983-2015 (2007).

Program, meant to reduce SO_2 and NO_x. The second is the Applicability Determination Index that contains a database of regulatory interpretations of EPA as to whether owners or operators of a point source must be regulated by a particular rule or if their monitoring and/or recordkeeping requirements (alternative monitoring) can be different than prevailing standards.[64] The third area focuses on asbestos demolition and renovation to make sure that renovation and demolition sites comply with NESHAP.[65] The fourth area is the Mobile Source Program that regulates emissions standards for motor vehicles and equipment, including fuel standards for domestic and imported fuel.[66] The fifth area is the creation of standards for HAPs under NESHAP and maximum achievable control technology (MACT) standards to reduce toxic emissions.[67] The sixth focuses on NSR/PSD through permitting requirements to achieve BACT or lowest achievable emission rate (LAER) standards that will not violate NAAQS.[68] The seventh area of compliance monitoring centers on accidental releases that requires owners and operators of facilities producing hazardous substances to identify hazards, design and maintain safe facilities, and minimize the consequences of accidental releases.[69] The eighth area focuses on NSPS for new stationary sources.[70] The ninth area focuses on CFCs and ozone-depleting substances through phaseout of the production and import of certain substances, requirements for the service and disposal of stationary refrigeration and air conditioning, servicing of motor vehicle air conditioning, and proper labeling of products that contain ozone-depleting substances. EPA also regulates and certifies residential wood heaters, because they collectively produce a significant amount of PM in the United States.[71]

64. U.S. EPA, *Resources and Guidance Documents for Compliance Assistance*, https://www.epa.gov/compliance/resources-and-guidance-documents-compliance-assistance (last updated Jan. 18, 2022).
65. U.S. EPA, *Overview of the Asbestos NESHAP*, https://www.epa.gov/asbestos/overview-asbestos-national-emission-standards-hazardous-air-pollutants-neshap (last updated Feb. 9, 2022).
66. U.S. EPA, *Mobile Source Compliance Monitoring Program* (2020), https://www.epa.gov/compliance/mobile-sources-compliance-monitoring-program (last updated Nov. 30, 2021).
67. West Virginia Dep't of Envtl. Protection, *MACT NESHAP Standards*, https://dep.wv.gov/daq/Air%20Toxics/Pages/MACTNESHAPStandards.aspx (last visited Apr. 6, 2022).
68. U.S. EPA, *RACT/BACT/LAER Clearinghouse (RBLC) Basic Information* (2020), https://www.epa.gov/catc/ractbactlaer-clearinghouse-rblc-basic-information (last updated Nov. 2, 2021).
69. U.S. Government Accountability Office, Accidental Release Prevention Requirements (1996), https://www.gao.gov/assets/200/197749.pdf.
70. Wisconsin Dep't of Nat. Resources, Air Program Fact Sheet (2019), https://dnr.wi.gov/files/PDF/pubs/am/AM513.pdf.
71. U.S. EPA, *Clean Air Act (CAA) Compliance Monitoring*, https://www.epa.gov/compliance/clean-air-act-caa-compliance-monitoring (last updated July 13, 2021).

Criminal violations of the CAA are negligent or knowing violations.[72] Negligent violations involve undertaking actions without reasonable care that violate any of the provisions of the CAA.[73] Knowing violations are intentional actions that demonstrate willful intent to violate any provision of the CAA. [74] Investigators focus on criminal enforcement when evidence of a crime suggests that a particular individual, company, or other organization violated the CAA in such a manner. The CAA contains provisions for punishing criminal offenses of clean air laws. We list these in Table 2. We include the violation, statute, and the maximum penalties for negligent actions and maximum penalties for knowing actions in columns 1-4, respectively.[75] The first criminal provision is for owners and/or operators of a stationary source that constructs or modifies an existing source that does not meet NESHAP standards. The second is violation of NESHAP standards for asbestos during demolition and removal. Anyone that disturbs at least 260 linear feet on pipes, 160 square feet on other facility components, or 35 cubic feet off facility components of asbestos is required to follow NESHAP workplace standards for demolition and remediation of asbestos containing materials, as well as disposal of said materials.

Violating stratospheric ozone protection provisions refers to the importation, production, or disposal of materials containing CFCs or other products containing ozone-depleting substances. In practice, this often deals with refrigerants or industrial or consumer devices containing refrigerants. Making false statements to EPA investigators or on official documents is punishable under the CAA. Tampering or rendering inaccurate any monitoring device or method is a criminal offense under the CAA as is failing to notify officials or report a crime, or knowing/negligent actions that endanger another person by causing HAPs to be released into the ambient air and put another person in immediate danger of death or serious bodily injury. During a period of federally assumed enforcement, violating a SIP is a criminal offense, as is remaining in violation after a 30-day notice of the violation. Operating a new stationary source of pollution in violation of NSPS can be charged as a criminal offense, as is violating provisions of an operating permit or violating an emergency order issued by EPA.

72. U.S. DOJ, *Environmental Crimes Section*, https://www.justice.gov/enrd/environmental-crimes-section (updated July 2, 2021).
73. Amanda Burns et al., *Environmental Crimes*, 50 Am. Crim. L. Rev. 857-952 (2013).
74. U.S. EPA, *Basic Information on Enforcement*, https://www.epa.gov/enforcement/basic-information-enforcement (updated Feb. 22, 2022).
75. For table data, see U.S. EPA, *Criminal Provisions of the Clean Air Act*, https://www.epa.gov/enforcement/criminal-provisions-clean-air-act (updated March 30, 2022).

Table 2. Criminal Provisions of the CAA

Violation	Statute	Negligent Penalty Max	Knowing Penalty Max
NESHAP	42 U.S.C. 7413(1)		5 years and/or fines
Asbestos NESHAP	42 U.S.C. 7413(1)		5 years and/or fines
Violating Stratospheric Ozone Protections	42 U.S.C. 7413(1)		5 years and/or fines
False Statements	42 U.S.C. 7413(1)		2 years and/or fines
Tampering with a Monitoring Device	42 U.S.C. 7413(1)		2 years and/or fines
Failure to Notify or Report	42 U.S.C. 7413(1)		2 years and/or fines
Knowing or Negligent Endangerment	42 U.S.C. 7413(c)(4) & (5) 42 U.S.C. 7412(b)(1)	1 year	15 years and/or fines
Violating SIP	42 U.S.C. 7413(c)(1)		5 years and/or fines
Violating NSPS	42 U.S.C. 7413(c)(1)		5 years and/or fines
Violating Operating Permits	42 U.S.C. 7413(c)(1) 42 U.S.C. 7661(1)-(2) 42 U.S.C. 7661a(a)		5 years and/or fines
Violating an Emergency Order	42 U.S.C. 7413(c)(1)		5 years and/or fines

Most of these criminal provisions at their core focus on permitting issues at regulated facilities, including ensuring monitoring equipment is properly working, ensuring that responsible parties provide timely and accurate reporting to stay in compliance with the law, as well as abiding by EPA orders and the mandate to report any known violations in a timely manner and not knowingly endanger workers or bystanders in their operations. Other provisions are more historical. Provisions for stratosphere O_3 center on the need to phase out CFCs and other refrigerants and regulate applications that use ozone-depleting chemicals today. These provisions exist because of the ubiquitous nature of CFCs in a variety of applications up to the 1980s. The same is the case for asbestos rules, as the material was applied in so many residential, commercial, and industrial applications. EPA realized there would be negligent and willful violations of the CAA when asbestos-containing materials in ceilings, floors, and pipes needed to be removed. This problem escalated in the 1990s and early 2000s as renovations to old buildings occurred and public health was negatively impacted.[76]

In the section below, we analyze all 377 prosecutions that occurred under the CAA stemming from EPA investigations from 1983-2019. We discuss how EPA has investigated a series of criminal violations and how those violations are prosecuted. We will be able to examine their compliance monitoring strategy in the context of developing an understanding of the themes in the CAA since 1983, as well as how criminal provisions of the CAA are applied across time and space.

II. Themes in Clean Air Act Prosecutions

Figure 2 provides context to the total number of CAA cases investigated by EPA that have been criminally prosecuted since 1983. These are shown in the figure by fiscal year, but that alone does not always represent when they were initiated or the time it took to investigate, bring charges, prosecute, and sentence offenders. It does give an idea of how many are settled each year. There were very few criminal prosecutions prior to 1983, so looking at this figure gives one a fairly solid idea of how the process of investigating and prosecuting these crimes grows with institutionalization.[77] During the 1980s, we find only 11 cases adjudicated under the CAA. In the 1990s, this grows to 67 prosecutions. Then, in the first nine years of the new century, we see 116, and from 2010-present we code 183 settled prosecutions. Altogether prosecutions start to grow in the Clinton era and drop in the Bush era after 9/11, tracking up and down until Barack Obama is elected to office.

This trend line reflects the growing sophistication of the criminal enforcement apparatus through Ronald Reagan, George H.W. Bush, and William Clinton. Prosecutions start to rise under George W. Bush but go through peaks and valleys. Prosecution begin to rise during Obama's presidency, even after the 2009 financial crisis, but start to dip again after 2014 and plateauing below the Bush numbers of the mid-2000s. During the Trump Administration, the total number fell rapidly from 21 in FY 2017 (through October of that year) to 11 in 2018, but this had risen to 10 by January 1, 2019.

We start to look at the total number of prosecutions across space, by exploring total prosecutions settled in every U.S. state and territory since 1983 in Figure 3. A total of 55 prosecutions were settled in New York, making this the high point for total prosecutions in the state. As we progress with

76. Jacques Dunnigan, *Linking Chrysotile Asbestos With Mesothelioma*, 14 Am. J. Indus. Med. 205-09 (1988).

77. *See* Celia B. Campbell-Mohn, Sustainable Environmental Law (West Publishing Co. 1993).

Figure 2. Total Annual CAA Criminal Prosecutions Adjudicated Since 1983

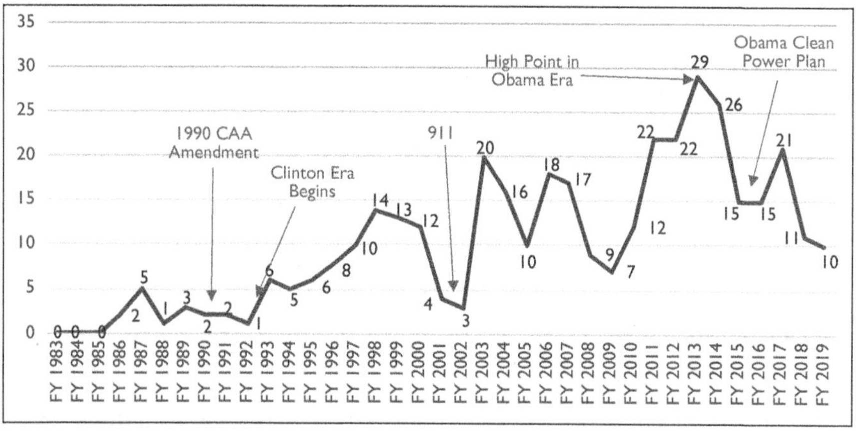

the analysis below it will become apparent that this number reflects a serious interest in asbestos-related prosecutions in the state in the 1990s and early 2000s. A total of 22 prosecutions were settled in Florida; 25 in Ohio; 27 in Pennsylvania; 27 in Texas; 18 in California and Missouri; and 21 in Michigan. We found no cases settled in Arkansas, Mississippi, New Hampshire, South Dakota, or Wyoming. Two cases were settled in Washington, D.C. and Puerto Rico. Only one case was settled in Delaware, Massachusetts, Maine, North Dakota, New Mexico, and Vermont, respectively during this time period. Examining these figures shows that prosecutions were concentrated in only 10 states that registered double-digit numbers since 1983. To put it another way, 62% of prosecutions occurred in 10 states and 57% of prosecutions occurred in the 8 highest totaling states listed above.

To understand how the CAA was used in criminal investigations and prosecutions, it is important to examine how it was used in conjunction with a variety of other federal environmental status to charge and prosecute defendants. For the CAA, the most common companion charging statutes were the CWA (8 prosecutions), TSCA (8 prosecutions), RCRA (4 prosecutions), CERCLA (14 prosecutions), and one case using FIFRA plus the CAA. Otherwise, a few prosecutions were undertaken in conjunction with the Hazardous Materials Transportation Act (HMTA), or state environmental laws, but most CAA criminal prosecutions were stand-alone or in conjunction with other Title 18 violations.[78] A case example is against Mlinton Delwyn

78. 9 U.S.C. §5101. Regulates the transportation of hazardous waste and other materials in intrastate, interstate, and foreign commerce under the U.S. Department of Transportation (DOJ). The Act

Figure 3. Total CAA Criminal Prosecutions by U.S. State and Territory Since 1983

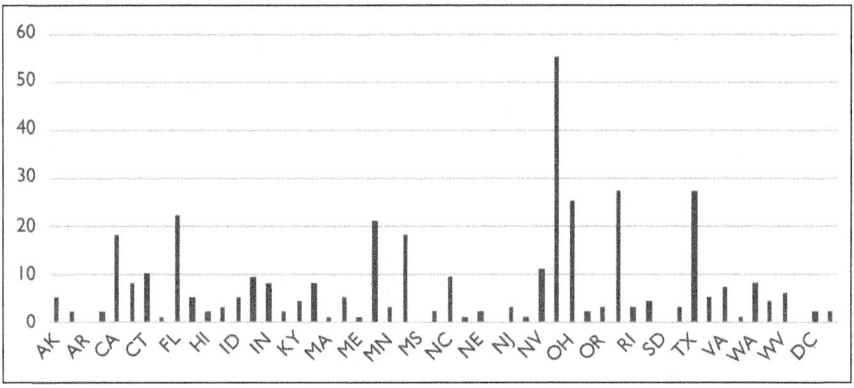

Smith and co-defendant Clinton James Matthews. Both defendants worked at Express Auto Sales in Durham, North Carolina.[79] Both cheated emissions testing devices, by clean scanning and using a vehicle manufactured between 1996-1999 that would not generate an identification number. The defendants conspired to pass at least 917 vehicles via false inspection for profit.[80] Another example was the prosecution of George Webber, along with co-defendants Michael Phelps Jr. and Stephen Jones for illegally removing asbestos from the basement of a home in East Liverpool, Ohio. They obtained asbestos covered pipes from a landfill and removed the asbestos with the intent to sell the pipes for scrap.[81]

Case examples of Howard Norman Angell, Daniel Bell, and Motiva Corporation illustrate CAA prosecutions that also relied on the CWA to charge

---

was passed in response to problems with the majority of hazardous waste being shipped via truck throughout the United States and increases in accidents and need for special disposal sites for this material.

79. Related prosecutions at the facility also occurred. *See* News Release, U.S. DOJ, Emissions Inspector Sentenced for Falsely Passing Vehicle Inspections (Feb. 20, 2013), https://www.justice.gov/usao-ednc/pr/emissions-inspector-sentenced-falsely-passing-vehicle-inspections.

80. E.D. N.C. 5:12-CR-193-1. The investigation was conducted by the United States EPA, Criminal Investigation Division, North Carolina State Bureau of Investigations, and the North Carolina Division of Motor Vehicles, License and Theft Bureau. The defendants were charged with conspiracy and under the CAA for cheating emissions testing. The defendants were each sentenced to 36 months of probation. Matthews was ordered to pay a fine of $1,300.

81. United States v. Webber, No. 4:09-CR-152 (N.D. Ohio). Webber was sentenced to 24 months of probation, the first 4 months to be served as home confinement, and was ordered to pay restitution in the amount of $9,515 to the company that paid for the asbestos cleanup. Jones was sentenced to 24 months of probation, the first 6 months to be served as home confinement, and ordered to pay $9,515 in restitution to the company that paid for the cleanup at the residence. Phelps was sentenced to 24 months of probation, the first 6 months to be served as home confinement, and ordered to pay restitution in the amount of $9,515 to the company that paid for the cleanup.

and prosecute defendants.[82] Angell illegally removed three underground storage tanks at private residences in Washington State.[83] He was not registered by the state to perform such removals. In the process, about 13,000 gallons of gasoline and/or gasoline-contaminated water discharged into Henderson Bay. He also illegally removed about 14,000 square feet from a building in the city of Seattle.[84] Bell was the environmental manager for Koppers Industries, Koppers Woodward Coke Plant in Dolomite, Alabama.[85] He instructed employees to tamper with monitoring devices and he falsified discharge monitoring reports.[86] A storage tank at the Motiva Corporation's facility in Delaware ruptured.[87] The tank discharged sulfuric acid into a nearby stream killing fish and marine life and eight workers were injured and one went missing after the acid caught fire.[88]

The use of TSCA alongside the CAA can be illustrated with the prosecutions of Dennis Marchuk, Ambers Scott Rind, and IEMC Environmental Group.[89] Marchuk was president of Strathaven Realty in Marcus Hook, Pennsylvania. He and his partner Jeanne Alvarez were in a limited part-

82. No. S:99-00065 (S.D. W. Va.). Another example is the prosecution of James Bragg, who owned and operated the Oakes Subdivisions Sewage Treatment Plant in Grandview, West Virginia. He did not operate the plant between spring 1996 and fall 1998 and failed to file appropriate DMRs during that time period and also violated his permit. Bragg was sentenced to six months' incarceration followed by six months' home confinement and 12 months of probation for violating both the CWA and the CAA. It is not clear in the case summary what aspect of the CAA was violated.

83. Julie McCormick, *Gig Harbor: Man Pleads Guilty for Contaminating Bay*, Kitsap Sun, Dec. 13, 1997, https://products.kitsapsun.com/archive/1997/12-13/0021_gig_harbor__man_pleads_guilty_to_.html.

84. United States v. Angell, No. 97-CR-453 (Dec. 10, 1997) For the illegal removal of asbestos he was charged under the CAA and the CWA for the illegal discharge. He was also charged under state law for performing work as an unregistered contractor. Angell was sentenced to 24 months' incarceration and 36 months of supervised release for the federal violations. Angell was sentenced to three months' incarceration, six months of probation, and ordered to pay $5,800 in restitution for the state violations.

85. News Release, U.S. EPA, Koppers Industries Inc., Sentenced to Pay $3 Million, Serve Probation (Jan. 8, 2003), https://archive.epa.gov/epapages/newsroom_archive/newsreleases/6f5371ef045320708525704b0064c2b1.html.

86. United States v. Koppers, No. CR-02-S-0300-S (N.D. Ala. Dec. 13, 2002). Bell was charged with making false statements under the CAA and Koppers was charged as a co-defendant under the CWA for illegal discharge and the CAA. Bell was sentenced to 36 months of probation, ordered to pay a $100 special assessment fee, and ordered to pay a $2,000 federal fine. The company was sentenced to 36 months' probation, ordered to pay a special assessment fee of $1,200, restitution of $900,000, and a fine in the amount of $2.1 million.

87. Josh Cable, *$23.7 Million Motiva Settlement Brings "Tragic Chapter" to Close*, EHS Today, Oct. 27, 2005, https://www.ehstoday.com/archive/article/21908105/237-million-motiva-settlement-brings-tragic-chapter-to-close

88. United States v. Motiva Corp., No. 05-CR-021-SLR (D. Del. Mar. 17, 2005). Motiva was charged with the illegal discharges into the water under the CWA and the other leak into the air under the CAA. Motiva pled guilty was sentenced to 36 months of probation, ordered to pay a $525 special assessment fee, and a $10 million federal fine.

89. News Release, U.S. EPA, Three West Virginia Plead Guilty to Asbestos Crimes (Nov. 27, 2002), https://archive.epa.gov/epapages/newsroom_archive/newsreleases/c667c3ea843dc0ab85257052004f416f.html.

nership (Marcus Hook Business & Commerce Center Ltd.) that contracted with Robert Tann and Michael Kelly of K&T Enterprises to remove friable asbestos materials from buildings owned by the company.[90] They removed and excavated asbestos without a permit releasing it into the ambient air and failed to notify the government of the release.[91] Rind removed asbestos from a building in Martinsburg, West Virginia, and illegally dumped it on a nearby farm.[92] IEMC Environmental Group was contracted to remove asbestos from the Hess department store at the Fayette Mall in Lexington, Kentucky.[93] They illegally removed the material, contaminating the property.[94]

RCRA was used as a co-charging statute against defendants in conjunction with the CAA in four prosecutions. These cases typically involve illegal storage, transport, or disposal of hazardous substances alongside prosecutions for illegal air emissions. Case examples include: Spectro Alloys; Gerald Cohen; and Mark Kamholz. Spectro Alloys operated a secondary aluminum processing facility in Rosemount, Minnesota, where it melts down scrap metal into aluminum alloys.[95] The company submitted false reports to EPA and the Minnesota Pollution Control Agency that it complied with its air permit. It also failed to report its own testing indicating it was creating

---

90. Lee Linder, *Four Charged With Environmental Violations in Delaware County Development*, AP News (1991), https://apnews.com/article/3538f42230f557643ae23466adc92445.
91. United States v. Marchuk, No. 91-000669 (E.D. Pa. Dec. 15, 1991). The defendants were charged with conspiracy, failure to notify under CERCLA, illegal storage and disposal under TSCA, and under the CAA for the asbestos violations. Marchuk was sentenced to 24 months' incarceration, 36 months' supervised probation, and fined $25,000. Alvarez was sentenced to 36 months' supervised probation and 100 hours of community service. Kelly was sentenced to 12 months of probation, 120 hours of community service, and fined $3,000. Tann was sentenced to 24 months of probation and 150 hours of community service.
92. United States v. Rind, No. CR:04-JUN-2002 (N.D. W. Va. June 4, 2003). Rind was prosecuted for the illegal removal and disposal of the asbestos under the CAA and TSCA, and he made false statements to investigators. He was sentenced to 36 months of probation, a $5,000 fine, and ordered to pay $25 in fees.
93. News Release, U.S. EPA, PA Kentucky Environmental and Management Companies Sentenced for Illegal Asbestos Abatement (Oct. 20, 1997) https://archive.epa.gov/epapages/newsroom_archive/newsreleases/0900a9f8e6f8aa0385256536005335e1.html
94. No. 96-25-S (E.D. Ky.). The company and five co-defendants were charged with the illegal abatement. IEMC Environmental Group was sentenced to 60 months of probation and to pay a $200 fine. IES Lead Paint was sentenced to 60 months of probation and a $200 fine. Barri Shurelds was sentenced to 51 months' incarceration, 36 months of probation, and a $50 fine. Jose Eusebio was sentenced to 6 months' incarceration, 12 months of probation, and a fine of $50. Samuel Robinson was sentenced to 10 months' incarceration, 24 months of probation, and a $50 fine. Sean Shurelds was sentenced to 24 months of probation and ordered to pay a fine of $50.
95. *Spectro Alloys Pleads Guilty*, Recycling Today, June 12, 2012, https://www.recyclingtoday.com/article/spector-alloys-doj-fine-statement/.

excessive dioxins and furans.[96] Cohen owned Lawrence Aviation,[97] and he was sentenced for illegal storage of hazardous waste and operation of diesel engines without a permit at his facility.[98] The Tonawanda Coke Corporation release coke over gas containing benzene through an unreported pressure relief valve and did not use permit-required pollution control devices.[99] Prior to an EPA inspection of the facility in 2009, Kamholz, the company's environmental control manager, instructed an employee to conceal the pressure release valve. The company also stored, treated, and disposed of hazardous waste without a permit.[100]

CERCLA was the most prevalent co-charging statute at 14 prosecutions completed since 1983. CERCLA cases under the CAA center on failure to notify provisions for the release of a hazardous substance. This was typically paired with an illegal asbestos removal/disposal operation. Case example prosecutions illustrating this pattern include: Kenneth Baez-Alers; Nicholas LaPenta; and Lester Mancuso.[101] Baez-Alers was a project manager for AIREKO Construction that contaminated a building in Puerto Rico when illegally abating asbestos-containing materials.[102] LaPenta was the owner of Antonio's Ristorante. He caused asbestos to be removed from the building

96. No. 12-110 (JRT) (D. Minn.). The company was charged with making false statements. The company was sentenced to 24 months of probation and a criminal fine of $500,000. Spectro must also retain a full-time environmental health and safety manager, report all emissions testing, and maintain procedures for accurate reporting. In a parallel civil case, the company agreed to install pollution control equipment and a civil penalty of $600,000.

97. The company and Lawrence Cohen were later ordered to pay significant penalties to remediate what became a Superfund site. *See* Carl MacGowan, *Lawrence Aviation, Owner Ordered to Pay $48.1 Million for Cleanup*, Newsday, Apr. 15, 2019, https://www.newsday.com/long-island/suffolk/lawrence-aviation-port-jefferson-station-superfund-1.29843630.

98. United States v. Cohen, No.2:06-CR-0596 (E.D.N.Y. Sept. 6, 2006). Cohen was sentenced to 12 months and a day of incarceration, 36 months of probation, and ordered to pay restitution totaling $105,816.

99. News Release, U.S. DOJ, Court of Appeals Affirms Tonawanda Coke Convictions (Jan. 11, 2016), https://www.justice.gov/usao-wdny/pr/court-appeals-affirms-tonawanda-coke-convictions.

100. United States v. Tonawanda Coke Corp. & Mark L. Kamholz, No. 10-CR-219-S (W.D.N.Y. Mar. 28, 2013). The defendants were charged under the CAA for the unpermitted releases and under RCRA for the illegal storage, transport, and storage of hazardous wastes without a permit. Kamholz was charged with obstruction for trying to conceal the illegal relief valve and hinder the investigation. Kamholz was sentenced to 12 months and a day of incarceration, 12 months of probation, 100 hours of community service, and ordered to pay a $20,000 fine. Tonawanda Coke Corporation was sentenced to 60 months of probation, ordered to pay $12.2 million in community service payments, and ordered to pay a fine of $12.5 million.

101. News Release, U.S. DOJ, AIREKO Construction Company Indicted for Violations of the Clean Air Act (July 13, 2015), https://www.justice.gov/usao-pr/pr/aireko-construction-company-indicted-violations-clean-air-act.

102. United States v. Baez-Alers, No. 13-871 (DRD) (D.P.R. Dec. 11, 2013). Baez-Alers was sentenced to serve 12 months of probation. The case centered on CAA violations for the asbestos and failure to notify under CERCLA. In a related case AIREKO Construction Company was sentenced to pay a $1.5 million fine and complete a three-year term of probation. The company will pay $172,020 to fund a baseline medical examination and follow-up tests for victims exposed to asbestos fibers.

and did not notify government officials of the illegal abatement. He also made false statements to investigators about the illegal removal.[103] Lester, Paul, Ronald, and Steve Mancuso were prosecuted for operating an asbestos removal business.[104] Their crimes included: improper removal of asbestos; illegal disposal; and manufacturing fraudulent documents. The defendants were charged with conspiracy, violations under the CAA for the illegal removal of asbestos and failure to notify under CERCLA.[105]

David Grummer was prosecuted in California for violating the CAA and FIFRA.[106] Grummer managed an environmental services company that contracted with cities in San Diego County to manage household hazardous waste collection facilities. He took chemicals and pesticides to sell online for profit and shipped them via FedEx, while not properly labeling the packages as hazardous materials.[107] Additionally, federal officials found child pornography on Grummer's computer while executing a search warrant, and he was charged with the unlawful use of a pesticide under FIFRA; the sale of a Class I ozone-depleting substance to an uncertified individual under the CAA; a hazardous materials violation for transporting hazardous waste via FedEx without a proper declaration; and later receipt and possession of child pornography.

Taking all of the prosecutions under the CAA since 1983, we are now able to organize these cases into a meaningful typology. We examined each prosecution and arranged them by theme, based on what we feel is the central issue in the prosecution (see Figure 4). In total we are able to organize 375 prosecutions based on this categorization.[108] Our analysis of all crimes that were investigated by EPA, sent for prosecution, and settled shows that the

---

103. United States v. LaPenta, No. 00-CR-67 (N.D.N.Y.). The defendant was charged under CERCLA with failure to notify, false statements, and the asbestos release under the CAA. LaPenta paid a $5,000 fine and his co-defendant, NPLA Corporation, was fined $20,000.

104. Press Release, U.S. DOJ, Three Upstate New York Men Sentenced to Prison for Environmental Crimes (June 9, 2010), https://www.justice.gov/opa/pr/three-upstate-new-york-men-sentenced-prison-environmental-crimes.

105. United States v. Mancuso, No. 08-CR-00611 (N.D.N.Y. Nov. 9, 2008). Lester Mancuso was sentenced to 36 months incarceration and 36 months of probation. Steven Mancuso was sentenced to 44 months' incarceration and 36 months of probation. Paul Mancuso was sentenced to 78 months' incarceration, 36 months of probation, and ordered to pay restitution to EPA in the amount of $17,972.68, as well as pay a $20,000 federal fine. Ronald Mancuso was sentenced to 36 months of probation.

106. United States v. Grummer, No. 08CR4402-DMS (S.D. Cal. Apr. 24, 2008). On Feb. 23, 2009, Grummer was sentenced to 18 months' incarceration, 36 months of probation, a $3,000 fine, and ordered to pay $92,410 in restitution on the environmental charges. He was later convicted and sentenced on the child pornography charges.

107. *Oceanside Man to Serve 24 Years in Child Porn Case*, CBS8.COM, Aug. 23, 2010, https://www.cbs8.com/article/news/oceanside-man-to-serve-24-years-in-child-porn-case/509-e36bc3a6-1d23-4159-a772-1debe2c55f64.

108. United States v. Chavez, No. 088-362 (D. Cal. Apr. 25, 1988) and United States v. Janiak, No. 93 CR-58 (EBB) (D. Conn. Apr. 14, 1993). In two against principal defendants Paul Chavez and Thomas

Figure 4. Major Themes in CAA Criminal Prosecutions Since 1983

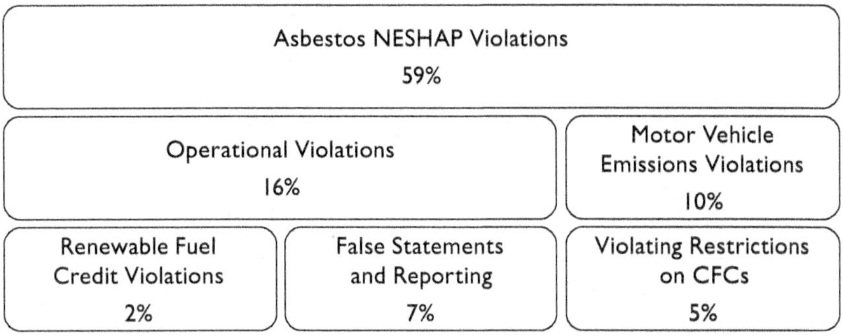

criminal prosecution of environmental crimes under the CAA focuses on the following six themes: (1) asbestos NESHAP violations; (2) operational violations; (3) motor vehicle emissions violations; (4) renewable fuel credit violations; (5) false statements and reporting; and (6) and violating restrictions on ozone-depleting substances. The numbers are rounded.

Asbestos was an almost ubiquitous material used in a variety of applications in the United States.[109] It was used for insulation in attics, pipes, furnaces, and walls, roofing and siding, textured paint, heat-resistant fabrics, and brakes and clutches in motor vehicles. EPA passed a final rule banning asbestos-containing materials in 1989 for new products containing asbestos.[110] EPA faced a difficult choice on deciding what should be done with a material present in almost all homes in the United States in some form, particularly those built in the 20th century. It chose to allow it to remain in situ and if disturbed it must be properly removed, remediated, and disposed of in a manner that protects occupants and workers and is properly permitted.[111] The Asbestos Hazard Emergency Response Act (AHERA) requires schools and government buildings to develop an asbestos management plan and inspect facilities for any asbestos-containing materials.[112] These actions created a significant market for asbestos abatement, as well as a large oppor-

Janiak it is not possible to discern the exact nature of the crime with the information provided in the database, which is why we have 375/377 cases represented.

109. Peter W.J. Bartrip, *History of Asbestos Related Disease*, 80 Postgraduate Med. J. 72-76 (2004).

110. U.S. EPA, Asbestos Manufacture, Importation, Processing, and Distribution in Commerce Prohibitions (1989), https://www.epa.gov/sites/production/files/documents/nps57f.pdf.

111. U.S. EPA, *Protect your Family from Exposures to Asbestos*, https://www.epa.gov/asbestos/protect-your-family-exposures-asbestos (updated March 28, 2022).

112. 15 U.S.C. §2651. U.S. EPA, *Asbestos Laws and Regulations*, https://www.epa.gov/asbestos/asbestos-laws-and-regulations (last updated Sept. 15, 2021).

tunity for criminal behavior, given the savings incurred through illegal abatement and disposal operations.

The CAA contains criminal provisions for punishing individuals and companies for illegal asbestos abatement. These provisions include companies that disturb any asbestos-containing material of at least 260 linear feet on pipes or 160 square feet or 35 cubic feet on other components in a facility. Criminal sanctions are present for companies or owners of companies that fail or cause employees to fail to abide by workplace standards or disposal standards when removing this hazardous material. Other provisions relevant to asbestos involve failure to notify provisions that can apply to individuals that do not properly inform governmental officials of asbestos removal and knowing/negligent endangerment clauses applied to releasing a hazardous substance in the ambient air and either negligently or knowingly putting another at risk of death or serious bodily injury.

We found that a majority of criminal prosecutions undertaken since 1983 that utilize the CAA were related to asbestos violations. A total of 221 prosecutions or 59% of the cases dealt with illegal removal and/or disposal, negligent/knowing endangerment violations, or failure to notify or report. These numbers clearly show that EPA investigations and federal criminal prosecutions centered on asbestos-related crimes more than any other criminal act. Within this broader category we find the following examples of defendants prosecuted for asbestos crimes: failure to obtain proper accreditation for asbestos remediation workers; selling fraudulent asbestos abatement certificates; performing asbestos abatement in violation of NESHAP workplace standards; improper demolition of a structure that contains asbestos-containing material; improper removal of asbestos-containing material; improper disposal of asbestos-containing material; and failure to notify of removal of asbestos-containing material.

We track the historical trajectory of these prosecutions in Figure 5. Before EPA made a final ruling on asbestos in 1989 there had been only two criminal prosecutions of asbestos-related crimes. This starts to slowly pick up in the 1990s with a high point of 9 prosecutions settled in 1998 and 40 cases settled throughout the 1990s. From 2000-2009, the government settled twice that amount (80 cases) and went on to complete 96 prosecutions by the beginning of 2020. Forty-seven asbestos cases were prosecuted in New York (21% of total) making it the largest player in this area. A total of 23 cases were prosecuted in Pennsylvania and 17 in Ohio, but New York was, by a good margin, the leader in these prosecutions historically. Looking at this phenomenon by regional office, Region II pursued 50 prosecutions and

Figure 5. Annual CAA Asbestos Criminal Prosecutions Since 1983

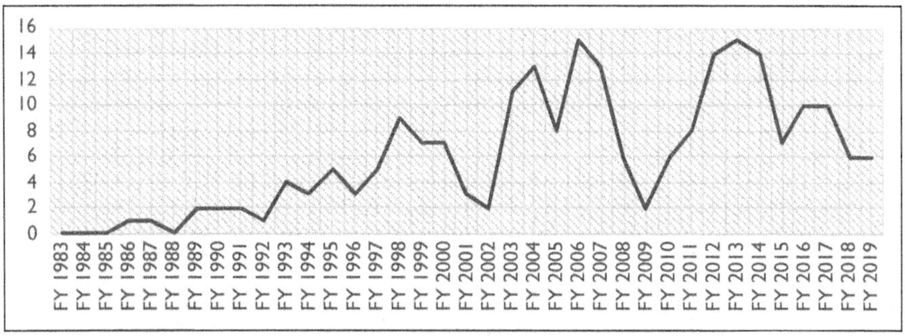

Region V pursued 43—making those regions responsible for 42% of asbestos-related prosecutions since 1983.

The CAA requires any company undertaking remediation work to certify their workers, take proper precautions, notify government officials, and obtain a permit prior to asbestos abatement. The notification and permitting requirements are tools prosecutors can use to pursue cases against unpermitted operations, as they would generally either fail to obtain a proper permit or notify officials. The release of hazardous materials and failure to notify can also be prosecuted under CERCLA as noted in the prior case examples discussed in the chapter.

The first three asbestos-related prosecutions in 1986, 1987, and 1989 against Peter Vileisis, Irwin Pearlman, and Alex Feinman, provide excellent examples of the range of cases prosecutors would come to pursue over time. Vileisis owned Waterbury House Wrecking Company and removed asbestos from the Old Pin Shop in Oakville, Connecticut. He failed to provide notice to EPA of the demolition and improperly removed the material during the job. He was indicted on August 1, 1985, along with the owner of the shop, Maurice Fabiani, for illegally releasing asbestos into the ambient air and improper removal.[113] EPA's Region III office issued an administrative order to Pearlman and Salvatore Williams to cease asbestos removal work at a former school building owned by Williams in a residential area of Pittsburgh, Pennsylvania. Pearlman ignored the order and removed the boiler and heat-

113. United States v. Vileisis, No. N-85-46 (D. Conn. Aug. 1, 1985). The charges against the company were dropped. Vileisis was sentenced to 12 months' suspended sentence, 60 months of probation, a $25,000 fine, a $25 penalty assessment, 1,000 hours community service and must attend at his own expense, seminars on proper asbestos remediation practices. Fabiani was sentenced to 12 months' incarceration (all but 30 days suspended), 60 months of probation, a $25,000, a $25 penalty assessment, and 1,000 hours community service.

ing systems violating NESHAP workplace standards for removing asbestos, including failure to notify and improper removal.[114] Feinman and Gregory Boone were charged in Pennsylvania on December 9, 1988, with conspiracy, knowingly disposing of asbestos in an unpermitted facility, and failure to notify under CERCLA.[115]

The most prevalent asbestos-related crimes center on improper remediation of these hazardous materials. These involve companies ripping out insulation, tiles, or dry scraping ceilings, and/or improperly disposing of the material. These crimes more often than not involve companies or contractors that put workers at risk by not providing them with either proper training or equipment. A few case example prosecutions include: Cuyahoga Wrecking Corporation; RAL Properties; and Miami Beach Ocean Resort. Cuyahoga Wrecking had purchased buildings from LTV Steel in Campbell, Ohio.[116] The company demolished the structures containing asbestos and failed to notify the government of the demolition.[117] They were charged under the CAA for violating asbestos NESHAP regulations, as well as CERCLA for failure to notify.[118] RAL Properties was sentenced in Ohio in 1993 for ille-

114. United States v. Pearlman, No. 86-246 (W.D. Pa. Dec. 30, 1986). The defendants were charged under the CAA for violating NESHAP standards in CAA removal failing to comply with an EPA administrative order. Each of the defendants was ordered to pay a $1,000 fine.

115. United States v. Feinman, No. 88-543 (E.D. Pa. Dec. 28, 1988). Feinman was sentenced to 12 months' incarceration. Co-defendant Gregory Boone was sentenced to 12 months' incarceration and 60 months of probation.

116. William K. Rashbaum & Charles V. Bagli, *Demolition Man*, N.Y. Times, Aug. 2, 2009, https://www.nytimes.com/2009/08/02/nyregion/02demo.html.

117. The company and owner Thomas Schwab have a checkered past. *See* Scott Glover & Luisa Yanez, *Wrecking Company Owner to Surrender*, Sun Sentinel, May 21, 1997, https://www.sun-sentinel.com/news/fl-xpm-1997-05-21-9705200456-story.html.

118. United States v. Cuyahoga Wrecking Corp., No. 4-89-CR-0281 (N.D. Ohio Sept. 21, 1989), The corporation pled guilty to the CAA and CERCLA counts and was ordered to pay a fine of $1,000,000 with $800,000 held in abeyance. Co-defendant Paul Buckley was sentenced to 36 months of probation, 300 hours community service, and a $5,000, as well as a $100 Special Assessment. Richard Salvati was sentenced to probation for 12 months and fined $1,000. Lawrence Button was sentenced to 24 months of probation and fined $3,000. The corporation was also prosecuted on two separate occasions in the 1980s, once for similar CAA violations and another for RCRA violations: The company and five co-defendants were charged in 1988 with conspiracy to defraud the EPA for violating structures containing asbestos in violation of NESHAP standards, as well as giving false statements, and failure to notify under CERCLA. The company was sentenced to pay a $250,000 fine. Co-defendant Leonard Capizzi was sentenced to 18 months' incarceration, Chester Reiss Sr. was sentenced to serve six months incarceration, James Abbajay was sentenced to serve 2 months' incarceration, and Samuel Torok was sentenced to serve 6 months' incarceration. The company and five co-defendants were prosecuted under RCRA for conspiracy and transporting, storing, and disposing of hazardous waste without a permit. Cuyahoga and Overland Corporations were both sentenced to pay a $100,000 fine. Co-defendant Ernest Martin was sentenced to 36 months of probation, 100 hours of community service, pay $50 to the Crime Victim's Fund, and to pay a fine in the amount of $3,000. Publicker Industries, Inc. was sentenced to pay a $50,000 fine. Samuel Runfola was sentenced to 36 months of probation, 60 months incarceration (suspended), 250 hours of community service, pay a $100 assessment to the Crime Victim's Fund, and pay a $5,000 fine. Virgil Cummings was sentenced to 48

gally removing and disposing of asbestos-containing material. The owner of the company, Michael Laska and his assistant, co-defendant Steve Howell, were remodeling a building owned by Laska known as the Old Swift Building. The two defendants removed asbestos, failed to notify authorities, and conspired to conceal the crime.[119] On April 5, 1991, inspectors with Dade County Environmental Resource Management received a complaint that the Sea Isle Hotel in North Miami Beach, Florida, was removing asbestos without proper handling. Sampling revealed the presence of asbestos in a large amount of material on-site and it became apparent material had already been removed off-site. The owner of the hotel, Miami Beach Ocean Resort Inc. failed to notify government officials of the removal or receive proper permits.[120] A good example of AHERA at work was the prosecution of Mountain States Insulation. In 1996, the company and its secretary Patricia Persons were charged under AHERA for illegal removal of asbestos from schools. Persons did not obtain proper accreditation for the company's workers prior to remediation activities. She gave false statements to investigators when question about the activities.[121]

The second most frequently occurring set of prosecutions at 16% of the total was what we label as operational violations. We tried to organize these crimes around illegal emissions releases, tampering with emissions equipment or monitoring devices, and other unpermitted releases. This category includes: chemical or solid/hazardous waste spills; illegal release of refrigerants; illegal release of air emissions without a permit or over-permitted levels; tampering with pollution monitoring controls or failing to install proper emissions control equipment; operating without a risk management plan; and operating without a permit.

Case examples include: Amitech U.S.A.; Joel Patterson; Corey Blake Beard; and MFA Incorporated. Prompted by a citizen complaint, an inspection of the Amitech U.S.A. plant in Louisiana revealed it had not been

---

months of probation, 48 months incarceration (42 months suspended), and ordered to pay a $4,000 fine.

119. United States v. RAL Prop., No. 91 (s)-V-3-1 (N.D. Ohio Sept. 30, 1992). Laska was sentenced to seven months incarceration, seven months of home detention, a special assessment fee of $100, and fined $3,000. Howell was sentenced to 24 months of probation, and ordered to pay a special assessment fee of $50.

120. No. 94-246-CR (M.D. Fla.). The company was charged on May 20, with violations of the CAA pled guilty to the charge in the information on the same day and was sentenced to a $100,000 fine.

121. United States v. Persons, No. 4:96CR00005-01. (D. Idaho Nov. 1, 1996). The company was sentenced to 36 months of probation and fined $19,000. Persons was sentenced to six months incarceration, 36 months of probation and fined $6,000.

operating with appropriate emissions controls since 2002.[122] The control equipment on-site had never been functional. The company was charged in May 2006 with making false statements and unpermitted releases of styrene into the ambient air.[123] Joel Patterson owned Joel Patterson Air Conditioning Recycling in Fort Myers, Florida, and was in the business of recycling air conditioners. Investigators discovered his employees cut refrigerant lines and emitted chemicals into the ambient air, rather than properly disposing of them.[124] Beard was an air conditioner thief that stole units to dismantle and strip the copper and aluminum. He and three co-defendants were prosecuted for releasing the emissions into the ambient air and conspiracy.[125] The defendants admitted they dismantled 35 commercial air conditioning units at 14 locations. MFA in Martinsburg, Missouri, was charged under the CAA when an employee loading anhydrous ammonia between two tanks at the facility leaked when a hose separated during the operation burning the employee. Investigations of the facility showed lack of inspections and maintenance that caused the connection failure leading to the unpermitted release of a hazardous substance.[126]

The third most common set of crimes prosecuted under the CAA are what we categorize as motor vehicle emissions violations. This category focuses on a range of crimes involving attempts to circumvent emissions controls on motor vehicles including: illegal importation or smuggling of non-conforming vehicles into the United States; illegal importation of non-conforming engines; mislabeling vehicles as conforming to emissions standards; manufacturing and selling vehicles with emissions-testing cheating devices; and issuing vehicle registrations for vehicles that failed emissions testing. We place 37 prosecutions or about 10% of overall prosecutions in this category.

122. *Amitech USA, L.L.C.*, ViolationTracker, https://violationtracker.goodjobsfirst.org/violation-tracker/la-amitech-usa-llc.

123. No. 06-96-RET-SCR (M.D. La.). The company was sentenced to 24 months of probation, ordered to pay a $400 special assessment fee, pay $1,070,000 in federal fines and $100,000 in restitution. Co-defendant William McCann the plant's manager was sentenced to 60 months of probation, a $25 special assessment fee, $25,000 in restitution, and a $50,000 federal fine.

124. No. 02-CR-00063-JES-ALL (M.D. Fla.). Patterson was charged with 15 counts of knowingly releasing refrigerant gas and was sentenced to 36 months of probation, including 6 months home detention, and a $100 special assessment fee.

125. No. 2:10-cr-024 (N.D. Ga.). Beard was sentenced to time served, 36 months of probation, 240 hours of community service, and a $1,000 special assessment. Justin Joyner was sentenced to time served, 36 months of probation, 240 hours of community service, and a $200 special assessment. Daniel Arnot was sentenced to time served, 36 months of probation, 240 hours of community service, and a $1,300 special assessment. Sabrina Arnot was sentenced to 36 months of probation. Beard, Daniel Arnot, and Joyner must pay $13,000 in restitution to the victim in the case Dunlap Stainless located in Gainesville, Georgia.

126. No. 407CR00550TIA (E.D. Mo.). The company was sentenced to pay $100,000 federal fine, $604,000 in judicially mandated fines, and a $125 assessment fee.

Case examples include: Hyundai Construction Equipment Americas; Dennis Alston; Olga Mata; John Arthur Clark; Louis Demeo; Tanveer Anwar; and Volkswagen AG. Hyundai was prosecuted under the CAA for knowingly importing construction equipment into the United States that did not meet emissions standards. During a phase-in period for new standards, the company participated in a program to report the number of non-conforming engines, but falsified reports showing they had not exceeded its allowance.[127] A consultant retained by the company warned them they were in non-compliance, but the company persisted in importing non-conforming engines in violation of the law and its employees conspired to hide this fact.[128] Alston and six co-defendants lied to EPA to illegally import non-conforming vehicles into the United States. They were prosecuted for conspiracy, false statements, and importing goods into the United States by means of false statements.[129] Mata registered numerous vehicles that failed emissions testing and created false bills of sale. She was charged under the CAA for false statements and mail fraud because the falsified sales documents were mailed to the Missouri Department of Revenue.[130]

Clean scanning involves scanning cars by registering emissions with one car for another that would not pass and certifying it.[131] These situations arise in non-attainment areas that require vehicle emissions testing, typically at the time a motor vehicle needs to be annually registered. A clean scanner charges a fee to a customer to ensure their car passes an emissions test and receives a passing certificate. A common scenario would be placing a tailpipe probe in a passing car and using the data to certify a non-passing car. Clean scanning operations were responsible for 27 or about 73% of the cases in this category and the prosecutorial strategy involved charging under false statements provisions of the CAA. Clark ran a clean scanning operation with his co-defendant Herschel Clark Jr. The Clarks clean scanned more than 100

127. David Allison, *Feds Charge Hyundai Construction Equipment Americas in 'Conspiracy' to Fraudulently Avoid EPA Rules*, Atlanta Bus. Chron., Sept. 18, 2018, https://www.bizjournals.com/atlanta/news/2018/09/28/feds-charge-hyundai-construction-equipment.html.

128. United States v. Hyundai Constr. Equip. Americas Inc., No. 1:18-CR-00379 (N.D. Ga. Sept. 28, 2018). The company was sentenced to pay a $1,950,000 fine.

129. No. 85-236 (S.D. Tex.). Alston was sentenced to six months of probation, ordered to pay restitution in the amount of $3,800, and a $24,000 fine. Phillip Anthony Williams was sentenced to 36 months of probation and ordered to perform 80 hours of community service. Edward Wiatt was sentenced to 150 hours of community service and ordered to pay a $1,500 fine. Brigitte Laurus was sentenced to 12 months of probation. Freddie and Donald Fincher were each sentenced to a $10,000 fine. Norbert Gall's sentence is not listed in the case summary.

130. United States v. Mata, No. 2014R00704 (E.D. Mo. 2016). Mata was sentenced to 14 months in prison.

131. *Texas AG Stops Auto Dealer From "Clean Scanning" Vehicle Emissions*, Claims J., 2010, https://www.claimsjournal.com/news/southcentral/2010/05/10/109705.htm.

vehicles at Clark Tire and Wheel in Imperial, Missouri, and charged fees to customers to fraudulently obtain passing emissions tests.[132] Demeo was prosecuted in Nevada for clean scanning and up charging customers $10-$100 for the service.[133] Anwar was also prosecuted in North Carolina for clean scanning alongside co-defendant Jassim Jubiri. Anwar was the owner of Eagle Auto Repair in Charlotte, North Carolina. According to investigators, between January 2010 and May 2011, he clean scanned 1,008 vehicles. Jubiri worked at Central Auto Inspection and Repair in Charlotte. Between August 2010 and March 2012, he clean scanned 534 vehicles. Both were charged with conspiracy under the CAA.[134]

Volkswagen AG and a series of co-defendants in related cases were prosecuted for an emissions-rigging scheme, where the company's engineers added software to clean diesel vehicles to help them pass emissions testing when the same fuel mileage would not be possible under normal driving conditions. The company installed the software when it realized its vehicles could not meet emissions standards and knowingly defrauded U.S. consumers for the better part of a decade for model years 2009-2016.[135] The $2.8 million criminal penalty was the second-largest criminal penalty assessed by EPA in its history.[136] The company also agreed to a $1.5 billion payment to set civil claims by EPA and U.S. Customs and Border Protection.[137]

132. United States v. Clark Jr., No. 4:10CR00432AGF (E.D. Mo. 2011). The defendants were charged with making false statements under the CAA. Jon Clark was sentenced to 24 months of probation and a $1,500 federal fine. Hershel Clark was sentenced to 36 months of probation, of which 12 months is to be served in home confinement, 100 hours of community service, and a special assessment fee of $100.

133. No. 2:10-CR-005 (D. Nev.). Demeo was sentenced to 36 months of probation.

134. Anwar was sentenced to 4 months in prison and 4 months of home confinement and was ordered to serve 50 hours of community service and prohibited from conducting vehicle inspections in the future. Juburi was sentenced in August 2013 to 18 months' incarceration, 36 months of probation, ordered to pay a $100 special assessment, and pay a $15,000 fine. In March 2015, Jubiri was sentenced to 40 months in prison and 36 months' supervised release for violating his probation on the previous charge with felon in a possession of a firearm under Title 18.

135. United States v. Volkswagen AG, No. 16-CR-20394 (E.D. Mich. 2017). The company was charged with conspiracy, wire fraud, obstruction, and importation of merchandise by false statements and ordered to pay $2.8 billion. Related cases include: James Robert Ling an engineer involved in the conspiracy was sentenced to 40 months in federal prison, and two years of supervised release. Oliver Schmidt the manager of the company's Environmental and Engineering Office was sentenced to 84 months in prison and a $400,000 fine. IAV GmbH, the company that designs automotive systems, was part of the conspiracy and was ordered to pay a $35 million fine.

136. A series of executives were also indicated and ended up on the EPA's Fugitive List. *See* Jasper Jolly, *Former Head of Volkswagen Could Face 10 Years in Prison*, GUARDIAN, Apr. 15, 2019, https://www.theguardian.com/business/2019/apr/15/former-head-of-volkswagen-could-face-10-years-in-prison. *See also* U.S. EPA, EPA FUGITIVES (2020), https://www.epa.gov/enforcement/epa-fugitives.

137. News Release, U.S. DOJ, Volkswagen AG Sentenced in Connection With Conspiracy to Cheat U.S. Emissions Tests (Apr. 21, 2017), https://www.justice.gov/opa/pr/volkswagen-ag-sentenced-connection-conspiracy-cheat-us-emissions-tests.

Seven percent of the CAA prosecutions or 28 cases total focus historically in our judgment on false reporting issues. In many of these prosecutions, defendants were charged with false reporting or false statements under the criminal provisions of the CAA. We placed the prosecutions in this category if we determined that the focus of the investigation involved giving false statements to investigators or in a document. We included cases that center on: falsifying lab testing results; submitting false records or reports; submitting falsified shipping logs; and failure to report failure of emissions control devices. These sub-categories make up the range of cases we included in this category.

Case examples that illustrate this range include: Kinder Morgan Bulk Terminals; Mullins Rubber Products; Erler Industies; John Littlehale; William Nowak; and Jet Pep. Kinder Morgan was prosecuted for falsifying reports. Its baghouse pollution control system to capture PM was not properly functioning, but the company certified on reports that it was fully operational. The pollution control devices were dysfunctional from about 2001-2008, but from August 2006-2007, employees certified on official forms that the equipment was fully functional. The company failed to notify EPA that they were not in compliance with their air permit.[138] Mullins Rubber Products falsified reports of their emissions data from 1995-2001 for each of its six annual compliance reports thus emitting volatile organic compounds (VOCs) at much higher levels than would be allowed under its permit. The company was charged with knowing violations of the CAA, as well as false statements.[139] Erler Industries, located in North Vernon, Indiana, submitted false quarterly VOC reports to regulators.[140] Littlehale was the vice president of a printing firm. He conspired to construct and operate a printing press in a manner that would subvert its air pollution control device. He lied on the company's air permit application claiming an oxidizer would be installed to eliminate most emissions. That oxidizer was never installed.[141]

---

138. No. 8:10 CR 76 T 30 TGW (M.D. Fla.). The company was charged with false statements and failure to notify under the CAA. They were sentenced to 24 months of probation, order to pay a $750,000 fine, and a $250,000 community service payment.

139. No. 3-03-CR-146 (S.D. Ohio). The company was sentenced to 36 months of probation and ordered to pay a $100,000 federal fine. The owner and co-defendant, William R. Mullins Sr. was sentenced to 4 months' incarceration, 36 months of probation, and was ordered to pay a federal fine in the amount of $350,000 and $50,000 in restitution.

140. No. 1:08-CR-00109-WTL-KPF (S.D. Ind.). The company was charged with making false statements. The company was sentenced to 12 months of probation, $125,000 in restitution, and ordered to pay a federal fine in the amount of $1 million.

141. No. 03-01-CR-01 H/N (S.D. Ind.). Littlehale was charged with making false statements and conspiracy. He was sentenced to 18 months' incarceration, 24 months of probation, ordered to perform 50 hours of community service, and pay a $4,000 federal fine. His co-defendant Roger Taylor was

The CAA requires testing and certification of wood-burning stoves so that they meet emissions standards for PM. At the time, Nowak owned Energy and Environmental System Performance Corporation in Washington State, one of four facilities in the United States used to certify the emissions performance of wood-burning stoves. Between December 1992-1994, the company performed testing on 21 stove models. Washington State had higher emissions standards than federal standards. Nowak admitted he falsified testing data on 10 of the 21 models because they would fail state testing requirements. These stoves received federal certification based on the false lab data. Investigators estimated that in 1996, a total of 53,000 stoves were sold with invalid certificates.[142] Jet Pep conducted commercial fuel blending tests for companies. They did not properly test the fuel blends and made false statements to the contrary.[143]

In 5% of cases, defendants engaged in violating CAA restrictions on ozone-depleting substances. EPA rules restricting CFCs and other chemicals, particularly refrigerants, created a series of opportunities for illegal behavior. As CFCs were phased out and replacements were found in consumer, commercial, and industrial applications, these crimes abated. Fifteen of the 20 prosecutions in this category were settled by FY 2000 with 60% of prosecutions in this category settled between 1996-1999. Most of these prosecutions centered on dichlorodifluoromethane known as freon-12. Motor vehicle air conditions prior to 1994 almost universally relied on R-12 as a refrigerant in the United States. After R-12 was phased out and replaced with R-134a, old air conditioning systems would require retrofitting to use the new refrigerant. While owners were not required to retrofit, they would have to pay for it and a black market in R-12 developed, which explains the timeline of these prosecutions. R-22 has more recently been phased out, but a few later prosecutions focus on illegal activity related to R-22 or hydrochlorofluorocarbons (HCFCs) as a consequence. Prosecutions in this category include: illegal importation; smuggling; and distribution/selling, purchasing, mislabeling, or installing substitutes for restricted refrigerants.

Case examples that illustrate prosecutions in this category include: Robert Pennell; Joseph Kodell; Glenn Shortt; Jerry Gentry; and E-Air. Pennell and his co-defendant Sam Alfano conspired to smuggle 513 tons of Freon hidden

---

charged with misprision of a felony and was sentenced to 6 months' home confinement, 60 months of probation, and ordered to perform 500 hours of community service.

142. No. CR-96-218C (W.D. Wash.). Nowak pled guilty to knowing violations that he submitted false testing data to EPA. He was sentenced to 36 months of probation and 240 hours of community service.

143. No. CR-03-S-0127NE (N.D. Ala.). The company was sentenced to 36 months of probation, a special assessment fee of $400, and a federal fine of $200,000.

in shipping containers into the United States via New Jersey and Miami. They were charged in May 1995 under the CAA and for smuggling.[144] Kodell was prosecuted for illegally distributing 1,297,695 million pounds of banned refrigerants as president of Florida Motor Oil Distributors, Inc. He was charged under the CAA, for conspiracy and tax fraud.[145] Shortt was prosecuted for installing a substitute for R-12 in motor vehicle air conditioners that was flammable and a dangerous refrigerant substitute (HC-12a). It is illegal in the United States to swap the refrigerants.[146] Gentry was charged in 2001 for knowing violations of the CAA for relabeling R-22 canisters as R-12. He then resold them to motor vehicle repair shops throughout the United States.[147] E-Air was prosecuted for the illegal sale and distribution of products containing HCFC-22.[148] EPA banned the sale and distribution of products containing the refrigerant as of January 1, 2010.[149]

The Energy Independence and Security Act of 2007 developed incentives for companies to develop biodiesel and other renewable fuels. To incentivize production, companies would generate renewable identification numbers (RINs) that would be sold in the emerging market for such credits that would be required for other companies not meeting production quotas. The system generated incentives for making fraudulent claims for renewable fuel production to falsely claim RINs or to engage in tax fraud.[150] We find eight prosecutions undertaken since 2013 that focus on fraudulently claiming tax credits

144. No. 95-0365-CR-RYSKAMP (S.D. Fla.). Pennell was sentenced to 12 months' incarceration, 36 months of probation, and ordered to make restitution in the amount of $3.4 million. Half of the prison sentence will be served at home with a monitoring device. Alfano was sentenced to 14 months' incarceration, 36 months of probation, and fined a total of $3,423,035.

145. No. 97-8095COUNJARO (S.D. Fla.). Kodell was sentenced to 12 months' home confinement, 36 months of probation, a $200 special assessment fee, a $5,000 federal fine, and to pay $6,334,020 in back taxes to the IRS.

146. U.S. EPA, *Unacceptable Substitute Refrigerants*, https://www.epa.gov/snap/unacceptable-substitute-refrigerants (last updated May 3, 2021). United States v. Shortt, No. EDCR 98-3-RT (Cal. Oct. 28, 1998). Shortt and co-defendants Dennis Henckel and Randy Lee Christensen were prosecuted for knowing violations of the CAA. Shortt and Henkel were both sentenced to 36 months of probation. Christensen was sentenced to 36 months of probation and 100 hours of community service.

147. No. CR-01-1007-PHX-MHM (D. Ariz.). Gentry was sentenced to 24 months of probation and ordered to pay a federal fine of $1,500.

148. Press Release, U.S. DOJ, International Distributor Pleads Guilty and Is Sentenced for Illegal Sale and Distribution of Refrigeration Equipment Containing Ozone-Depleting Substances (June 20, 2014), https://www.justice.gov/usao-sdfl/pr/international-distributor-pleads-guilty-and-sentenced-illegal-sale-and-distribution.

149. No. 1:14-CR-20392-CMA (S.D. Fla.). E-Air was sentenced to 60 months of probation and ordered to pay a $200,000 federal fine. The company was required to make community service payments totaling $75,000 and reimburse U.S. Customs and Border Protection for the costs incurred in storing illegal merchandise. They were also required to implement and enforce a comprehensive environmental compliance plan.

150. Pub. L. No. 110-140 (2007). The Act focused on increasing CAFE standards, to increase biofuel research and production, and generate new initiatives for energy efficiency in appliances, lighting, and buildings.

for renewable energy production or fraudulently reporting the production of biodiesel and renewable fuels and selling/trading the associated RINs.

Rodney Rashawn Hailey owned Clean Green Fuel in Baltimore, Maryland. He registered with EPA's Renewable Fuel Standards program as a producer of biodiesel.[151] Between March 2009 and December 2010, Hailey claimed 23 million gallons of biodiesel production and then claimed and sold 35 million RINs to both brokers and oil companies. Hailey never developed a facility to produce biodiesel. He was charged under the CAA for false statements, wire fraud, and money laundering in November 2011 and convicted in June 2013.[152] William Bradley, Dean Daniels, Richard Smith, and Brenda Daniels produced low-grade fuel and claimed credits for production of biodiesel that met EPA standards. The defendants sold over $15 million worth of RINs obtained from their fraudulent activities and claimed $7 million in fraudulent tax credits.[153]

III. Penalties in Clean Air Act Prosecutions

In Figure 6 we start to explore how defendants were punished in CAA prosecutions since 1983. We examine each case and look for criminal charges beyond the environmental charges in the case. Our analysis shows that the most common criminal charge was false statements. In 21% of cases, defendants were charged with false statement, false reporting, or falsifying documents. This occurred in 78 prosecutions. In 18% of the cases, at least one defendant was charged with conspiracy. In 8% of the prosecutions, at least one defendant was charged with some type of fraud, and in 2% of cases, a defendant was charged with obstruction.

Case example prosecutions of false statements and obstruction include: John Meyer; David Marshall; Wade Bertelson; All World Cycles Inc.; and Watkins Street Project. Meyer was prosecuted under the CAA for illegally importing cars under a five-year emissions exemption and reselling them. He was prosecuted for false statements.[154] Marshall was certified to remove

151. Alison Matas, *Md. Man Gets 12 ½-Year Term in Biodiesel Credit Fraud*, BALT. SUN, Feb. 2, 2013, https://www.baltimoresun.com/news/environment/bs-gr-rodney-hailey-20130222-story.html
152. United States v. Hailey, No.1:11-CR-00540-WDQ (D. Md. Nov. 8, 2011). Hailey was sentenced to 12 years and 6 months' incarceration and ordered to pay restitution of approximately $ 42.2 million and forfeit $9.1 million in proceeds from the fraudulent activities.
153. United States v. Smith, No. 2:15CR44 (S.D. Ohio Feb. 23, 2015). Dean Daniels was sentenced to 63 months of incarceration. Bradley was sentenced to 51 months of incarceration. Smith was sentenced to 41 months of incarceration. Brenda Daniels was sentenced to 366 days' incarceration. The defendants were ordered to pay $23 million in restitution.
154. No. 87-10060M (E.D. Mo.). Meyer was sentenced to 24 months of probation, ordered to pay $2,600, and fined $10,000.

Figure 6. Common Criminal Charges in CAA Criminal Prosecutions

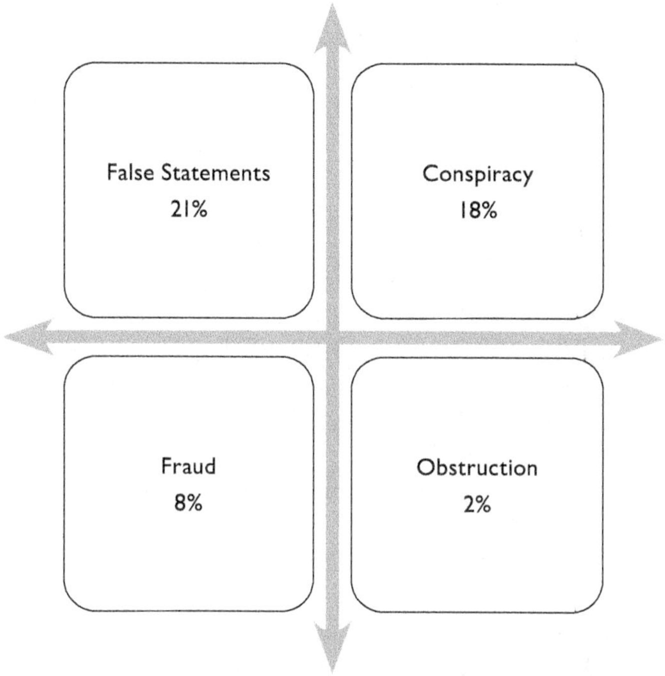

asbestos in West Virginia, but his license was revoked. He was prosecuted for making false statements.[155] Bertelson and his co-defendants were indicted for failing to properly remediate asbestos, issuing false asbestos training certificates, and submitting false certificates to the Illinois Department of Public Health.[156] All World Cycles and owner Tory Stone were importing motorcycle parts that were assembled as kits, when he advertised them as being

155. No. CR-00001-001 (N.D. W. Va.). Marshall was sentenced to 15 months' incarceration, 36 months' supervised release, and was ordered not to perform asbestos demolition work in the future.

156. No. 99-400005-001 (C.D. Ill.). Bertelson and Robert Rapp were each sentenced to 15 months' incarceration, 36 months of probation, ordered to pay a special assessment fee of $100, and a federal fine of $1,800. Talbot was sentenced to 24 months of probation. Dale Roseman was sentenced to 9 months' incarceration, 12 months of probation, ordered to pay a $25 special assessment fee, and a $3,000 federal fine. Gregory Corder was sentenced to 24 months of probation, ordered to pay a special assessment fee of $1,600, a federal fine in the amount of $5,000, and restitution in the amount of $1,600. Curry Environmental was sentenced to 60 months of probation, ordered to pay a special assessment fee of $1,200, and a $1 million federal fine. Darren Wright was sentenced to 5 months' incarceration, 24 months of probation, and ordered to pay a $100 special assessment fee. Timothy Coutts was sentenced to 4 months' incarceration, 36 months of probation, and ordered to pay a $100 special assessment fee. Cook was sentenced to 6 months' home confinement, 36 months of probation, and ordered to pay a $20,000 federal fine.

manufactured in his shop. He did not file a certificate of conformity with EPA as required under the CAA.[157] Watkins Street Project illegally demolished a factory in Chattanooga, Tennessee, which contained large amounts of asbestos. The defendants were charged with obstruction, conspiracy to violate the CAA, and false statements.[158]

Case example prosecutions of conspiracy include: John A. Deck; Louisiana Pacific Corporation; and William Threatt Jr. Deck and his co-defendants dumped 400 truckloads containing asbestos at an open property in Frankfort, New York. The defendants conspired to conceal the illegal dumping, recruited co-conspirators, and falsified a New York State Department of Environmental Conservation permit, including forging an official signature on the permit. The defendants were charged with conspiracy, as well as wire fraud and false statements.[159] Louisiana Pacific Corporation was prosecuted for tampering with emissions controls and conspiring to falsify data.[160] They were charged with conspiracy, tampering with a monitoring device, false statements, and wire fraud.[161]

Case example prosecutions for fraud include: Daniel Black; Jason Scardecchio; and Kevin Pilgrim. Black was president of Blackstone Business Enterprises. He authorized the cleanup of a four-story building in Jamestown, New York, and instructed workers to remove steam pipes covered in asbestos. Investigations revealed he failed to report income for the job and other income. He was charged under the CAA for illegal asbestos removal

157. No. SACR 05-101(A)–CJC (C.D. Cal.). Stone and the company were charged with obstruction and evading reporting requirements, as well as false statements and failure to pay a fee as required to the U.S. government. The company was sentenced to 12 months of probation and ordered to pay a $400 special assessment fee. Stone was sentenced to 12 months of probation and ordered to pay a $25 special assessment fee.

158. No. 1:09-CR-144 (E.D. Tenn.). The company was sentenced to 36 months of probation, ordered to pay $30,000 in federal fines, and $28,000 in restitution. Gary Fillers was sentenced to 36 months of probation, which includes 6 months' home detention. James Mathis was sentenced to 36 months of probation. Donald Fillers was sentenced to 48 months' incarceration, 36 months of probation, and ordered to pay $20,000 in federal fines, to be shared with Mathis and Watkins Street. David Wood was sentenced to 20 months' incarceration and 36 months of probation.

159. No. 5:09CR469 (N.D.N.Y.). Deck was sentenced to 15 months' incarceration and ordered to pay restitution, joint and several with the other defendants in the amount of $492,494.44. Julius DeSimone was sentenced to 60 months of probation, including 6 months' home confinement, restitution, joint and several with the other defendants in the amount of $492,494.44. Donald Torriero was sentenced to 36 months' incarceration, 36 months of probation, and restitution, joint and several with the other defendants in the amount of $492,494.44.

160. *Louisiana-Pacific to Pay Fines in Pollution Case*, L.A. TIMES, May 28, 1998, https://www.latimes.com/archives/la-xpm-1998-may-28-fi-54204-story.html

161. United States v. Louisiana Pac. Corp., No. 95-CR-215 (D. Colo. June 14, 1995). The company was sentenced to 60 months of probation, $235,000 in restitution, $500,000 in community project fines, and $36.5 million in other fines. Robert Mann was sentenced to 6 months' incarceration, 36 months of probation, and fined $10,000. Dana Dulohery was sentenced to 10 months' incarceration, 36 months of probation, and fined $15,000.

and tax fraud.[162] Scardecchio was prosecuted for the illegal abatement of asbestos at Trinity Church in Collegeville, Pennsylvania, and was prosecuted under TSCA for mail fraud and knowingly violating the CAA.[163] Pilgrim and six co-defendants were employees of AAR Contractors. The company engaged in a long-term conspiracy to defraud individuals by providing false laboratory analyses, as well as illegal asbestos demolition and disposal. The defendants were charged with a litany of criminal offenses, including: mail fraud; conspiracy; false statements, obstruction, and perjury; and negligent violations of the CAA.[164]

In Figure 7 we aggregate all of the penalties assessed across all individual and company defendants since 1983. We include incarceration (months), probation (months), fines (including all monetary penalties as assessed such as fines, special assessments, fees, forfeited assets due to fraud or other crimes, and community service payments), as well as community service (total hours). Our finding shows that overall totals are skewed by a few large penalty cases, but total fines assessed to individual defendants totaled almost $475 million. Philip Joel Rivkin was sentenced to 121 months in prison, three years of supervised release, and $138 million in penalties, including $87 million in restitution and forfeiture of $51 million in illegal gains from the operation. The prosecution of Eric Farbent and his co-conspirators Raul and Alex Salvagno over illegal asbestos testing and abatement amounted to over $72 million in penalties. Taking these two cases into consideration cut the penalties assessed to individuals in half.[165] For companies, the fines and penalties

162. United States v. Black, No. 1:10-CR-00303-RJA (W.D.N.Y. Mar. 1, 2011). Black was sentenced to 12 months and a day of incarceration, 24 months of probation, a $30,000 federal fine, $191,669 in restitution to the IRS, $205,000 to OSHA, and $25,000 to the New York State Department of Labor.

163. No. 05-CR-00472 (E.D. Pa.). He was sentenced 12 months and one day of incarceration, 36 months of probation, a special assessment fee of $300, and restitution of $11,805.

164. No. 5:05-CR-49 (N.D.N.Y.). In the trial against AAR, Pilgrim also gave false testimony under oath. Pilgrim was sentenced to 10 months' incarceration, 24 months of probation, and ordered to pay a special assessment fee of $100. Sheon Dimaio was sentenced to 42 months' incarceration, 24 months of probation, and order to pay a $200 special assessment fee. Bradford Hall was sentenced to 8 months' incarceration, 24 months of probation, and ordered to pay a $100 special assessment fee. Gerald Lindquist was sentenced to 30 months' incarceration, 24 months of probation, and ordered to pay an assessment fee of $400. Gary Alvord was sentenced to 15 months' incarceration, 24 months of probation, ordered to perform 200 hours of community service, and ordered to pay a $400 special assessment. Robert O'Brey was sentenced to 15 months' incarceration, 24 months of probation, ordered to perform 200 hours of community service, and ordered to pay a $300 special assessment. Anthony Mongato was sentenced to 18 months' incarceration, 24 months of probation, and ordered to pay a $300 special assessment fee.

165. United States v. Rivkin, No. 14-603M/H14-250 (S.D. Tex. Mar. 7, 2016). Rivkin was prosecuted for defrauding the biofuel credit program. He was sentenced to pay $87 in restitution and had to forfeit $51 million in illegal gains. United States v. Farbent, No. 02-CR-51 (N.D.N.Y. Feb. 21, 2000). The Farbent case is tied into the prosecution of AAR Contracting, which engaged in a 10-year conspiracy to provide fraudulent laboratory analysis for and demolition of asbestos throughout New York State.

Figure 7. Total Penalties Assessed in CAA Criminal Prosecutions Since 1983

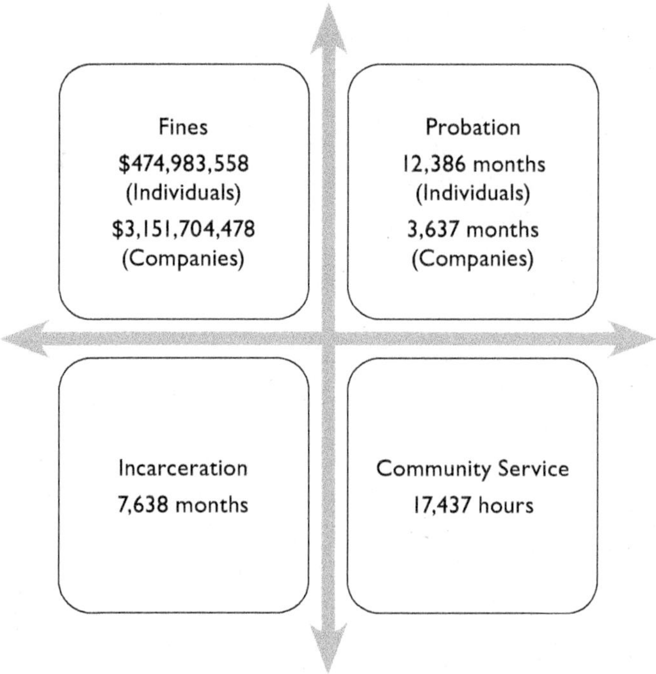

totaled over $3 billion. The Volkswagen AG case greatly skews this number. Eliminating it changes total penalties to companies to about $1.35 billion.

We find that individual defendants were assessed a grand total of 12,386 months of probation at sentencing. This amounted to 259 cases since 1983 where at least one individual defendant was given probation time as punishment. In contrast, we find 176 cases prosecuted since 1983 where individual defendants were assessed a total of 7,638 months of incarceration. We find 69 cases of home confinement assessed at sentencing and a total of 17,437 hours of community service assessed to defendants in CAA prosecutions. Companies were assessed probation in 86 cases amounting to a grand total of 3,687 months.

While Farbent was not assessed such substantial financial penalties, the owners of AAR—Raul and Alex Salvagno—were assessed substantial penalties in restitution and forfeiture, as was AAR and co-defendant Thomas Reed. The cases are given the same legal citation in EPA's database, but while having some intertwining information also appear separately.

IV. Conclusion

Criminal provisions in the CAA center on unpermitted air emissions.[166] We see these provisions mostly at work at stationary sources, where the Act sets forth criminal guidelines to enforce air permits, monitoring equipment, SIPs, and ensuring both workers and other bystanders are not injured because of hazardous emissions. Our analysis of trends in these prosecutions tells us quite a lot about how prosecutors have used CAA criminal provisions historically and give great insight into how the government enforces serious violations of clean air laws.

The most evident trend is the significant effort put forth to punish asbestos violations. As an almost universal building material at mid-century with a longer history of human use and known health effects, prohibiting the manufacture and use of asbestos opened up natural opportunities for negligent and willful crimes.[167] We find that the majority of CAA prosecutions focus on asbestos directly (59%) and many more are related to asbestos even if it is not the sole focus of the investigation and prosecution. Among the many problems of regulating air emissions is that the physical manifestation of toxic air pollution is both hard to measure and capture. Illegal discharges into waterways can be seen, often smelled, and easily measured. Air emissions often disappear into the atmosphere before investigators understand the criminal behaviors that created excess emissions. We still find about 16% of cases focusing on the central theme of operational issues, predominately at stationary sources of pollution large and small.

With asbestos crimes, investigators have the unique ability in CAA criminal cases to see the physical evidence.[168] While they do not always witness friable asbestos floating in the air or workers and other bystanders breathing in the harmful fibers, testing for the presence of asbestos is straightforward and the physical evidence is often extremely difficult to completely remove from an unpermitted operation. This physical evidence gives investigators a decided edge in pursuing a criminal investigation and strong evidence for prosecutors to pursue criminal charges if warranted. The extent of the historical problem with asbestos removal continues to be a serious one, given

166. U.S. EPA, *Criminal Provisions of the Clean Air Act*, https://19january2017snapshot.epa.gov/enforcement/criminal-provisions-clean-air-act_.html (Jan. 18, 2017).

167. W.R. Barclay, *Landmark Perspective: Asbestos. An Industrial Asset With a Health Cost*, 252 J. Am. Med. Ass'n 96 (1984); Kevin Browne & Robert Murray, *Asbestos and the Romans*, 18 Lancet 445 (1990).

168. Methods for testing for the presence of asbestos in criminal investigations focus on the "bulk material test method" instituted in 1993, giving the Agency broad regulatory discretion under asbestos NESHAP. *See* Robert M. Howard et al., *The EPA's Prosecution of Clean Air Act Asbestos NESHAP Cases Based Upon Nonbinding Bulk Material Test Methods*, 44 San Diego L. Rev. 173-230 (2007).

improper removal always exposes people to known danger, the public is very much aware of the dangers, and there is little dispute in the connections.[169] Requirements to notify officials of abatement, the need for training and certifying workers and companies, the physical evidence, the often public nature of removing asbestos from residential, commercial, and industrial applications, and the need to file appropriate paperwork, and need to dispose of the material create many opportunities to catch and prosecute criminals. We also found the paper chase to be central to CAA prosecutions. Mandating regular reporting, permitting, disclosure, and other requirements provide opportunities for prosecutors to demonstrate intent and secure physical evidence of wrongdoing. Lying to investigators or false reporting on permits, reports, or other documents are the focus of about 7% of the cases, although as we have demonstrated such crimes are present in 21% of the overall cases. It is fair to say that improperly removing asbestos and lying about doing so are to be avoided by environmental criminals, but polluting factories are mostly safe from prosecution.

169. EPA's risk assessments for asbestos have also been critiqued. *See* Suresh H. Moolgavkar et al., *A Review and Critique of U.S. EPA's Risk Assessments for Asbestos*, 44 Critical Rev. Toxicology 499-522 (2014).

Chapter 3. We Didn't Permit That Discharge: The Criminal Enforcement of the U.S. Clean Water Act

I. Enforcing the U.S. Clean Water Act

Access to water undergirds all human societies.[1] Whether it is used for agriculture, drinking, cooking, or pleasure, water imbues deep practical and spiritual meaning in our lives. Modern societies rest on a careful balance of using water as a shared resource for personal, commercial, and industrial applications.[2] Deep-well irrigation helped the American Southwest and California's Central Valley emerge as major agricultural centers. Pumping water from the San Joaquin Delta and elsewhere in northern California keeps the denizens of Los Angeles happy and their gardens green, while damming major rivers, such as the Colorado or Rio Grande, supplies sprawling metropolises in the desert. Water chlorination and the development of municipal wastewater treatment facilities provide seemingly unlimited clean drinking water and help fight back the public health scourges of typhoid, cholera, and dysentery; thus, our mastery of water seems ascendant.[3]

We do, however, take water for granted in the United States and have for some time. Rivers, lakes, and streams are great vehicles for getting rid of unwanted things. Whether it is garbage, effluent, animal waste, or toxic chemicals, Americans have been destroying our waterways at an ever-esca-

1. Vujica Yevjevich, *Water and Civilization*, 17 Water Int'l 163-71 (1992).
2. Brian Clark Howard, *California Drought Spurs Groundwater Drilling Boom in Central Valley*, Nat. Geo., Aug. 16, 2014, https://www.nationalgeographic.com/news/2014/8/140815-central-valley-california-drilling-boom-groundwater-drought-wells/.
3. Land subsistence in California's Central Valley has continually accelerated as agribusiness drains aquifers faster than they can be replenished. Maximum subsistence was as high as 28 feet in 1970. The only solution has been deeper wells and greater subsistence. Many smaller communities will increasingly be abandoned and the long-term outlook for extensive agriculture is grim. *See San Joaquin Valley, California: Largest Alteration to the Earth's Surface*, *in* U.S. Geological Serv., Land Subsidence in the United States (Devin Galloway et al. eds., 1999), https://pubs.usgs.gov/circ/circ1182/pdf/06SanJoaquinValley.pdf (full report available at https://pubs.usgs.gov/circ/1999/1182/report.pdf)

lating rate.[4] We take for granted clean water from our tap that doesn't sicken us.[5] One example, typhoid fever, is caused by bacterial infections of salmonella resulting from poor sanitation. While it infects more than 10 million people worldwide, it is mostly prevented in the United States with the chlorination of drinking water. It was a scourge of industrializing America, killing many notable people, such as Theodore Roosevelt's mother, Wilbur Wright, and Peter V, the king of Portugal from 1853-1861. Not even fame could save the children of the rich and powerful as both Abraham Lincoln and former governor and senator from California, Leland Stanford, lost sons to typhoid fever.[6] Only when we witness public health crises fed by poor decisions, such as the Flint water crisis or witness the current megadrought in the western United States that causes water rationing and the perpetual sinking of the Central Valley due to abuse of deep-well irrigation, are we reminded that our relationship with water is critical and unsustainable.[7]

Damming rivers, pumping water, and generating unlimited potable water has blinded us to our most important and intimate relationship with the natural world.[8] Not only did poor sanitation lead to disease and death, burgeoning factories in the late 19th century treated waterways as highways for

4. John Hoornbeeket et al., *Implementing Water Pollution Policy in the United States: Total Maximum Daily Loads and Collaborative Watershed Management*, 26 Soc'y & Nat. Resources 420-36 (2013).
5. Alan C. Burton & J. Frederick Cornhill, *Correlation of Cancer Death Rates With Altitude and Within the Quality of Water Supply of the 100 Largest Cities in the United States*, 3 J. Toxicology & Envtl. Health 465-78 (1977).
6. Jersey City, New Jersey was the first municipality in the United States to undertake routine disinfection of drinking water. The infectious disease death rate per hundred thousand for typhoid fever and cholera was drastically reduced from about 800 at the turn of the 20th century to 0.1 cases with a majority stemming from international travelers. *See* Centers for Disease Control & Prevention (CDC), *History of Drinking Water Treatment*, https://www.cdc.gov/healthywater/drinking/history.html (last visited May 6, 2022). The World Health Organization (WHO) estimates between 11 and 21 million cases of typhoid fever occur annually. *See* WHO, *Typhoid*, https://www.who.int/immunization/diseases/typhoid/en/ (last visited May 6, 2022). Industrialization and urbanization brought cholera pandemics in the 19th century. John Snow, one of the founders of modern epidemiology, was credited with making the connection between cholera and poor sanitation (fecal-oral route of disease transmission). *See* Michael A.E. Ramsay, *John Snow, MD: Anesthetist to the Queen of England and Pioneer Epidemiologist*, 19 Proc. Baylor U. Med. Ctr. 24-28 (2006), https://www.ncbi.nlm.nih.gov/pmc/articles/PMC1325279/.
7. The Flint water crisis was precipitated by cost saving measures put into place when the municipalities were essentially put into receivership by the state. The city declared a state of financial emergency in 2011 and to save money it switched to the polluted Flint River as the primary source of the city's water supply instead of Lake Huron. The water corroded the pipes and lead leeched into the water supply, as well as a variety of toxic metals made their way into the water supply. The switch began in April 2014 and by summer warning signs were already emerging. Threats to public health include shorter term effects from ingesting an array of chemicals, bacteria, and most pressing the effects of lead exposure on children are devastating. Longer term effects, such as higher rates of cancer and other illnesses, are likely to be pronounced. *See* Melissa Denchak, *Flint Water Crisis: Everything You Need to Know*, https://www.nrdc.org/stories/flint-water-crisis-everything-you-need-know (Nov. 8, 2018).
8. Elisabeth A Graffy, *Expert Forecasts and the Emergence of Water Scarcity on Public Agendas*, 19 Soc'y & Nat. Resources 465-72 (2006).

toxic pollution and bodies of water as trash dumps for industrial waste well into the mid-20th century.[9] Many cite the Cuyahoga River fire of 1969 as one defining event that united the modern environmental movement, when in fact it caught fire at least 12 times prior to 1968.[10] It was apparent in the early 20th century how quickly industrialization was destroying the American wilderness and at the same time polluting our rivers and bodies of water beyond repair.[11]

The Federal Water Pollution Control Act of 1948 was the first federal law that demonstrated federal interest in addressing water pollution.[12] The Act did not provide much enforcement authority but provided technical assistance to state and local governments.[13] The evolution of federal interest evolved in the 1950s and 1960s to amend the Act in 1956 and 1961 and then led to the creation of the Water Quality Act of 1965 and Clean Water Restoration Act of 1966.[14] An increased recognition of the scope of the problem of water pollution and the difficulty and necessity of creating standards to regulate and permit discharges from various municipal and industrial sources, paired with public outrage over a series of focusing events, such as the Santa Barbara oil spill and Cuyahoga River fire in 1969 provoked public outrage over the slow pace of change.[15] These events resulted in the Water Quality

9. National Oceanic & Atmospheric Administration (NOAA), *A Brief History of Pollution*, https://oceanservice.noaa.gov/education/tutorial_pollution/02history.html (last visited May 6, 2022).

10. The Cuyahoga River was a major industrial corridor at the time before deindustrialization started taking place in the 1970s. It caught on fire a total of 13 times over the previous century. *See* Ohio History Connection, *Cuyahoga River Fire*, https://ohiohistorycentral.org/w/Cuyahoga_River_Fire (last visited Feb. 28, 2022).

11. The Conservation Movement recognized the vastly disappearing wilderness the United States had only recently acquired in the 19th century. In addition, there is an acknowledgment of the rapidly escalating post-World War II chemical industry's effect on humans, animals, and the natural environment. This movement has helped by focusing on events and gaining media attention, which prompts greater federal involvement in cleaning up waterways.

12. Edmund S. Muskie, *The Meaning of the 1977 Clean Water Act*, EPA Journal (July/Aug. 1978), *available at* https://archive.epa.gov/epa/aboutepa/meaning-1977-clean-water-act.html.

13. To this day what constitutes "waters of the United States" and thus EPA's regulatory reach under the CWA is still in dispute. *See* Jacob Finkle, *Jurisdictional Determinations: An Important Battlefield in the Clean Water Act Fight*, 43 Ecology L.Q. 301-36 (2016). Kayla A. Currie, *Clear Waters Ahead? The Clean Water Rule Attempts to Bring Clarity to the Scope of the Clean Water Act*, 47 Cumberland L. Rev. 191-226 (2016).

14. Elliott P. Laws & Lawrence R. Liebesman, *The Water Quality Act of 1987: A Major Step in Assuring the Quality of the Nation's Waters*, 17 ELR 10311 (Aug. 1987).

15. A blow out on Union Oil's offshore platform resulted in somewhere around 100,000 barrels of oil washed up on the beaches of Santa Barbara County. It remains the largest oil spill off the California coast and the images of the waste and dead sea life helped to act as a focusing event for long-brewing frustrations over federal inaction to deal with water pollution. Two years later a collision between two oil tankers in San Francisco Bay resulted in about 800,000 gallons of oil being dumped in the bay. *See* K.C. Clarke & Jeffrey J. Hemphill, *The Santa Barbara Oil Spill: A Retrospective, in* 64 Yearbook of the Association of Pacific Coast Geographers 157-62 (Darrick Danta ed., Univ. of Hawaii Press 2020), http://www.geog.ucsb.edu/~kclarke/Papers/SBOilSpill1969.pdf and *Tanker Collision*

Improvement Act of 1970 and then finally the Federal Water Pollution Control Act Amendments of 1972 that make up the modern CWA.[16] This Act, which was revised in 1977 and then 1987, gave EPA significant authority to develop a regulatory framework for discharges of pollutants into the waters in the United States.[17]

The CWA is the primary vehicle used by EPA to regulate the surface waters of the United States.[18] Its broad focus has centered historically on two issues, providing federal funding for the construction of municipal sewage treatment plants and developing regulatory requirements for municipal and industrial entities that discharge pollution.[19] The Act was supremely important in helping to develop and regulate municipal wastewater facilities in the United States in the 1970s and to develop a permitting system for all entities that discharges into the waters of the United States.[20] The Act contains six titles or sections to define its parameters.[21] We lay these out in Table 3.

Dumps a Huge Oil Spill in San Francisco Bay, N.Y. Times, Jan. 19, 1971, https://www.nytimes.com/1971/01/19/archives/tanker-collision-dumps-a-huge-oil-spill-in-san-francisco-bay.html.

16. *The Pros and Cons of Federal Jurisdiction Over Local Waters*, 95 Cong. Dig. 16-31 (2016).
17. The legal citation for this evolution follows: 1948 Federal Water Pollution Control Act, Pub. L. No. 80-845, 62 Stat. 1155; 1956 Water Pollution Control Act, Pub. L. No. 84-660, 70 Stat. 518; 1961 Amendments, Pub. L. No. 87-88, 75 Stat. 203; 1965 Water Quality Act, Pub. L. No. 89-234, 79 Stat. 903; 1966 Clean Water Restoration Act, Pub. L. No. 89-753, 80 Stat. 1246; 1970 Water Quality Improvement Act, Pub. L. No. 91-224, 84 Stat. 91; 1972 Amendments, Pub. L. No. 92-500, 86 Stat. 816; 1977 Clean Water Act, Pub. L. No. 95-217, 91 Stat. 1567; 1981 Municipal Wastewater Treatment Construction Grants Amendments, Pub. L. No. 97-117, 95 Stat. 1623; 1987 Water Quality Act, Pub. L. No. 100-104, 101 Stat. 7; 2014 Water Resources Reform and Development Act, Pub. L. No. 113-121, 128 Stat. 1273. For a legal review of the history and major statutory provisions of the CWA, see Claudia Copeland, Clean Water Act: Summary of the Law (2016).
18. America's Water Infrastructure Act of 2018, Pub. L. No. 115-270 (enacted Oct. 23, 2018), further amends the CWA to provide further oversight, research, and investment in water infrastructure projects, drinking water, and other actions. *See* U.S. EPA, *America's Water Infrastructure Act of 2018 (AWIA) Overview*, https://www.epa.gov/ground-water-and-drinking-water/americas-water-infrastructure-act-2018-awia (last updated Sept. 8, 2021).
19. U.S. EPA, *Clean Water Act Section 502: General Definitions*, https://www.epa.gov/cwa-404/clean-water-act-section-502-general-definitions (last updated Apr. 20, 2022).
20. National NPDES Stormwater Center, *What is NPDES?*, https://npdes.com/npdes (last visited May 6, 2022). U.S. EPA, *Pretreatment Standards and Requirements-General and Specific Prohibitions*, https://www.epa.gov/npdes/pretreatment-standards-and-requirements-general-and-specific-prohibitions (last updated Oct. 11, 2021).
21. The CWA can be used as a regulatory and permitting vehicle outside of discharges. For example, domestic oil and gas pipeline permitting does not require environmental analysis, the CWA and NEPA are often used in conjunction to require the U.S. Army Corps of Engineers (the Corps) to conduct such an analysis when the pipelines cross regulated waters. *See* Alexander Arkfeld, *Nationwide Permit 12 and Domestic Oil Pipelines: An Incompatible Relationship?*, 82 Wash. L. Rev. 1991-2024 (2017).

Table 3. Major Statutory Provisions of the CWA

Title	Description
I	Sets Goals and Policies for Pollution Control and Grant Programs
II	POTW Construction Grant Program
III	Development of Standards for Programs and Enforcement
IV	Permits for Point Sources, 404, and Biosolids
V	Citizen Suit and Whistleblower Protections
VI	Clean Water State Revolving Fund (CWSRF)

Title I sets goals and policies and establishes grant and pollution control programs. Title II establishes the basis for grants to subsidize the construction of municipal wastewater treatment plants. Title III manages standards and enforcement and establishes the need for discharge permits and technology-based standards for treatment plants such as effluent standards and NSPS, the national water quality inventory, water quality standards program, and the nonpoint source management program, as well as enforcement provisions for civil and criminal penalties.[22] Title IV establishes permit and licensure requirements for point sources and state certification requirements.[23] Title V contains the citizen suit provisions and whistleblower protections.[24] Title VI establishes the Clean Water State Revolving Funds (CWSRF) Program that replaced the original construction grants program for municipal wastewater facilities.[25] Broadly speaking, Titles II and VI focus on funding

22. EPA regulates nonpoint source pollution, but it cannot directly regulate and permit nonpoint sources themselves, causing a significant oversight issue for the Agency. *See* U.S. EPA, *Economic Incentives*, https://www.epa.gov/environmental-economics/economic-incentives (last updated Sept. 29, 2021).
23. Permitting authority can be devolved to the states and in the case of §404 permits for obstructing waterways or impacting wetlands. *See* Adam Blalock, *The Process for Assuming Clean Water Act Section 404 Permitting Authority and an Overview of the States Seeking Assumption*, 43 Admin. & Reg. L. News 15-18 (2018).
24. Citizen suit provisions in the CAA and the CWA were innovative tools to have citizens and environmental groups that represent them to challenge the actions of regulatory agencies such as EPA under these laws or compel them to meet their legal obligations under an Act and have provided examples for other countries. *See* Ozge Atil, *Adopting the Citizen Suit Provision of the United States Clean Water Act as a Tool for Water Pollution Enforcement in Turkey*, J. Transnat'l L. & Pol'y 75-123 (2017).
25. The CWA does not empower EPA to regulate drinking water. The Safe Drinking Water Act (SDWA) gives EPA authority to set drinking water quality standards for public water systems in the United States (42 U.S.C. §300f). The Act does not authorize EPA to regulate bottled water or private wells serving under 25 people. It gives the agency authority to regulate injection wells. EPA uses Maximum Containment Levels (MCLs) as the primary mechanism to determine the legal threshold for a substance allowed in public water systems. These standards regulate the following: microorganisms, disinfectants, disinfection byproducts, inorganic chemicals, organic chemicals, and radionuclides. EPA has authority to set quality standards for over 170,000 public waters systems in the United States, but it is often criticized for its limited focus on what it actually regulates, given the significant number of chemicals and compounds that make their way to POTWs.

    U.S. EPA, Understanding the Safe Water Drinking Act (EPA 816-F-04-030 June 2004), *available at* https://www.epa.gov/sites/production/files/2015-04/documents/epa816f04030.pdf.

the construction of municipal wastewater plants known as publicly owned treatment works (POTWs), while the other provisions set out regulatory requirements.[26]

The CWA empowered the Agency to regulate point source pollution from stationary sources such as power plants, concentrated animal feeding operations (CAFOs), factories, POTWs, and industrial stormwater systems, including discharges from construction sites among others. Arguably, this is the most successful and widest reaching tool in the CWA tool belt. Point source means "any discernible, confined and discrete conveyance, including but not limited to any pipe, ditch, channel, tunnel, conduit, well, discrete fissure, container, rolling stock, concentrated animal feeding operation, or vessel or other floating craft, from which pollutants are or may be discharged." This term does not include agricultural stormwater discharges and return flows from irrigated agriculture.[27]

Regulatory authority over point source pollution allows EPA to require point source polluters to have a permit through the national pollutant discharge elimination system (NPDES).[28] The NPDES sets limits on what can be discharged from the point source, how much, as well as establishing monitoring and reporting requirements. Today, no point source may discharge

26. A major innovation in the CWA, as well as the CAA and RCRA, is the provision for citizens' lawsuits. The CWA gives individuals and organizations the ability to bring legal action if they feel government, in this case primarily EPA, is not complying with the statute's requirements. The concept undergirding the citizen suit provision harkens back to the complex nature and discretion given to EPA to comply with congressional mandates under the major federal environmental statutes passed in the 1970s. To bring suit you must be a person affected by the alleged non-compliance and gain standing. The test of standing focuses on whether there was identifiable and real damage to the individual, that the cause can be established, and a reasonable remedy can be found through litigation. This is often known as: injury in fact, causation, and redressability. Such provisions are very important, but it is often difficult to achieve standing and it is a costly process. This has become a vehicle for environmental groups, such as Sierra Club and Public Citizen to file lawsuits on behalf of clients, but as one can imagine complex litigation often results. A good example might be members of an environmental justice (EJ) community live near a shipping channel and the pollution coming from industrial sources across the fence line have negatively affected their health. They have to establish the pollution and their health problems are related, the problem stems from non-compliance with the CAA, and the courts can find a reasonable solution. Meeting these burdens is often very difficult. EJ communities can also bring suit under civil rights provisions of federal law, which is an equally difficult task. Arguably, the citizen suit provisions have spawned a larger legal industry dedicated to protecting corporate clients from litigation than individuals. *See* Hunton Andrews Kurth, *Clean Water Act Citizen Suits: Defense Litigation and Settlement Strategies*, Strafford CLE Webinar (Mar. 19, 2014), http://media.straffordpub.com/products/clean-water-act-citizen-suits-defense-litigation-and-settlement-strategies-2019-03-14/presentation.pdf.

27. U.S. EPA, *NPDES State Program Information*, https://www.epa.gov/npdes/npdes-state-program-information (last updated Oct. 11, 2021). Any facility that discharges directly into the waters of the United States requires an NDPES permit, but agricultural stormwater discharges and discharges from irrigated agriculture are exempt from being legally defined as a point source for permitting purposes.

28. U.S. EPA, *National Pollution Discharge Elimination System (NPDES)*, https://www.epa.gov/npdes (last updated Apr. 28, 2022).

pollutants into surface water without an NPDES permit.[29] Perhaps the greatest success with this program is the Agency's ability to regulate municipal wastewater treatment plants.[30] In the 1970s, municipalities lacked funding and expertise to develop such plants. EPA helped local governments fund them and then regulate their operation through NPDES. Originally Title II of the CWA provided grant funding to states under a formula allocation. The federal government paid 75% of the cost of this program, which was subsequently reduced in 1981 to 55%. By 1984, Congress had appropriated about $41 billion under this program making it the largest non-military public works program since the development of the Interstate Highway System. Later, Congress replaced the grants program with the CWSRF once it was determined the initial phase of financial support was no longer needed.[31]

Nonpoint source pollution is any source of water pollution that does not meet this legal definition of point source pollution listed above.[32] Nonpoint source pollution is generated from a range of sources from rainfall to snowmelt, land runoff, drainage, or seepage and the Agency has less authority to regulate these kinds of pollution. EPA does monitor and collect data through such programs as the National Nonpoint Source Monitoring Program.

29. U.S. EPA, *History of the Clean Water Act*, https://www.epa.gov/laws-regulations/history-clean-water-act (last updated May 27, 2021). One area the Agency has been vocally criticized for is the acceptance of biosolids. Critics often simply refer to this as a rebranding of toxic sludge. While pretreatment standards are effective at eliminating many pathogens and other chemicals, NPDES permits do not capture the thousands of chemicals that enter our waterways and end up at POTWs, such as pharmaceuticals, certain organic and inorganic compounds, and many known substances that are hazardous to human and/or animal health and the environment. One could argue this is a reasonable practical solution or a deal with the devil for what to do with billions of pounds of effluent with no practical purpose. An industry has developed around selling these fertilizers or giving them away to farms and agribusinesses. Perhaps the better question is what to do with toxic sludge otherwise and the truth is EPA would need to develop much stricter standards to require NPDES permit holders to reduce an array of substances in pretreatment or require POTWs to deal with the issue. Another option is to simply inject it into the bedrock like fracking companies routinely do, which is not a viable solution, although the fracking industry has developed in great part because they were exempted from the CWA and SWDA on these grounds. Known as the fracking loophole, this allowed the United States to become, as of 2020, the world's largest oil producer again, but at great environmental cost whose full damage is yet unknown. *See* John Stauber & Sheldon Rampton, Toxic Sludge Is Good for You (Common Courage Press 2002).

30. U.S. EPA, *Pretreatment Standards and Requirements-General and Specific Prohibitions*, https://www.epa.gov/npdes/pretreatment-standards-and-requirements-general-and-specific-prohibitions (last visited Oct. 11, 2021).

31. Water Infrastructure Financing: History of EPA Appropriations, Cong. Res. Serv. CRS Rep. 96-647 (Apr. 10, 2019). Congress no longer wanted to fund the bulk of the infrastructure development cost and effectively stopped the program as conceived in its heyday, replacing it with a loan program. It is often forgotten today how inexperienced and incapable a significant number of municipal governments were at managing complex wastewater systems and funding them by the 1970s.

32. U.S. EPA, *Basic Information About Nonpoint Source (NPS) Pollution*, https://www.epa.gov/nps/basic-information-about-nonpoint-source-nps-pollution (last updated July 8, 2021) [hereinafter *NPS Pollution*].

Related programs, such as the 319 Nonpoint Management Program provides grants to states, territories, and tribes related to assessing the success of nonpoint implementation projects. Funding for FY 2019 totaled $165.4 million, which is not terribly extensive given the scope of the problem.[33]

Enforcing the CWA often starts at the state level.[34] Over time, EPA has empowered states in the permitting process. In the NPDES program, state regulators issue permits directly in all states except Idaho, Massachusetts, New Hampshire, and New Mexico. Tribal governments and U.S. territories are not afforded this ability.[35] Not only do states issue most of the civil enforcement violations to permitted facilities, but they engage in most of the day-to-day monitoring of facilities.[36]

The CWA is enforced through a compliance monitoring strategy. EPA focuses on three areas under the Act.[37] The first area centers on wastewater management issues. This covers a range of problems stemming primarily from NPDES permits. This includes ensuring regulated entities engage in timely and accurate reporting through discharge monitoring reports (DMRs), do not violate permit limits, engage in proper pretreatment, manage, and report unlawful discharges, and the like. Wastewater management includes stormwater, debris, soil and sediment, and other pollutants that wash down storm

33. U.S. EPA, *319 Grant Program for States and Territories*, https://www.epa.gov/nps/319-grant-program-states-and-territories (last updated Feb. 2, 2022). The amount of resources that EPA provides to states, territories, and tribal governments for this purpose is infinitesimally small, given the scope of the problem. *See NPS Pollution*, *supra* note 32.

34. U.S. EPA, *Basic Information on Enforcement*, https://www.epa.gov/enforcement/basic-information-enforcement (last updated Feb. 22, 2022). Theodore M. Hammett & Joel Epstein, Local Prosecution of Environmental Crime xiv (National Inst. of Justice 1993). As previously noted in Chapter 1, only 25 environmental crimes were prosecuted by the federal government prior to 1983. States engage in the bulk of compliance monitoring and enforcement of all federal environmental statutes and that has more and more over time extended to permitting itself. The former can be troublesome, given many states do not have the resources for stringent monitoring, but EPA may not have a choice with constrained budgets. The Agency can be criticized for how much oversight it likely is not able to offer of those state agencies it oversees and delegates significant permitting authority for its signature programs under the CWA. States and EPA rely on civil remedies almost exclusively in many areas. See David M. Uhlmann, *Environmental Crime Comes of Age: The Evolution of Criminal Enforcement in the Environmental Regulatory Scheme*, 4 Utah L. Rev. 1244 (2009).

35. Legal and congressional fights over determining federal authority for waters in the United States is ongoing. *See* Cameron Secord, *Uncertain Waters: The Legal Implications of the "New Waters of the United States" Rule on the Energy Sector and a Potential Remedy Within Administrative Law*, 54 Hous. L. Rev. 963-94 (2017). *See also* Jessalin Powell, *Clean Water or a Guilty Conscience? The Newly Proposed Rulemaking to Rescind and Replace the Clean Water Act Rule Has Ethical and Professional Implications for EPA Attorneys*, 43 J. Legal Prof. 87-100 (2018).

36. U.S. EPA, *National Pretreatment Program*, https://www.epa.gov/npdes/national-pretreatment-program (last updated July 12, 2021).

37. U.S. EPA, *Clean Water Act (CWA) Compliance Monitoring*, https://www.epa.gov/compliance/clean-water-act-cwa-compliance-monitoring (last updated July 13, 2021). Other areas can be investigated and enforced through a civil or criminal process, but this three-prong strategy covers most of the general scenarios investigators would encounter.

drains. EPA monitors CAFOs, POTWs, construction sites, and any entity with an NPDES permit and monitors overflows to make sure pretreatment standards are met, facilities do not interfere with water monitoring equipment in the pretreatment process, and ultimately do not engage in unlawful/unpermitted discharges. Typical violations involving wastewater management issues revolve around recordkeeping and reporting and illegal or unpermitted discharges from a variety of sources.

The second section of their compliance monitoring strategy is what is known as §404 permitting.[38] This section regulates the dredging, filling, or alteration of waterways, such as lakes, streams, rivers, estuaries, and wetlands.[39] The U.S. Army Corps of Engineers (the Corps) issues §404 permits to prevent losses to wetlands and to ensure illegal dredging and filling of waterways does not occur.[40] Developers require these permits if their projects impact a wetland.[41] If they must fill in a wetland, they can buy what are known as offsets, where they purchase credits for a restoration project that enhances a conservation area to mitigate in a broader, national sense what they are doing locally. Mitigation banking developed to serve this need.[42] Banks buy or create credits for the restoration, creation, or enhancement of aquatic resources they can sell to developers. Developers buy these credits to help secure a §404 permit. The Regulatory In-Lieu Fee and Bank Tracking System (RIBITS) tracks banks engaged in this marketplace.[43]

In-lieu mitigation is another option where the permittee works with a mitigation sponsor (a public agency or nonprofit organization) where the sponsor collects funds from multiple permittees from various projects and pools that

---

38. Michael C. Blumm & Elisabeth Mering, *Vetoing Wetland Permits Under Section 404(c) of the Clean Water Act: A History of Inter-Federal Agency Controversy and Reform*, 33 UCLA J. Envtl. L. & Pol'y 215-308 (2015).
39. What qualifies as filling or altering waterways or fill itself is always subject to scrutiny. *See* Nathaniel Browand, *Shifting the Boundary Between the Section 402 and 404 Permitting Programs by Expanding the Definition of Fill Material*, 31 B.C. Envtl. Aff. L. Rev. 617-47. (2004) and Thomas Hanley, *A Developer's Dream: The United States Claims Court's New Analysis of Section 404 Takings*, 19 B.C. Envtl. Aff. L. Rev. 317-52 (1991).
40. Rebecca Lave, *Stream Mitigation Banking*, 5 Wire's Water 1-7 (2018).
41. John Fumero et al., *Waters of the United States: A New Era for Federal Wetland Jurisdiction*, 94 Fla. B. J. 48-50 (2020).
42. Judicial review is available for final Agency actions under the CWA. *See* Roberto Borgert, 2018, *What About* Bell?: *Overcoming the Presumption in Favor of Requiring Finality in the CWA's Direct-Review Provision*, 85 U. Chi. L. Rev. 145-91 (2018).
43. U.S. Army Corps of Eng'rs, *RIBITS*, https://ribits.ops.usace.army.mil/ords/f?p=107:2. Real estate develops typically do a Phase I environmental assessment of a site. It has become common practice, however, to look at the impact on wetlands and the need to determine whether a §404 permit is necessary. In good American fashion this has spawned a lucrative cottage industry in the legal profession. *See* Peter Stark Strassner et al., *Do you need a Section 404 permit for your real estate development?*. ThompsonCoburn.com, Sept. 12, 2016, at https://www.thompsoncoburn.com/insights/publications/item/2016-09-12/do-you-need-a-section-404-permit-for-your-real-estate-development.

money to create another aquatic resource site to compensate for the wetland loss.[44] The final option is permittee-responsible mitigation, where the individual or organization requesting the permit is responsible for funding a mitigation scheme to offset the habitat loss caused by the development.[45] Broadly speaking, §404 offenses typically result from unlawful dredging or filling of wetlands without a permit. Common examples include: companies developing a subdivision; commercial or industrial facilities that impact wetlands without a proper permit; or individuals and companies altering waterways without a permit through removing soil, dredging, damming, or other methods of impacting waterways or wetlands.[46]

The third area of compliance monitoring under the CWA is the prevention of oil spills and spill prevention.[47] The CWA prohibits the discharge of oil in U.S. waters.[48] The CWA was enhanced with the passage of the Oil Pollution Act (1990) to help EPA manage the response to discharges of hazardous substances.[49] EPA requires owners and operators of oil facilities to implement plans to prevent discharges. Regulated facilities must have a facility response plan for facilities that store and use oil, as well as a spill prevention control and countermeasures plan.[50] A spill prevention control and countermeasures plan regulates the prevention, preparedness, and response to oil discharges at nontransportation-related facilities. Illegal actions related to the prevention of oil spills include ships illegally discharging oil in the navigable waters of

---

44. James M. McElfish Jr., *It's Legal: What's New in Environmental Law*, 72 PLANNING 18-21 (Aug./Sep't 2006).
45. Obtaining a §404 permit is a financial and regulatory hurdle for developers that have strong interests in clear guidelines with low costs, but it can be difficult to quantify offsets when applying for a permit to show the applicant is going to properly mitigate their environmental damage. *See* Jon Schutz, *The Steepest Hurdle in Obtaining a Clean Water Act Section 404 Permit: Complying with EPA's 4040(b)(1) Guidelines' Least Environmentally Damaging Practicable Alternative Requirement*, 24 UCLA J. ENVTL. L. & POL'Y 235-57 (2005). Nicola Ulibarri & Jiarui Tao, *Evaluating Environmental Permitting Process Duration: The Case of the Clean Water Act Section 404 Permits*, 62 J. ENVTL. PLAN. & MGMT. 2124-44 (2019).
46. Legal problems can arise when individuals and companies purchase property that was illegally filled without a permit. *See* John Webster Kilborn, *Purchaser Liability for the Restoration of Illegally Filled Wetlands Under Section 404 of the Clean Water Act*, 18 B.C. ENVTL. AFF. L. REV. 319-57 (1991).
47. Michael J. Wray & Rachel Reese, *Does a Good Deed Go Unpunished? The Availability of Responder Immunity in an Oil Pollution Response*, 8 TEX. J. OIL, GAS, & ENERGY L. 349-82 (2013).
48. Katherine A. Swanson, *The Cost of Doing Business: Corporate Vicarious Criminal Liability for the Negligent Discharge of Oil Under the Clean Water Act*, 84 WASH. L. REV. 555-79 (2009).
49. David H. Sump, *OPA 90: Twenty-Five Years of Judicial Interpretation*, 39 TUL. MAR. L.J. 439-69 (2015).
50. Of course, an industry arises to provide such plans for any facility that has a capacity to store oil products exceeding 1,320 gallons. This involves a variety of applications, such as oil production and reclamation facilities, electrical power substations, marinas, auto dealerships, generators, farms and ranches, asphalt plants, and bulk oil storage facilities. *See* Spillco, *SPCC Plans for All Industries*, https://spillco.net/spcc-plan/ (last visited May 6, 2022).

the United States, and recordkeeping, reporting, and unpermitted discharge issues from facilities that store and transport oil.[51]

Criminal violations of the CWA tend to either be negligent violations or knowing violations.[52] The former tends to be the lesser evil and involves actions committed by individuals, municipalities, companies, or other organizations, where they did not undertake reasonable care in their actions that resulted in the violation of a federal environmental statute. Knowing violations are willful violations of a statute, where an entity acted intentionally to break the law. Criminal charges under the CWA rest on a beyond a reasonable doubt standard and prosecutors and investigators choose cases where they feel the crime is best categorized as a criminal violation and that guilt can meet this high standard. Civil cases rest on a preponderance of the evidence standard that guilt is more likely true than not, a lower standard.[53] Criminal provisions under the CWA fall into a smaller set of categories focused on whether an individual or company engaged in negligent or knowing violations of the Act and maximum punishments increase for the latter. In Table 4 we organize criminal provisions of the CWA with penalties.[54] We organize this by 12 scenarios laid out by EPA, as well as maximum penalties for each negligent and knowing violation.

If an individual directly discharges into the waters of the United States without a NPDES or §404 permit, a negligent violation can land them in prison for a maximum of one year and/or a $2,500-$25,000 per day penalty (see first row in Table 4, next page).[55] For a knowing violation, a defendant can receive up to three years and $50,000 per day.[56] These penalties increase for second offenses. Unlawfully discharging oil or hazardous substances receives similar penalties as does the failure to report discharges (see row 3 in the Table 4). Other violations of CWA pretreatment standards and local pretreatment standards (we combined these two categories in the table), as well

51. Lawrence I. Kiern, *Liability, Compensation, and Financial Responsibility Under the Oil Pollution Act of 1990: A Review of the Second Decade*, 36 Tul. Mar. L.J. 1-64 (2011).
52. Stephen J. Darmody, *The Oil Pollution Act's Criminal Penalties: On a Collision Course With the Law of the Sea*, 21 B.C. Envtl. Aff. L. Rev. 89-145 (1993).
53. U.S. EPA, *Basic Information on Enforcement*, https://www.epa.gov/enforcement/basic-information-enforcement (last updated Feb. 22, 2022).
54. U.S. EPA, *Criminal Provisions of the Clean Water Act*, https://www.epa.gov/enforcement/criminal-provisions-clean-water-act (last updated Nov. 18, 2021). This page contains extensive information from EPA on all criminal provisions and penalties under the CWA and is the basis for Table 4.
55. Szonja Ludvig, *Is the Clean Water Act's Diligent Prosecution Bar Jurisdictional?*, 5 Brigham Young U. L. Rev. 1408 (2013).
56. The reach of the CWA typically makes a permit holder liable for discharges under the permit alone if those charges were reasonably contemplated at the time of issuance and the permittee discloses said discharges. *See* Mae Manupipatpong, *ICG Hazard: Permitting Away the Clean Water Act*, 43 Ecology L.Q. 449-71 (2016).

Table 4. Criminal Provisions of the CWA

Violation	Statute	Negligent Penalty Max	Knowing Penalty Max
Direct Discharge to waters of the United States	33 U.S.C. 1319(1) & (2)	1 year and/or $2,500 - 25,000 per day	3 years and/or $5,000 - 50,000 per day
Discharge of Oil or Hazardous Substance	33 U.S.C. 1319(1) & (2) & 1321 (b)(3)	1 year and/or $2,500 - 25,000 per day	3 years and/or $5,000 - 50,000 per day
Failure to Report Oil or Hazardous Discharge	33 U.S.C. 1321(b)(5)	5 years and/or fines under 18 U.S.C. 3571	
Discharge to a POTW Violating Pretreatment (or Local Pretreatment)	33 U.S.C. 1319 (1) (A) & (2)(A)	1 year and/or $2,500 - 25,000 per day	3 years and/or $5,000 - 50,000 per day
Discharge to a POTW Causing Harm to the System	33 U.S.C. 1319(1) (B) & (2)(B)	1 year and/or $2,500 - 25,000 per day	3 years and/or $5,000 - 50,000 per day
Discharge to a POTW causing Pretreatment Violation	33 U.S.C. 1319 (1) & (2)	1 year and/or $2,500 - 25,000 per day	3 years and/or $5,000 - 50,000 per day
CWA Knowing Endangerment	33 U.S.C. 1319(3)	–	15 years and/or $250,000
CWA False Statements	33 U.S.C. 1319(4)	–	2 years and/or $10,000
Tampering with a Monitoring Device or Equipment	33 U.S.C. 1319(4)	–	2 years and/or $10,000
Rivers and Harbors Act Violations	33 C.F.R. 320-323	1 year and/ or $100,000 ($200,000 corporations)	
Ocean Dumping Act	33 U.S.C. 1411		5 years and/or $250,000
Act to Prevent Pollution from Ships	33 U.S.C. 1908(a)		10 years

as causing a discharge from a POTW that causes harm to the facility. There are criminal provisions for knowing endangerment, where an action by a person "knowingly puts another at risk of imminent danger of death or serious bodily injury," which is one of the more serious criminal provisions in the Act. Violations carry up to 15 years in prison and/or a $250,000 fine; for subsequent provisions this can be doubled. Making false statements or tampering with a pollution control monitoring device are also potential criminal violations, as are impacting the navigable waters of the United States without a permit (Rivers and Harbors Act), transporting materials from the United States with intent to dump into ocean waters without a permit or in violation of regulations (Ocean Dumping Act), or illegal discharges of waste, oil, and other hazardous substances from ships via the Act to Prevent Pollution From Ships (APPS).[57]

In the section below, we analyze all 828 prosecutions that occurred under the CWA from 1983-2019. We discuss how EPA has worked with federal prosecutors to enforce the provisions of the Act, as well as what provisions they chose to enforce, and penalties meted out to environmental criminals. We discuss if they followed their broader compliance monitoring strategy and the themes that develop in their prosecutions over almost 40 years of criminal enforcement actions, as well as how penalties were applied under the provisions in Table 4.

II. Themes in CWA Prosecutions

We explore how the CWA was used as a criminal enforcement tool in Figure 8 (next page), which shows the total number of prosecutions under the Act by fiscal year over the last 37 years. A prosecution can typically span multiple years, so the year it is settled is not generally indicative of when it began. We can track these from when the OECA was created and Anne Gorsuch was removed from office in 1984 to a high point in the Clinton era of 50 annual prosecutions in 1998. We find a total of 53 prosecutions settled in the 1980s, which rises fairly dramatically to 219 in the 1990s, and then 288 total prosecutions from 2000-2009, and finally 268 prosecutions until 2019. We can see dips in prosecutions both after the 2009 financial crisis, as well as the years after the Trump presidency begins. All analysis here and below comes from EPA's database.[58]

57. 16 U.S.C. §1431 (Ocean Dumping Act). Also known as the Marine Protection, Research, and Sanctuaries Act (MPRSA), it prohibits the transportation of materials from the United States or to the country for purposes of dumping it the ocean without a permit. For an enforcement discussion, see Robert B. Parrish et al., *Criminalization of Maritime Casualties Circa 2013*, 87 Tul. L. Rev. 995-1023 (2013). 33 U.S.C. §1905 (Act to Prevent Pollution From Ships). The Act implements the provisions of the International Convention for the Prevention of Pollution From Ships (MARPOL). The goal is to minimize global ocean pollution. For a discussion of enforcement, see Taylor Dunne, *MARPOL Annex VI: Disproportionate Burden or Necessary Regulations for the Greater Good? How Pollution Controls on the Shipping Industry Are Currently Affecting and Will Continue to Affect Maritime Commerce and the Global Environment*, 44 Tul. Mar. L.J. 193-216 (2019).

58. U.S. EPA, *Summary of Criminal Prosecutions Database*, https://cfpub.epa.gov/compliance/criminal_prosecution/index.cfm (last updated May 9, 2022).

Figure 8. Total Annual CWA Criminal Prosecutions Adjudicated Since 1983

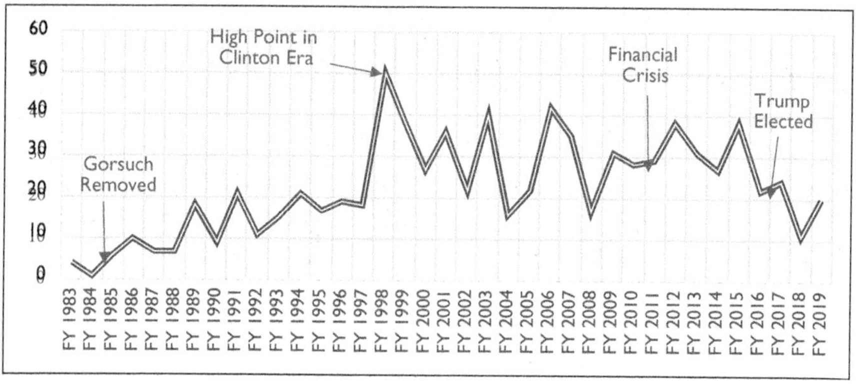

If we break these results down by U.S. state in Figure 9, Louisiana, California, and Ohio have the largest number of total prosecutions at 62, 61, and 54, respectively over this time period. Maine has no prosecutions and Vermont and Wisconsin have one prosecution. The average number of prosecutions across the states over time is 16.34. We find that four prosecutions were completed in Washington, D.C., five cases in Puerto Rico, and one in the U.S. Virgin Islands over the last 37 years.[59]

If you examine CWA prosecutions, they often occur in conjunction with other federal charging statutes. We find nine case examples where the CAA and the CWA are used together. Kenneth Morrison discharged about 1,000 gallons of oil into the Schuylkill River in June 1993. Morrison attempted to build a sand berm to contain the oil instead of notifying officials of the discharge. He was charged for not just the discharge, but also for failing to notify officials of the discharge.[60] He pled guilty to two counts and was sentenced to 12 months and a day incarceration on each count, to run concurrently and was ordered to pay $50,000 in restitution and a $100 special assessment fee. In a different case, a man named James Bragg owned the Oaks Subdivision Sewage Treatment plant in Grandview, West Virginia. Between 1996-1998, Bragg did not operate the plant and while he did apply for and receive an NPDES permit, he did not submit DMRs and violated fecal coliform limits on at least 10 occasions. He was charged with knowing violations of the CWA, as well as the CAA. He was sentenced in 1999 to

59. In the case against Ahmed Hujabre, it is not possible to determine the U.S. state or territory of the prosecution from the case summary. Web search identifies Hujabre as the plant manager at PCS Nitrogen in Louisiana. *See Plant Worker Pleads Guilty*, HOUMATODAY, Dec. 27, 2002.

60. United States v. Morrison, No. 2:17-cr-00130-PPS-APR (N.D. Ind. Dec. 6, 2019).

Figure 9. Total CWA Prosecutions by U.S. State and Territory

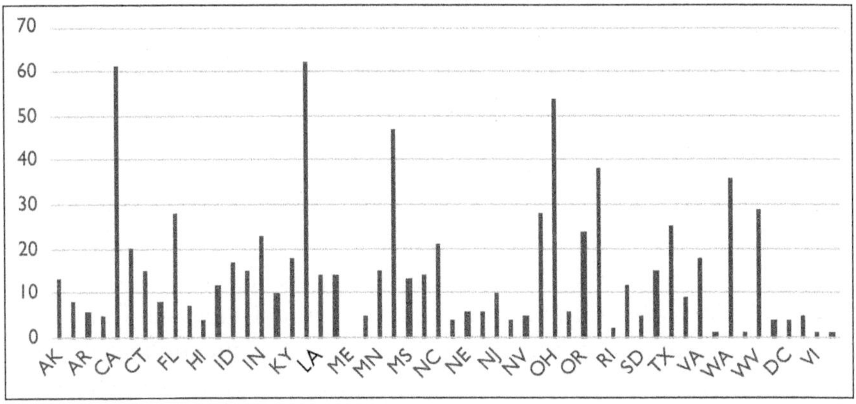

6 months' incarceration, 6 months' home confinement, and 12 months of probation.[61]

Prosecutors used CERCLA + the CWA in 13 cases. These cases tended to involve illegal discharges of hazardous materials and the defendants failed to notify officials of the offense, which the latter is a violation of CERCLA. HCI Chemtec Inc. spilled 20,000 gallons of sodium hydroxide from the company's Kansas City plant in September 1995.[62] Investigators estimated about 134,000 pounds were discharged into the Missouri River. The defendants were charged with conspiracy, false statements, illegal discharge, and failure to notify officials of the release of a hazardous substance. HCI was sentenced to 36 months of probation, $21,200 in restitution, and fined $175,000. Co-defendant Andre Rober was sentenced to 24 months of probation, a $25 special assessment fee, and a $1,000 fine. Marc Peterson was sentenced to 36 months of probation and fined $1,000. Fred Garner was sentenced to four months incarceration, a $100 special assessment fee, and fined $100.[63]

Wagner Construction JV was prosecuted and sentenced in 2008 for a large spill of Plasti-Kote (a mixture of acrylic polymer and xylene) that spilled on the ground and into a creek at the company's facility in Lakeside, California. The company admitted a worker spilled the chemicals when operating a forklift that was moving 55-gallon drums. A call to 911, however, alerted investigators who found very high levels of toluene in the drums. Investigators found about 11 roll-off containers (large dumpsters with wheels that can

61. Bragg v. West Virginia Coal Ass'n, 248 F.3d 275, 291 (4th Cir. 2001).

62. Press Release, U.S. EPA, Company and Employee Sentenced for Caustic Soda Spill, July 25, 1997, https://archive.epa.gov/epapages/newsroom_archive/newsreleases/99b87d77b963b075852564df005c9261.html.

63. United States v. HCI Chemtech, No. 4:76 CR00156-001 (W.D. Mo.).

be loaded on a tractor trailer) of soil were contaminated with toluene on-site. The company was closing its facility and moving to Tampa, Florida, and illegally disposed of the chemicals on the ground at the Lakeside facility. The company and two co-defendants were charged under the CWA for negligent actions related to the illegal disposal, charged under RCRA for illegal storage and disposal of the hazardous waste, and charged under CERCLA for failure to notify. The company was sentenced to 24 months of probation, a $125 special assessment fee, restitution in the amount of $7,503 to the San Diego County Department of Environmental Health Services, Hazardous Materials Management Division for the spill cleanup, and was ordered to pay a $20,000 federal fine. Co-defendant Guillermo Garcia and Ivan Oliver was sentenced to 24 months of probation, 4 months' home confinement, and ordered to pay a $1,000 fine. Another co-defendant, Ivan Oliver, was sentenced to 24 months of probation and 15 months' incarceration.[64]

In 57 cases prosecutors used RCRA and CWA together in the prosecutions. RCRA governs storage, transport, and disposal of hazardous materials, so these cases typically involve a violation of one or more of those violations plus illegal discharge under the CWA. Gabriel Lefave was arrested while dumping waste in the East Mojave National Preserve in California. He along with two other co-defendants and his company Fluid Polymer were indicted for the illegal transportation and disposal of the material.[65] The defendants were charged under RCRA for conspiracy and for the illegal transport and disposal without a manifest. In addition, they were charged under the CWA for the illegal discharge. Lefave was sentenced to 60 months of probation and ordered to pay a $3,750 fine. Fluid Polymers was sentenced to pay a $49,898 fine. Co-defendant Gene Lefave was sentenced to 46 months' incarceration, 12 months of probation, and fined $39,898.[66]

EPA investigators along with investigators from the Missouri Department of Natural Resources determined that Usona Metal Finishing Company stored hazardous waste solvents at its facility in Cuba, Missouri, and illegally disposed of them in the sanitary sewer system.[67] These substances included nitric acid and methyl ethyl ketone, which is a liquid solvent used in surface coatings, adhesives, printing ink, and magnetic tapes. The company and its owner Paul Fredericks were charged under the CWA for the illegal discharge

64. No. 07CR3443-IEG (S.D. Cal.).
65. Press Release, U.S. EPA, Nevada Company and Employees Indicted, Aug. 29, 1997, https://archive.epa.gov/epapages/newsroom_archive/newsreleases/b915eb05882a0b218525650200670c80.html.
66. No. CR-95-8 (C.D. Cal.).
67. U.S. DOJ, Environmental Crimes Monthly Bulletin, March 2009, at https://www.justice.gov/sites/default/files/enrd/legacy/2015/04/13/LPS-190681-v1-ECS_Bulletin_2009_03_Block.PDF.

and charged under RCRA for storing, transporting, and disposing of hazardous waste without a permit. Both defendants were sentenced to 36 months of probation and each was ordered to pay $4,681.[68]

In two cases, prosecutors used the Toxic Substances Control Act (TSCA) and the CWA to prosecute defendants. TSCA governs toxic substances, particularly polychlorinated biphenyls (PCBs). These were very common in commercial and industrial applications before being phased out by the 1990s. One function in particular was their use in power transformers. Robert Derecktor was prosecuted for dumping transformers on his land and investigators dug up the material and found PCBs leaking in the ground.[69] He operated a shipyard building and repair business in Middleton, Rhode Island. He and his co-defendants were charged under TSCA for the illegal disposal of transformers leaking PCBs, charged under RCRA for the storage and disposal of hazardous wastes without a permit, charged under CERCLA for failure to report the release of a hazardous substance, and charged with the illegal discharge of pollutants under the CWA. Derecktor Inc. was sentenced to a $600,000 fine. Derecktor himself was ordered to pay a $75,000 fine and sentenced to 60 months of probation.[70] Thompson Center Arms and three co-defendants were prosecuted in 1985 for illegally disposing of hazardous waste in the Cocheco River in New Hampshire. The defendants were charged under the CWA for the illegal discharge, charged under TSCA for the illegal storage of PCBs, and charged under CERCLA for failure to notify of the hazardous release, as well as being charged with making false statements, and with conspiracy. Charges against the three co-defendants were dismissed. Thompson was sentenced to pay a $75,000 fine.[71]

The Federal Insecticide, Fungicide, and Rodenticide Act (FIFRA) and the CWA were used to prosecute defendants in three cases. Charles Lewis Thomas III and Pied Piper Pest Control Inc. dumped cypermethrin, an insecticide, in a park. They were charged with illegal discharge under the CWA and FIFRA for the misuse of a registered pesticide.[72] Thomas was sentenced to 24 months of probation and was ordered to pay a $25 special assessment fee. The company was sentenced to 24 months of probation, a $525 special assessment

68. No. 4:08CR565HEA (E.D. Mo.).
69. *A Rhode Island Shipbuilder and His Firm were Fined*, UPI, Dec. 30, 1986, https://www.upi.com/Archives/1986/12/30/A-Rhode-Island-shipbuilder-and-his-firm-were-fined/5280536302800/.
70. United States v. Robert E. Derecktor of Rhode Island Inc., No. 86-022 (D.R.I. 1986). Robert E. Derecktor of Rhode Island Inc. v. United States, 762 F. Supp. 1019 (D.R.I. 1991).
71. No. CR-92-200014 (W.D. Ark.).
72. *EPA Summons Pied Piper to Court*, EHS Today, Apr. 29, 2019, https://www.ehstoday.com/archive/article/21905699/epa-summons-pied-piper-to-court.

fee, $10,000 in restitution to Montgomery County and $15,000 in fines.[73] John Martin Anderson, president of A.C. Supply Inc., sold a registered pesticide (diclofop methyl) to non-certified applicators and then falsified records of the transaction. He was also charged for illegally discharging pesticides into the Big Horn River in Wyoming without an NPDES permit. He was charged under FIFRA for the illegal transaction, under the CWA for the illegal discharge, and charged with false statements for the false reporting. On November 20, 1984, Anderson was sentenced to 36 months of probation and must comply with all environmental laws for 18 months. He was ordered to contribute $5,000 to the Big Horn County Agricultural Extension Service or pay a $6,150 fine.[74] HPI Products Inc. along with co-defendant and owner of the company William Garvey and vice president of the company Hans Nielsen were prosecuted in Missouri for illegally storing hazardous waste generated in the pesticide manufacturing process and disposing of them in the municipal sewer system.[75] They were charged under the CWA, RCRA, and FIFRA for illegally storing and disposing of pesticides. HPI pled guilty and was sentenced to pay a $300,000 federal fine, and Garvey was sentenced to 12 months' incarceration and a $100,000 federal fine.[76]

Taking all of this information in, we find California, Louisiana, Florida, Missouri, and Ohio to have the most prosecutions over time. In some states like Maine, a federal environmental crime investigated by EPA has never been settled in our data. Truthfully, these numbers are quite low and there is a very low probability in any state of being prosecuted criminally for violating the CWA. When those prosecutions do occur, they appear to be either pure CWA prosecutions or done in conjunction with RCRA. Prosecutions with CWA in conjunction with FIFRA, CAA, CERCLA, or TSCA are decidedly rare across time and space. What themes do we actually see in these prosecutions over time? Do the major themes in prosecutions over time reflect EPA's compliance monitoring strategy, and if so how? We answer these questions in Figure 10.

Figure 10 shows a typology we created by analyzing all 828 cases CWA investigated by EPA and pursued by federal prosecutors since 1983. Upon analyzing all of the CWA prosecutions, we examined them for the primary crime

73. Berkley Reg'l Ins. Co. v. Murray, No. DKC-01-0563 (D. Md. Jan. 20, 2016).
74. United States v. Anderson, No. 84-00056 (D. Wyo. Nov. 20, 1984).
75. Sandy Smith, *HPI Products Inc. and Owner to Pay $150,000 in Environmental Penalties*, EHS Today, Nov. 18, 2010, https://www.ehstoday.com/environment/article/21911892/hpi-products-inc-and-owner-to-pay-150000-in-environmental-penalties.
76. United States v. HPI Products Inc. et al., No. 09-00023-01-CR-W-HFS (W.D. Mo. Mar. 22, 2010). Nielsen was sentenced to three years' probation and ordered to pay a $4,000 fine. The case summary did not specify the extent of his penalty and additional penalties resulting from a related civil settlement, but this can be found via web search.

Figure 10. Major Themes in CWA Criminal Prosecutions Since 1983

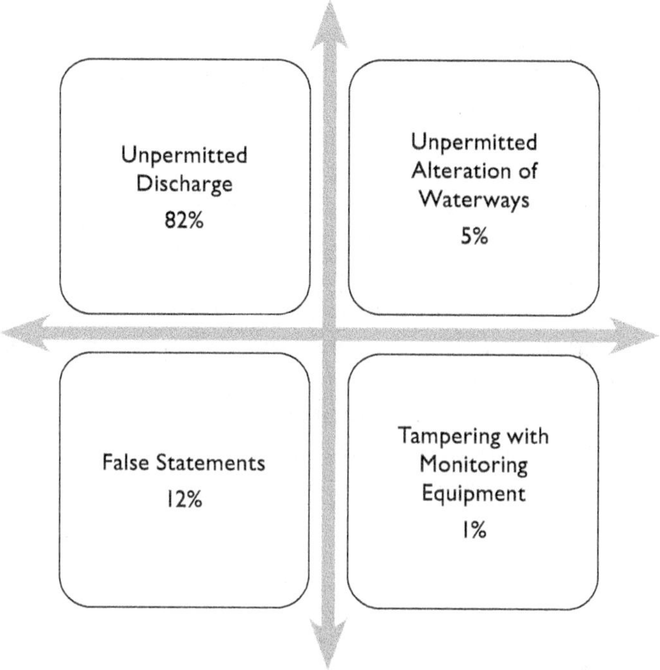

for which we felt the defendants were charged and prosecuted. All of these cases can be collapsed into four categories. We find four primary themes in the analysis, including unpermitted discharge, false statements, tampering with equipment, and unpermitted alteration of waterways. In many cases, defendants were charged with multiple crimes, but these categories reflect our judgment regarding the primary focus of the crime and scope of the prosecution.

Most of the criminal provisions of the CWA focus on unpermitted discharges. This could be from direct discharges, discharge of oil or hazardous substances, discharge from a POTW, or a discharge violating pretreatment standards (including local). We found that in 82% of cases or 680 total cases, the prosecution focused on one or more of these issues related to unpermitted discharges. When we further break these down, we find that 342 cases resulted from individual actions related to the unpermitted discharge of pollutants and in 338 cases it was company actions to discharge unpermitted pollutants that were at the center of the crime, investigation, and prosecution. In many cases, these were illegal stormwater discharges and unpermitted municipal wastewater overflows or actions resulting in POTWs violating pretreatment standards.[77]

In 15 cases, municipal governments were charged with unpermitted discharges.[78] In all but the Wheat Ridge Sanitation District, Municipality of Penn Hill, and Central Valley Water Reclamation Board (charged primarily with false reporting, focused on DMRs or other documents), the primary charge in our judgment involves an unpermitted discharge. The state or territory of the crime, date of sentencing, fine, and probation assessed to municipal governments are included in each respective column in Table 5.

Wheat Ridge Sanitation District is a public sanitation district near Denver, Colorado. Lenny Hart the acting superintendent was charged under the CWA for making false statements and illegal disposal under RCRA. Wheat Ridge was charged with illegal disposal and false statements. The city of Waldport wastewater treatment plant was out of compliance with its NPDES permit. In 1996, it discharged approximately 3.5 million gallons of contaminated water into Alsea Bay. This case is marked as unique, as it was the first time an Oregon municipality pled guilty to a federal environmental crime.

77. In two cases the primary nature of the CWA violation cannot be determined. These are a 1991 case against Paul Tudor Jones II and a 1992 case against Dexter Corporation. Defendant Jones was prosecuted under a series of sections in the CWA, but the case summary is not clear regarding the primary nature of the crime. The defendant owned Tudor Investment Corporation, which purchased over 3,200 in Dorchester County, Maryland, to develop a private hunting ground. Dexter Corporation's Windsor Locks facility manufactures specialty paper products. The summary claims they were charged with eight felony counts under the CWA and RCRA, but does not specify those counts or the sections in the statute to decide which quadrant the case could fit in Figure 3.

78. Puerto Rico Aqueducts and Sewer Authority (PRASA) is a government-owned corporation of Puerto Rico and not a municipal government. *See* United States v. City of Elkins, No. 2:96CR9 (N.D. W. Va. 1996); United States v. Wheat Ridge Sanitation Dist., No. 93 CR 91 (D. Colo. 1993); United States v. City of Post Falls, Idaho, No. CR96-00092-01 (D. Idaho 1997); United States v. St. Charles County, Missouri, No. 09701548 (E.D. Mo. 1998); United States v. City of Lake Ozark, Mo., No. 08-04036-01-CR-C-NKL (W.D. Mo. 2008); United States v. City of Madison, Ind., No. 4:09-CR-0024DFH-MGN (S.D. Ind. 2010); United States v. Washington Metro Area Transit Auth., No. 8:09-CR-00557-RWT (D. Md. Apr. 12, 2009); United States v. City of Pineville, La., No. 1:11-CR-00265 (W.D. La. Jan. 4, 2012); United States v. City of Waldport, Or., No. 98-60084-HO (D. Or. May 29, 1998); United States v. City of Venice, Fla., No. 8:05-CR-00190-EAK-EAJ (M.D. Fla. May 10, 2005); United States v. Wayne Cty. Airport Auth., No. CR-94-172 (E.D. Mich. June 6, 2006); United States v. Puerto Rico Aqueduct & Sewer Auth., No. 06CR00202 (PG) (D. P.R. June 22, 2007); United States v. Municipality of Penn Hill, (W.D. Pa. 1994); United States v. Central Valley Water Reclamation Bd., No. 88-CR-085W (D. Utah 1998); and United States v. City of Bethlehem, Pa., No. CR-97-102 (E.D. Pa. Mar. 7, 1997). The city was also required to install a new $250,000 sewer line, audit its sewage treatment plant, and develop a regulatory compliance program.

Table 5. Municipal Governments as Principal Defendants in Illegal Discharge Prosecutions

Defendant	State	Date	$ Penalty	Probation
City of Elkins	WV	1996	$5,000	None
Wheat Ridge Sanitation District	CO	1993	$35,000	None
City of Post Falls	ID	1997	$30,000	None
St. Charles County	MO	1998	$200,800	None
City of Lake Ozark	MO	2008	$50,000	60 months
City of Madison	IN	2010	$15,000	60 months
Washington Metropolitan Area Transit	MD	2009	$200,125	18 months
City of Pineville	LA	2012	$15,000	12 months
City of Waldport	OR	1998	$52,500	60 months
City of Venice	FL	2005	$111,200	None
Wayne County Airport Authority	MI	2006	$100,125	48 months
Puerto Rico Aqueduct and Sewer	PR	2006	$9,600,000	60 months
Municipality of Penn Hill	PA	1994	$150,000	60 months
Central Valley Water Reclamation	UT	1998	$1,100	None
City of Bethlehem Pennsylvania	PA	1997	$250,000	36 months

The Wayne County Airport Authority illegally discharged roughly 25 million gallons of water from a retention pond that contains stormwater runoff including deicing materials. The discharge was not reported. Investigators discovered the discharge two days later while investigating a fish kill and determined it occurred on May 16, 2001. In addition to fines and probation the defendant had to complete a force main project to connect the pond in question to a sanitary sewer line at an estimated cost of $8.5 million.

The most extensive prosecution was against the Puerto Rico Aqueducts and Sewer Authority (PRASA).[79] The defendant was found to have illegally discharged pollutants from nine wastewater treatment plants and five drinking water treatment plants. These crimes were part of a larger pattern of PRASA failing to maintain some 61 treatment facilities in Puerto Rico. The defendant pled guilty to 15 knowing violations of the CWA. In addition to

79. *EPA Charges Companies with Thousands of Violations of Clean Water Act*, EHS Today, Nov. 28, 2001, https://www.ehstoday.com/archive/article/21910441/epa-charges-companies-with-thousands-of-violations-of-clean-water-act.

60 months of probation, $6,000 in special assessment fees, and a $9 million criminal fine (the largest at the time for a public utility violating the CWA), it was required to spend $109 million on capital improvement projects and $10 million to correct discharges into Martin PeZa Creek. The prosecution was also connected to a related civil case.[80]

Many prosecutions involved employees of POTWs, such as Lawrence Ostler the superintendent of the Olympus Terrace Sewage Treatment Plant in Mukilteo, Washington. Ostler was charged and sentenced in 1989 for knowingly discharging pollutants from a point source into Puget Sound without an NPEDS permit.[81] Ostler was sentenced to 36 months of probation, 250 hours of community service, and a $5,000 fine for the crime. The illegal discharge was the central crime and focus of the prosecution with the permitting violation related to that crime in the case. John Auten was sentenced in Florida in 1990 for dumping about 20,000 tires into canals near West Palm Beach, Florida, between 1981 and 1987. He was charged under the CWA for the illegal discharge.[82] Auten was sentenced to 36 months of probation, ordered to make full restitution in the sum of $16,829.88 to Southern Florida Water Management, ordered to perform 100 hours of community service for each year of probation, and ordered to pay a special assessment of $50.

One of the more unique applications of the CWA to an unpermitted discharge was the prosecution of David Eugene Turner.[83] Turner operated two seasonal labor camps for migrant workers. He and his co-defendants recruited homeless men from shelters and the street to work in the camp and paid them in crack cocaine and untaxed beer and cigarettes. The CWA charge stemmed from the camp discharging raw sewage into the St. Johns River via a tributary without a permit, in addition to false statements, conspiracy to distribute cocaine, and illegal transportation of farm laborers among other charges. In one of the severest sentences in the dataset, the defendants were collectively sentenced to 626 months' incarceration, 324 months of probation, and monetary penalties exceeding $2.2 million.

80. This long-standing case dealt with PRASA's inability or unwillingness to fix its broken and dilapidated wastewater treatment facilities. *See* Press Release, U.S. EPA, Puerto Rico Aqueduct and Sewer Authority to Upgrade Sewage Infrastructure, Sewage Pollution in Martín Peña Canal, San Juan Bay, Condado Lagoon, and Atlantic Ocean will be Reduced, Sept. 15, 2015, https://archive.epa.gov/epa/newsreleases/puerto-rico-aqueduct-and-sewer-authority-upgrade-sewage-infrastructure-sewage-pollution.html; and Jake Varn, *Puerto Rico and the Complicated Path to Disaster Recovery*, Bipartisan Pol'y Ctr. Blog (Sept. 29, 2017), https://bipartisanpolicy.org/blog/puerto-rico-and-the-complicated-path-to-disaster-recovery/.

81. No. CR89-107W (W.D. Wash.).

82. United States v. Auten, No. 90-8032 (S.D. Fla.).

83. United States v. Turner, No. 3:05-CR-00159-TJC-MMH (M.D. Fla.). This was a very serious case that resulted in abuse to a significant number of individuals and the environment. *See* U.S. EPA, Criminal Enforcement Program, Evans Labor Camp (2011), https://www.epa.gov/sites/production/files/documents/oceft-overview-2011.pdf.

James Findlay was prosecuted under the CWA for extracting depleted uranium inside his apartment in Boise, Idaho, and discharging the waste into the public sewer system. The defendant was sentenced to one-year probation.[84] Victor Alan Buchanan was prosecuted in Alaska and sentenced in 2013 for discharging oily bilge water into St. Paul Harbor.[85] The defendant owned the commercial fishing vessel Chisik Island. The U.S. Coast Guard performed an inspection of the boat in Kodiak harbor. The inspection revealed the vessel was discharging oily bilge water and its Marine Sanitation Device was not secure causing the illegal sewage discharge. Buchanan was charged under the CWA and the Refuse Act, which forbids the depositing of refuse in the navigable waters of the United States without a permit. Buchanan was sentenced to 60 months of probation and a $50,000 fine. Duke Energy Business Services, Duke Energy Carolinas, and Duke Energy Progress Inc. were sentenced to pay a $68 million criminal fine and a $24 million community service payment to the National Fish and Wildlife Foundation. The companies had to certify they possessed sufficient reserves (approximately $3.4 billion) to manage any other legal obligations from their coal ash impoundments in North Carolina.[86]

Another high-profile case in this category was the prosecution of Transocean for its role in the Deepwater Horizon disaster.[87] Transocean paid $400 million in criminal fines and penalties. The company was found negligent when its employees failed to investigate the Macondo well that exploded. Transocean was sentenced to five years' probation and settled a $1 billion civil consent decree to resolve the federal government's claims under the CWA.[88]

84. United States v. Findlay, No. 1:17-CR-189-BLW (D. Idaho).
85. United States v. Buchanan, No. 3:12-CR-00036-SLG-JDR (D. Alaska 2013). *See* 33. U.S.C. §407.
86. No. 15-CR-00062, 67, 68 (E.D.N.C.). About 39,000 tons of coal ash spilled into the river and polluted the local environmental downriver. This was the third largest coal ash spill in U.S. history. The collapse came when a drainage pipe ruptured in a containment pond. Coal-fired power plants often generate significant waste with no great place to dispose of it. Companies typically create containment ponds, which is not a permanent solution. Companies are allowed to create encapsulated coal ash in a variety of applications by applying it to fly ash used in concreate applications and flue gas desulfurization material gypsum used in gypsum panels, i.e., also known as Sheetrock. Unencapsulated uses are commonly seen in highway embankments and as secondary fill material. The technical term for coal ash is coal combustion residuals. U.S. EPA, *Coal Ash Reuse*, https://www.epa.gov/coalash/coal-ash-reuse (last updated March 6, 2022). Jennifer Fernandez, *5 Years after Dan River Coal Ash Spill Duke Energy Close to Finishing State-Mandated Cleanup at Site*, Greensboro.com, Feb. 1, 2019, https://www.greensboro.com/news/state/5-years-after-dan-river-coal-ash-spill-duke-energy-close-to-finishing-state-mandated/article_de8d0fa9-43e8-5b83-85d1-b253683a0548.html.
87. No. 2:13-CR-00001-JTM-SS (E.D. La.).
88. The consent decree requires the company to perform a series of actions. *See* Transocean, *Macondo U.S. Consent Decree*, https://www.deepwater.com/macondo-us-consent-decree-compliance (last visited May 9, 2022).

Five percent of prosecutions are focused on the unpermitted alteration of waterways. This category makes up a host of issues related to companies and individuals that failed to get permits before dredging, building dams, filling in wetlands, and otherwise illegally altering waterways. Thirty-nine prosecutions were focused on these acts in our judgment. In 30 cases, individuals were the principal defendants charged for illegally dredging or filling waterways or wetlands. In nine cases, companies were charged with illegal dredging or filling activities. Many of these were focused on §404 permit issues and violations of the Rivers and Harbors Act, such as developing a wetland without a permit or a proper permit, dredging canals, altering the course of rivers, and other related actions.

Brusco Tug & Barge Inc. towed barges containing dredge material to Winter Island, a private Island located near the Sacramento-San Joaquin River Delta in Contra Costa County, California.[89] Between 2003-2007, employees illegally discharged dredging material without a permit on many occasions, often at night. On April 17, a Brusco manager also admitted to investigators he ordered an employee to dump 87,000 gallons of material in the waters surrounding Winter Island. The company was charged under the CWA and sentenced to 36 months of probation and a $750,000 fine.[90]

Thomas Warren Resch and Dwayne Bruce Smith were officers in a homeowner's association and local improvement district in California.[91] They wanted to free up land for real estate development that required draining a lagoon and altering a sandbar. They applied for a §10 permit under the Rivers and Harbors Act to make the alterations, which was denied. Each defendant was sentenced to 18 months of probation and a $5,000 fine.[92] John Hubenka constructed three earthen dikes along the Wind River near Riverton, Wyoming.[93] His actions altered the flow of the river impacting the Wind River

89. *Tugboat Company Manager Accused of Polluting Delta*, Bay City News Serv., July 8, 2009, https://www.eastbaytimes.com/2009/07/08/tugboat-company-manager-accused-of-polluting-delta/.

90. No. CR09 0728 SI (N.D. Cal.).

91. Jane Kay, *Two Fined: Drained Lake With Rare Fish*, S.F. Gate, Aug. 2, 2012, https://www.sfgate.com/news/article/Two-fined-Drained-lakes-with-rare-fish-3138679.php.

92. No. C 95-209 MAG (N.D. Cal.). Section 10 of the Rivers and Harbors Act deals with the construction of bridges, causeways, dams, or dikes. Section 404 under the CWA requires a permit for these kinds of activities. "Normal farming" activities are exempt, such as building stock ponds, drainage ditches, levees, dams, and dikes if they impact existing activities. Permits are required for new projects that impact wetlands or waterways. U.S. EPA, *Exemptions to Permit Requirements Under CWA Section 404*, https://www.epa.gov/cwa-404/exemptions-permit-requirements-under-cwa-section-404 (last updated Apr. 20, 2022).

93. For the related civil suit, see U.S. EPA, *John Hubenka and LeClair Irrigation District Clean Water Act Settlement*, https://www.epa.gov/enforcement/john-hubenka-and-leclair-irrigation-district-clean-water-act-settlement (last updated March 23, 2022).

Indian Reservation downstream. For his unpermitted actions, he was sentenced to 12 months of probation.[94]

A case against Robert Lucas Jr. illustrates the practical value of 404 permits for residential development. Lucas and his co-defendants developed Bill Hill Acres, a 2,600-acre subdivision in Pascagoula, Mississippi. They filled in a wetland without a permit and over 600 families purchased homes in the area. The high-water table caused streets to flood, septic systems to fail releasing raw sewage and creating chronic backflow issues.[95] Hancock County Land was also prosecuted in Mississippi for illegally filling in protected wetlands without a permit from the Corps.[96] The defendants were charged for illegally filling in wetlands, as well as mail fraud, conspiracy, and many other charges. Lucas was sentenced to 108 months' incarceration, 36 months' supervised release, a $15,000 fine, and $4,100 in special assessments. Robbie Wrigley and M.E. Thompson were each sentenced to 87 months' incarceration, 36 months' supervised release, charged a $15,000 fine, as well as $3,300 and $2,500 in special assessment fees, respectively. Big Hill Acres was sentenced to pay a $4.8 million fine, 60 months of probation, and order to pay a $7,600 special assessment. Consolidated Investments Inc. was sentenced to 60 months of probation, $500,000 in fines, and charged a $400 special assessment. The defendants were all sentenced to pay $1,407,400 in restitution to fund 454 mitigation credits.

A good amount of the enforcement of any federal environmental law comes down to the paper chase. With so many logs, reports, and other requirements, there are ample opportunities to find negligent violations under the CWA. In these cases, they can become knowing violations if defendants try to cover up a crime or alter required logs and engage in willful acts of covering up illegal discharges and other crimes. If they lie about any of these issues to investigators, then they may be charged with knowing violations. We find all of these in the data, where we catalog 99 cases as centered on false statements or false reporting. These cases make up 12% of total prosecutions. Although other cases under the unpermitted discharge category may contain false statements or reporting, we felt in our judgment these 99 cases centered

94. United States v. Hubenka, No. 04CR0004-1B (D. Wyo.). Hubenka was sentenced to serve 12 months of probation in 2004 for the CWA violations.

95. No. 1:04CR60GuRo-001 (S.D. Miss.). As with any failed capitalist enterprise, the cost of fixing the problem fell on government and residents. Tens of millions of dollars had to be appropriated from various sources to offset the drainage and sewage problems presented by chronic soil movement and water inundation issues. April M. Havens, *Big Hill Acres Getting Water, Sewer Help*, Gulf Live, Jan. 2, 2019, https://www.gulflive.com/mississippi-press-news/2010/04/big_hill_acres_getting_water_sewer_help.html.

96. No. 1:13CR35HSO-RHW (S.D. Miss.). HCL was sentenced to 24 months of probation and ordered to pay a $1 million fine.

on it as the focus of the crime. In 70 cases, the principal defendants were individuals that falsified reports, testing, or gave false statements to investigators. In 29 cases, companies were the principal defendants that engaged in false reporting, testing, or gave false statements.

We find three cases of false reporting involving municipalities. Pen Hill, Pennsylvania, was the principal defendant in a case of submitting false DMRs, along with co-defendants Matthew Girdick and Walter Baker. The defendants were charged with false reporting and illegal discharge.[97] The municipality was sentenced to 60 months of probation and fined $150,000. Girdick was sentenced to 5 years of probation, 4,480 hours community service, and a fine of $5,000. Baker was sentenced to 12 months' incarceration, 12 months' supervised release, and fined $5,000. The city of Bethlehem, Pennsylvania, was prosecuted for falsifying DMRs. John Lawrence, the wastewater treatment plant's chief chemist, lied on reports.[98] The city was sentenced to 36 months of probation, fined $250,000, and ordered to install a new $250,000 sewer line. During the probation period, the city was ordered to perform an environmental audit of its sewage treatment plan. Lawrence was sentenced to 36 months of probation, 120 hours of community service, and fined $2,000. William Grim was sentenced to 12 months of probation, 20 hours of community service, and fined $5,000.

Eric Donald Roth Sr. owned a laboratory in Festus, Missouri, called Analyst Consulting Laboratories Inc. The company provided testing to municipalities to help them comply with their NPDES permits. Roth and his company submitted false DMRs for five cities. They were investigated by EPA and prosecuted for false reporting, mail fraud, and false statements. Roth was sentenced to 4 months' incarceration and a suspended sentence on the false statements violation if he completed 5 years of probation and 200 hours community service.[99] Another case resting on false environmental testing involved defendant Samar Chatterjee. The defendant submitted false testing data for sanitary sewer connections, flow gauging, manhole inspections, and sewer survey reports to EPA for the Metropolitan Sanitary Sewer District of Greater Chicago. He was investigated and prosecuted for one count of conspiracy under the CWA, false statements, and mail fraud. Chatterjee was sentenced in 1999 to 48 months' incarceration, 60 months of probation, and $220,000 in restitution.

97. No. CR-94-172 (W.D. Pa.).
98. No. CR-97-102 (W.D. Pa.).
99. No. 85-00119 (E.D. Mo.), No. CR-87-656 (N.D. Ill.).

We find eight cases or 1% of the cases that involve tampering with a monitoring device or equipment. In many of these cases, tampering with a monitoring device and false statements often went hand in hand and defendants falsified DMRs to conceal the crime. The false reporting or false statements given to investigators were often the impetus for this to become a criminal investigation and prosecution. It is difficult to tell in many cases which are considered the central crime in the prosecution as they are so closely related. Only eight cases fall into this category because we were trying to be as stringent in our categorization as possible. In four prosecutions, the principal defendant was engaged in actions related to tampering with a monitoring device or equipment. In four prosecutions, a company was the principal defendant in a tampering case. Ore-Ida Food Inc. operated a wastewater treatment plant in Ontario, Oregon.[100] The environmental controls supervisor was Frank Jordan. Jordan was charged with tampering with a monitoring device, as well as falsifying reports.[101] Jordan was sentenced to 60 days of house arrest, 60 months of probation, 100 hours of community service, and a $5,000 fine. Ore-Ida Foods was sentenced in another case related to Jordan to 36 months of probation and a $1,000,000 fine. Three-quarters of a million dollars of the fine was suspended and reduced to $1 for every $1 expended to comprehensively rebuild the treatment plant.

Ketchikan Pulp Company was prosecuted for tampering with a monitoring device and sampling methods in violation of their NPDES permit.[102] They also discharged untreated waste into Ward Cove near Ketchikan, Alaska, bypassing its water treatment plant without a permit.[103] The defendant was sentenced to 60 months of probation and a fine of $1,250,000. Sea Watch International was prosecuted for tampering with a monitoring device. The tampering was discovered during a county inspection of the facility.[104] Sea Watch was sentenced to 60 months of probation, a $400 special assessment, and ordered to pay $25,000 to the Delaware Nature Society as community service.

We can plot the four themes we found since 1983 and examine the patterns in Figure 11. Three unpermitted discharge prosecutions were settled in 1983. This increases to 15 by 1989, 19 by 1991, and hits a high point of 45 in 1998, then declining to 16 in 2004, up to 30 in 2006 and 2015, then 9 by

100. U.S. EPA, *Ore-Ida Foods to Pay $1 Million for Polluting Snake River*, EPA J., Fall 1994, at 5, *also available at* https://www.epaalumni.org/userdata/pdf/1994-09-9100LD8J.PDF.
101. No. CR-91-414 (D. Or.), No. CR-94-0010 (D. Or.).
102. Russell Mokhiber, *Top 100 Corporate Criminals of the Decade*, CORP. CRIME REP., (n.d.), https://www.corporatecrimereporter.com/top100.html.
103. No. A95-025CR (D. Alaska).
104. No. CR:02-124 (D. Del.).

Figure 11. Tracking Four Major Themes in CWA Prosecutions Since 1983

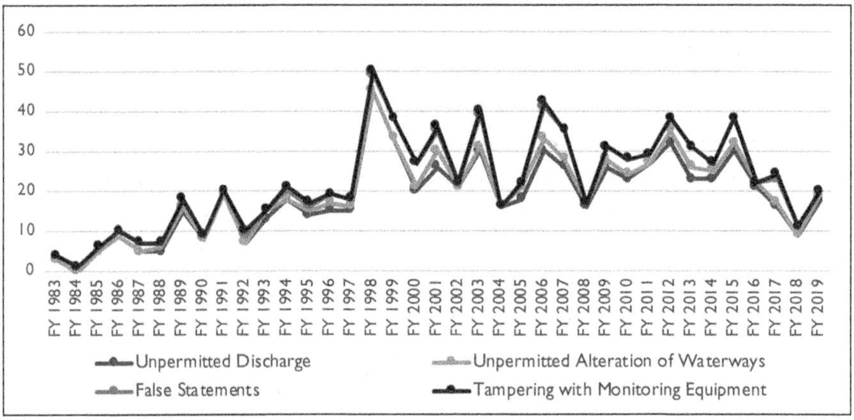

2018, and 18 again in 2019. Unpermitted discharge prosecutions averaged 18.38 prosecutions annually. A case centering on unpermitted alteration of waterways is not settled until 1988 and then reaches a high point of 4 in 2004, never rising about 3 thereafter. The average was 1.05 cases. Prosecutions centered on false statements increase from 1 in 1983 to a high point of 8 in 2003 and 2006. The average number of false statements prosecutions annually was 2.7. A case centered on tampering with monitoring equipment was not settled until 1992. Cases averaged .22 annually. The patterns overall fit fairly well with those found in Figure 10. The pattern of prosecutions over time focus on illegal discharge, false statements, records, and reporting, followed by illegally altering waterways, dredging, and filling cases, and finally tampering with monitoring devices and equipment.

III. Penalties in CWA Prosecutions

We now turn our analysis to showing the trends in punishments meted out to individual defendants and company defendants in criminal prosecutions. Figure 12 demonstrates the four most common categories of criminal charges we found in these prosecutions. In 16% of cases or 135 total cases, making false statements or giving false reports was by far the most common charge we found. In 86 cases or 10% of the prosecutions, defendants engaged in a criminal conspiracy to cover up their crimes. In 22 cases we found defendants charged with fraud, which includes mail, wire, tax, visa, and bank fraud. In 1% of cases, defendants were charged with obstruction in the case.

Figure 12. Common Criminal Charges in CWA Prosecutions

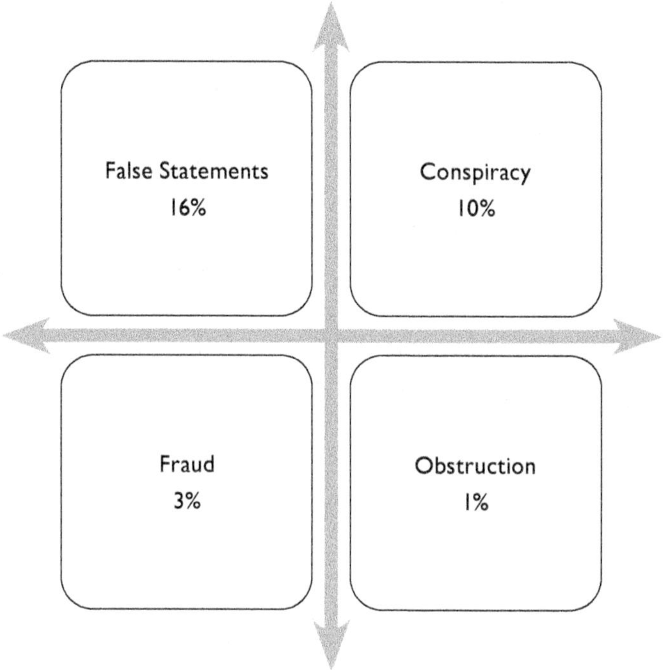

Altogether we find that 210 cases or 25% of total prosecutions involved one or more of these charges.

Mari Leigh Childs, a certified Wastewater Operator, created and submitted at least eight quarters of falsified laboratory analytical data and at least three falsified DMRs for both the Rising Sun and Chapman Subdivision wastewater treatment plants to the Mississippi Department of Environmental Quality.[105] She was charged with false statements for the falsified reports, as well as a knowing violation of the CWA.[106] Childs was sentenced in 2012 to 6 months' home confinement, 60 months of probation, and was ordered to pay a $200 special assessment and $34,900 in restitution.

Defendants John and Cody Tuma were charged for discharging untreated wastewater directly into the Red River without a permit. They also discharged untreated wastewater into the city of Shreveport municipal sewer system and obstructed an EPA inspection. They were charged with conspiracy, obstruction, and violating the CWA for the illegal discharge. Cody Tuma was sen-

105. U.S. DOJ, Environmental Crimes Section Monthly Bulletin 9 (Jan. 2012), https://www.justice.gov/sites/default/files/enrd/legacy/2015/04/13/jan_2012_508.pdf.

106. No. 3:11-CR-00135-WAP-SAA (N.D. Miss.).

Figure 13. Total Penalties Assessed in CWA Prosecutions Since 1983

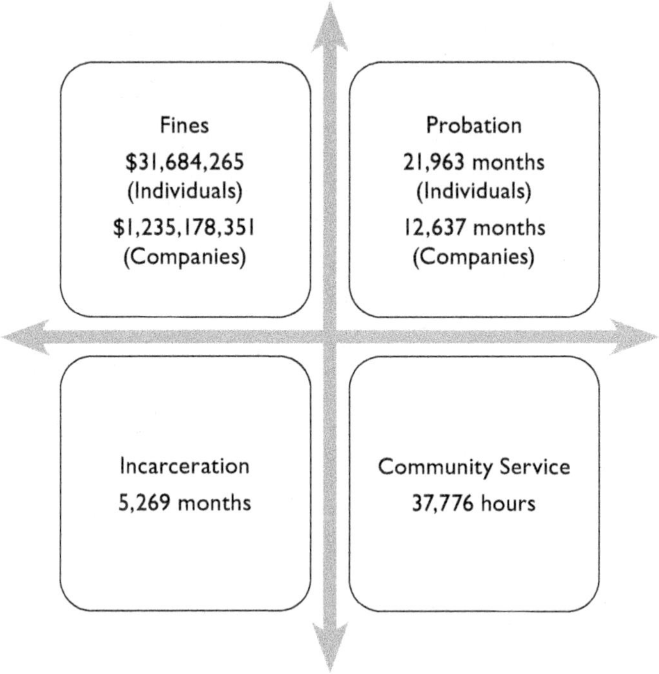

tenced in 2012 to 60 months of probation and 60 months' incarceration. John Tuma was sentenced to 36 months of probation and a $100,000 fine.[107] For about 10 years All Out Sewer and Drain Service Inc. dumped industrial, septic, and grease trap waste into the Longview, Washington, sewer system. They falsified reports during an investigation to obscure the extent of the illegal discharges. The defendants were charged under the CWA for the illegal discharges, false statements for the false reporting, and mail fraud. The company was sentenced to 36 months of probation and ordered to pay a fine of $250,000. Owner Ray Eugene Caldwell was sentenced to 27 months of incarceration and ordered to pay a fine of $250,000.[108]

Figure 13 displays the total penalties assessed to all violators of the CWA since 1983. We break these penalties down by individual defendants and company defendants. In 62% of the cases (517 total cases), individuals were assessed fines, assessments, and other penalties exceeding $31 million. In 461 cases or 56% of prosecutions, companies were assessed a total of over

107. No. 5:11-CR-00031 (W.D. La.).
108. No. CR 13-5308 BHS (W.D. Wash.).

$1.2 billion in fines and other financial penalties in the data. We also find a grand total of 37,776 hours of community service assessed to defendants, as well as other punishments including 641 months of home confinement and 454 months of home corrections. We do not include the prosecution of BP for their role in the Deepwater Horizon case in the figure. That case is not found by searching the database, only by web search, which violates our data collection protocols and it is not included in the totals. Including that case would raise the penalties to companies an additional $4 billion and raising total financial penalties assessed overall to over $5.2 billion.[109]

A substantial financial penalty case for both individuals and companies was the prosecution of West Indies Transport, West Indies Equipment, and Warren James Oelsner sentenced in 1996 in the U.S. Virgin Islands.[110] The defendants illegally imported Filipino laborers to perform dry dock work and shore-based operations. The workers lived in shipping containers and worked over 50 hours per week at below minimum wage. The defendants were charged with visa fraud, unlawful discharge of a pollutant, obstruction of navigable waters, and conspiracy to make false statements.[111] West Indies Transport was fined $3.520 million, West Indies Equipment was fined $1,520,500, and Warren Oelsner was sentenced to 37 months' incarceration, charged a fine of $559,500, and ordered to pay restitution in the amount of $1,440,450.

A case involving extensive probation was against Glenn Cooper and co-defendants Darrin Melerine, Dominic Bruno, Gregory Plaia, Richard Coffey, and Vincent Tamor. Cooper was the plant manager of the St. Bernard Parish public wastewater treatment facility in Louisiana. He instructed his employees to submit fraudulent water quality samples. The defendants were charged with a negligent violation of the CWA for submitting the falsified reports. Cooper was sentenced in 2000 to 60 months of probation and ordered to pay a fine of $10,000. Tamor, Bruno, Plaia, Melerine were sentenced to 36 months of probation and ordered to perform 50 hours of community service each, and Coffey was sentenced to 36 months of probation and ordered to perform 150 hours of community service.[112]

109. No. 2:12-CR-00292-DEK (E.D. La.). The CWA prosecution of BP for its role in the Deepwater Horizon disaster was the largest criminal penalty ever assessed against a defendant for a federal environmental crime. The company was also charged with manslaughter, obstruction, and other charges under the MBTA.

110. U.S. DOJ, West Indies Transport Co. v. United States Opposition (2001), https://www.justice.gov/osg/brief/west-indies-transport-co-v-united-states-opposition.

111. No. CR-93-195 (D.V.I.).

112. No. 99-419 (E.D. La.).The municipality was not named as a defendant in the case.

The most extensive incarceration time assessed at sentencing went to the previous case in Florida against David Eugene Turner and his co-defendants for operating a migrant labor camp, selling drugs and untaxed cigarettes, and illegally discharging pollutants into waterways. We counted over 52 cumulative years of incarceration assessed in the case. The case against Robert Lucas and Bill Hill Acres was also an extensive incarceration case with a cumulative total of over 23 years assessed at sentencing.[113] A Georgia case sentenced in 1999 against principal defendant Wilbur Duane Outhwaite, the Hanlin Group, and five co-defendants resulted in a significant number of years of incarceration at sentencing. LCP Chemicals, a division of the Hanlin Group contaminated their 550-acre facility near Brunswick, Georgia, with mercury and PCBs. Defendants were collectively sentenced to almost 18 years in prison.[114] The most extensive community service penalty came with the previously mentioned case against the municipality of Penn Hill, Pennsylvania. Girdick, the assistant director of the municipality's water control department, was sentenced to 4,480 months' community service.[115]

IV. Conclusion

This chapter provided an analysis of all CWA criminal investigators undertaken by EPA and the subsequent prosecutions that followed from 1983-2019. The first theme we uncovered was that while CWA prosecutions represent almost one-third of all criminal prosecutions, they are still quite infrequent. Across space and time, many U.S. states saw very few prosecutions and no prosecutions were settled in Maine. In a handful of states such as Vermont and Wisconsin we see only one or a few prosecutions undertaken since the institutionalization of the criminal enforcement division.

The second theme we find is that CWA prosecutions focus heavily on unpermitted discharges. Illegally discharging from a point source is the primary tool prosecutors used to convict environmental criminals in the data and the principal mechanism by which EPA investigators built their cases. While many of these illegal discharge cases stemmed from municipalities and companies violating or not possessing an NPDES permit and subsequently in many cases attempting to cover up the illegal discharges, these discharges also came from boats, midnight dumping, and other sources that

113. *Major Wetlands Criminal Prosecution Results in Defendants Receiving Jail Sentences, Paying Restitution*, Envt'l Protection, Dec. 1, 2005, at https://eponline.com/articles/2005/12/01/major-wetlands-criminal-prosecution-results-in-defendants-receiving-jail-sentences-paying-restitutio.aspx.
114. No. CR-298-11 (S.D. Ga.).
115. No. CR-94-208 (W.D. Pa.).

polluted sewers, stormwater systems, wetlands, rivers, lakes, and other waterways in the United States.

Related to illegal discharges were charges stemming from the paper chase of filling out DMRs and other paperwork. More than any other knowing violation, giving false statements to investigators, filling or altering DMRs or other false reporting represented the most common knowing crime we see in the data. We find that in 13% of cases, defendants engaged in such actions to conceal environmental crimes. Overall, about one-quarter of cases involve some knowing violation related to the environmental crime, including false statements, as well as obstruction, fraud, and conspiracy. Cases centered on tampering with a monitoring device or equipment also tend to fall into this category of defendants intentionally and willfully acting to conceal an environmental crime. These were not just individuals getting rid of waste in the middle of the night, but workers and executives of companies and municipal governments.

A third theme we find is that CWA prosecutions fit well within the boundaries of their compliance monitoring strategy. Our analysis shows for the first time that criminal enforcement efforts truly center on wastewater management issues and NPDES monitoring strategies. Municipal wastewater overflows, stormwater pollution, and pretreatment violations dominated this category. We did not see many criminal prosecutions of CAFOs on the whole or prosecutions related to the creation, transport, and sale of biosolids.[116] Prosecutions for lack of §404 permits that involved illegal dredging or filling or otherwise altering waterways occurred, as did prosecuting illegal oil spills, but these were not nearly as numerous as wastewater management on the whole.

While the CWA has made great strides in reducing pollution and managing wastewater, there are many loopholes that weaken its reach and ability to properly enforce the substance and spirit of the Act. The first comes from the delegation of regulatory power and data gathering that comes in our federal system of government. With limited funds, reliance on the states can be an easy means for EPA to divest authority for monitoring, enforcement,

116. Prosecuting biosolid manufacturers was not a theme we found in the analysis. One example case is that against George Alan Harmon owner of D&E Septic Service Inc. This case was not a prosecution of a biosolids company, but Harmon contracted with municipal wastewater treatment plants to transport waste to remove sludge to a licensed biowaste facility. Instead he dumped biosolids (sludge) and septage (partially treated sludge from septic tanks) on his own property. Investigators estimated that 500,000 gallons of sludge and septage had been illegally disposed of in this manner in 2003. He was prosecuted for illegal disposal of biosolids under Washington State law in 2004 and sentenced to serve 12 months' incarceration on the disposal of biosolids, 90 days for forgery, and 5.5 months for bail jumping, to run concurrently and ordered to pay a $500 special assessment fee (Washington CR04-1-00022-0).

and permitting.[117] The difficulty with this approach is that most states are even more severely underfunded and the data that comes to EPA is mostly industry self-reported.[118] States can provide exemptions or loopholes or simply fail to enforce EPA standards and it is not uncommon for states to have contentious relationships with EPA. Another weakness in compliance monitoring is that only major sources of pollution report data. Many companies do not report data, fail to obtain permits, or more commonly allowed them to expire. Civil penalties are weak and often have minimal deterrent effects or companies repeatedly pay fines and remain in noncompliance as a cost of doing business, rather than complying with the law.

The scope of the CWA is also more limiting than many observers imagine.[119] While thousands of companies operate without valid NPDES permits and others simply fail to come into compliance, regulating water pollution does not rise to the highest standard to protect public health, but to the standard of the best available control technologies. Older facilities often only retrofit their facilities when forced through consent decrees brought on by legal action or through criminal prosecution.[120] The CWA is ultimately a permitting statute on this front and only as strong as that principle and any goals of zero discharges of pollutants was arrested years ago.[121] A report by the Environmental Working Group in 2000 suggested that even then, according to EPA data, 40% of all U.S. waters are not fishable or swimmable. Nationwide at the time an analysis of NPDES permits showed that 1,690 facilities are operating without current permits and more than 770 major facility permits

117. One example here is with the prosecution of those that commit oil spills under the context of regulatory federalism or states having varied rules for illegal discharges. *See* Jennifer Lamb, *OPA or NOPA? Restoring Cooperative Federalism in Oil Pollution Enforcement*, 65 Emory L.J. 841-61 (2016). Tobias F. Bannon III, *A Cranberry Recipe for Citizen Rulemaking*, 37 B.C. Envtl. Aff. L. Rev. 127-57 (2010).

118. Limited resources and the nature of the regulatory oversight dilemma induces self-reporting. EPA has to balance between strict liability that provides forbearance for due diligence and absolute liability that provides no such relief but may induce non-compliance without it.

119. *See* K. Fukuyama & D. Marc Kilgour, *Self-Reporting Systems for Environmental Compliance*, 126 J. Water Resources Plan. & Mgmt. 3 (2000).

120. A related problem is that industrial polluters that discharge into sewer systems are indirect and not direct sources of pollution, thus exempting them from NPDES permits. POTWs only treat biological waste and not toxic chemicals. The latter should be dealt with through pretreatment from the facilities discharging into the public sewer systems, but only major POTWs with a daily flow exceeding five million gallons and have significant industrial inputs fall into this category and thus only ten percent of the country's POTWs are compelled by EPA to perform this function. *See* Craig Collins, Toxic Loopholes 68-69 (Cambridge Univ. Press 2012).

121. The same can be said regarding air emissions. Controlling air pollution via the CAA is wrought with the same challenges of lax state enforcement, minimal fines, regulatory loopholes, and self-reported data. The result is that ambient air pollution is likely much worse of a problem than what is reported by EPA data. *See* Joshua Ozymy & Melissa L. Jarrell, *Upset Events, Policy Drift, and the Regulation of Air Emissions at Industrial Facilities in the United States*, 2 Envtl. Pol. 451-66 (2012).

have been expired for 2 years, and 251 have been expired for 5 years.[122] A 2007 report from U.S. Public Interest Research Group (PIRG) found that 3,600 major facilities (57%) exceeded their permits at least once in 2005 for a total of 24,400 exceedances. For those exceeding their permits, major facilities did on an average at a rate of 263% of their allowed amount. At the time, 39% of rivers, 46% of lakes, and 51% of estuaries were deemed too polluted for fishing and swimming, showing outputs have worsened since 2000.[123]

Another major issue with the CWA is that its scope and reach can be severely limited by how its regulatory authority is applied to waterways.[124] The Trump Administration sought to weaken regulations on polluting in streams and wetlands through its Navigable Waters Protection Rule that limits the reach of CWA permits in ephemeral streams and wetlands not adjacent to protected waters.[125] This would mean freshwater streams, washes, and other marshes would lose federal protection; a similar tactic applied to different areas in the G.W. Bush Administration. This suggests 81% of streams in the Southwest could lose federal protections.[126] Changes to wording can greatly reduce what the Agency is both responsible for and thus what we can expect from the CWA.[127] The same can be said for criminal enforcement. Given the scope of the problem and that most criminal enforcement actions focus on unpermitted actions, so many problems go unaddressed both by the inability of the criminal enforcement apparatus to practically address them and the weakness and loopholes in the CWA that make such enforcement extremely difficult.

---

122. Environmental Working Group, Clean Water Report Card (2000), https://www.ewg.org/research/clean-water-report-card.
123. U.S. PIRG, Troubled Waters: An Analysis of 2005 Clean Water Act Compliance (2007), https://pincdn.s3.amazonaws.com/assets/3tktXoZDBxOWKaGyop20ew/US_Troubled_Waters_2007.pdf.
124. For issues with the application of the CWA to various regulatory situations, see Eric M. Dirth, *Successful Agriculture and Clean Water? A Workable Path for Regulating Drainage Districts and Point Sources Under the Clean Water Act*, 103 Iowa L. Rev. 1213-43 (2018). Natalia Cabrera, *Plain Meaning or Pragmatics? Differing Interpretations of the Clean Water Act's Jurisdictional Provisions*, 41 B.C. Envtl. Aff. L. Rev. 1-13 (2014). Robin Kundis Craig, *Dealing With Ocean Acidification: The Problem, The Clean Water Act, and State and Regional Approaches*, 90 Wash. L. Rev. 1583-658 (2015).
125. James R. Mihelcic & Mark Rains, *Where's the Science? Recent Changes to Clean Water Act Threaten Wetlands and Thousands of Miles of Our Nation's Rivers and Streams*, 37 Envtl. Eng'rg Sci. 173-77 (2020).
126. Anna M. Phillips, *California Will Be Hit Hard as Trump Administration Weakens Clean Water Protections*, L.A. Times, Jan. 23, 2020, https://www.latimes.com/politics/story/2020-01-23/california-will-be-hit-hard-as-trump-administration-weakens-clean-water-protections.
127. Charles P. Hawkins, *The Clean Water Rule: Defining the Scope of the Clean Water Act*, 34 Freshwater Sci. 1585-87 (2015). Robert W. Adler, *The Decline and (Possible) Renewal of Aspiration in the Clean Water Act*, 88 Wash. L. Rev. 759-812 (2013).

Chapter 4. You Should Have Warned Me: The Criminal Enforcement of the U.S. Resource Conservation and Recovery Act and Superfund

I. Enforcing the U.S. Resource Conservation and Recovery Act and Superfund

By the 1970s, it had become apparent that Americans and American companies were generating a substantial amount of waste with very few rules on how to transport it or get rid of it.[1] As the chemical revolution after WWII and related explosion in consumption was demonstrating, the country was in need of a reckoning for what to do with hazardous waste.[2] Certain media events began to focus critical public attention on the fact there were few rules for companies transporting deadly waste and materials on U.S. roads, the unmitigated disposal of hazardous waste in waterways, natural areas, and even in their backyards.[3]

RCRA was passed into federal law in 1976 to address escalating public concerns over the life cycle of hazardous waste.[4] RCRA is mostly known for affording EPA cradle-to-grave authority over waste. This means EPA is empowered via RCRA to develop rules and regulations over the generation, storage, transport, treatment, and disposal of solid hazardous waste.[5] Determining a national framework for these issues starts with RCRA and determines conditions for permitting the life cycle of these wastes.[6] EPA develops guidelines for states to permit the life cycle of waste from point of generation

1. U.S. Government Accountability Office, Hazardous Waste Disposal: A Staggering Problem (1981), https://www.gao.gov/products/116152.
2. Michael F. Hearn, *One Person's Waste Is Another Person's Liability: Closing the Liability Loophole in RCRA's Citizen Enforcement Action*, 42 McGeorge L. Rev. 467-69 (2011).
3. Press Release, U.S. EPA, EPA Schedules Emergency Cleanup at Valley of the Drums, Sept. 18, 1981, https://archive.epa.gov/epa/aboutepa/epa-schedules-emergency-cleanup-valley-drums.html .
4. Russell Phifer, *RCRA: The First 30 Years of Hazardous Waste Regulation*, 17 J. Chem. Health & Safety 4-7 (2010).
5. Thomas P. Eichler, *The Status of RCRA in the Mid-Atlantic States*, 26 Environment 2-3 (1984).
6. Lynn L. Bergeso, *EPA Proposes Standardized RCRA Permits*, 33 Pollution Eng'rg 24-27 (2001).

to disposal, which involves permitting 6,600 facilities and 20,000 process units.[7] The major statutory provisions speak to the authority granted to EPA in this area and can be found in Table 6.

Table 6. Major Statutory Provisions of RCRA

Title	Description
Subtitle A	Objectives, Definitions, and Financial Disclosure
Subtitle B	Office of Solid Waste and EPA Authority
Subtitle C	Control of Hazardous Waste "Cradle to Grave" Provisions
Subtitle D	Non-Hazardous Waste
Subtitle E	Secondary Materials and Markets for Recovered Materials
Subtitle F	Responsibilities of the Federal Government
Subtitle G	Whistleblower and Citizen Suits
Subtitle H	Research and Development
Subtitle I	Underground Storage Tanks
Subtitle J	Medical Waste

Subtitle A defines congressional intent, basic definitions used in the Act, as well as interstate cooperation and financial disclosure guidelines. Subtitle B establishes the Office of Solid Waste and agency authority in various areas. Subtitle C is one of the most important provisions of the Act, as it establishes EPA authority over the life cycle of hazardous waste. This includes regulating generators of waste, transporter, storage, treatment, and disposal facilities.[8] Another important requirement in this section is the development of record-keeping rules for individuals and companies in all of these areas.[9] Subtitle G provides provisions for citizen suits similar to the CAA and the CWA.[10]

7. U.S. EPA, *Resource Conservation and Recovery Act (RCRA) Overview*, https://www.epa.gov/rcra/resource-conservation-and-recovery-act-rcra-overview (last updated July 14, 2021); U.S. EPA, *RCRA Correction Action Cleanup Enforcement*, https://www.epa.gov/enforcement/rcra-corrective-action-cleanup-enforcement (last updated Aug. 12, 2021).
8. What qualifies as hazardous waste, mixture, derivative, or secondary waste and which of these is regulated under the Act is always an ongoing point of contention under RCRA. *See* Reed J. McCalib, *Opening the Gates of Cow Palace: Regulating Runoff Manure As Hazardous Waste*, 116 Mich. L. Rev. 501-21 (2017). Cadesby B. Cooper, *Toxic Solid Waste Leeching From Telephone Poles? Navigating Ambiguous Definitions in RCRA*, 41 B.C. Envtl. Aff. L. Rev. 14-29 (2014). Casey Roberts, *D.C. Circuit Affirms EPA Trend Towards Reducing RCRA Requirements for Recycling of Hazardous Secondary Materials*, 32 Ecology L.Q. 749-56 (2005). Jim Nickovich, *EPA Broadens RCRA Definiton of "Hazardous Waste" to Include Mixtures and Derivatives*, 31 Ecology L.Q. 781-85 (2004).
9. Of course, this has created an industry of lawyers, consultants, and trainers dedicated to helping companies comply (or avoid regulation) if they deal with hazardous waste. At the time of writing one can be trained on-site starting at $1,249 for EPA Hazardous Waste Personnel, but the best price was a simple regulatory compliance webinar for $189. Daniels Training Services Inc., *RCRA Training Options & Pricing*, https://danielstraining.com/rcra-training-options-pricing/ (2021).
10. Jonathan York, *The Next Step in Revitalizing RCRA: Maine People's Alliance and the Importance of Citizen Intervention in EPA Actions*, 35 Ecology L.Q 405-25 (2008).

In 1978, EPA set out to regulate hazardous wastes under Subtitle C and set aside certain wastes to further study health effects before promulgating regulations.[11] In 1980, Congress passed the Solid Waste Disposal Act Amendments.[12] These Amendments exempted wastes generated in large volume by extractive industries, such as drilling fluids and other byproducts of oil, natural gas, and geothermal industry exploration, development, and production, combustion waste from ore, such as coal, lead, phosphate rock, uranium, any fossil fuel combination waste, and cement kiln dust. These were all regulated as special wastes, rather than hazardous waste.[13] These amendments exempted most of the fossil fuel and extractive industries from more stringent regulations required if these substances were to be regulated as hazardous waste under RCRA.[14] For example, EPA did not issue a final ruling until 1988 exempting oil, gas, and geothermal energy wastes under Subtitle C. Due to concerns over the rapid growth of hydraulic fracturing, the Environmental Integrity Project filed suit claiming EPA failed to perform its discretionary duty to apply Subtitle D to these wastes. EPA entered into a consent decree to study these wastes and determined they did not fall under RCRA.[15]

Subtitle D deals with non-hazardous waste. This includes rules for landfills, such as a ban on open landfills and any other waste disposal facility. Rules for household trash and municipal solid waste, such as sludge from wastewater treatment plants or drinking water treatment facilities are developed here.[16] The basic goal of Subtitle D is to develop a framework for government

11. *Common Toxic Products Exempt From RCRA*, 29 Envtl. Sci. & Toxicology 301A-7A (1995).
12. Pub. L. No. 3001(b)(2)(A) and Pub. L. No. 3001(b)(3)(A). These important exemptions are known as the Bentsen and Bevill Amendments after their sponsors, Sens. Lloyd Bentsen and Thomas Bevill.
13. Lynn L. Bergeson, *Re-Re-Re Defining RCRA Solid Wastes*, 36 Pollution Eng'rg 32-33 (2004).
14. David L. Hippensteel, *The RCRA Exemption for Oil and Natural Gas Exploration and Production Wastes: What You May Not Know*, 6 Envtl. Geosci. 106-09 (1999).
15. U.S. EPA, *Management of Oil and Gas Exploration and Production Waste*, https://www.epa.gov/hw/management-oil-and-gas-exploration-and-production-waste#consentdecree (last updated Apr. 4, 2022). U.S. EPA, *Special Wastes*, https://www.epa.gov/hw/special-wastes (last updated July 6, 2021). In response to one of the largest coal ash spills in 2008 from a Tennessee Valley Authority (TVA) plant in Kingston, Tennessee, EPA began the process of studying and developing stricter rules for coal ash impoundments under Subtitle D. They issued a final rule in April 2015 that was amended in 2018 and public comments were still being taken as of April 2020 and the process is ongoing as industry seeks exemptions from the rule and the EPA is now asserting the possibility of making these more flexible. This is an excellent example of the life cycle of any regulating any hazardous substance with a substantial industry lobby that moves over many decades without resolution. *See* U.S. EPA, *Disposal of Coal Combustion Residuals From Electric Utilities Rulemakings*, https://www.epa.gov/coalash/coal-ash-rule (last updated July 30, 2021).
16. Michael Somers, *RCRA's New Causation Question: Linking Ubiquitous Wastes to Specific Defendants*, 38 B.C. Envtl. Aff. L. Rev. 193-217 (2011).

cooperation at all levels to manage non-hazardous waste.[17] EPA promulgates minimum criteria for the design, location, restrictions, and closure of any municipal or industrial waste landfill. EPA determines minimum standards for the incineration of non-hazardous waste and guidance and rules for state permit programs to comply with federal standards.[18]

While RCRA establishes a framework for permitting across the United States and provisions for the life cycle of hazardous waste, it does not sufficiently address the problem of remediation of such wastes. It started to become apparent in the 1970s that strewn across the United States were numerous unsafe sites containing hazardous waste that had to be remediated.[19] In many cases, the companies or individuals that created the problem were no longer in existence or could not afford to pay for the needed improvements, landowners faced issues with liability from nearby hazards, and many other issues persisted, meaning Congress needed a systematic solution to managing the complex and expensive problem of such remediation.[20] While RCRA is extremely important for professionalizing waste management across the country, RCRA has some significant shortcomings. "Special wastes" are exempted from the Act, as are drilling fluids, cement kiln dust, uranium ore, and other materials.[21] Creating significant problems is that under RCRA, prioritizing waste reduction is not a priority for EPA. For example, the outstanding increase in plastics pollution in the country and other problems created when reducing wastes is not a major mandate.[22] Broadly speaking, managing hazardous waste has ended up becoming a commercial endeavor in the United States and this has meant many unscrupulous individuals and

17. EPA has authority over enforcement actions and often does so in conjunction with the states or despite state actions. *See* Margaret May, *Tenth Circuit Upholds the EPA's Right to Overfile Under RCRA*, 30 Ecology L.Q. 777-81 (2003).
18. U.S. EPA, *Resource Conservation and Recovery Act (RCRA) Regulations*, https://www.epa.gov/rcra/resource-conservation-and-recovery-act-rcra-regulations#nonhaz (last updated May 3, 2021). As of 2017, EPA data shows that 267.8 million tons of municipal solid waste (MSW) was generated annually in the United States. Approximately, 35% was recycled or composted. These figures include typical waste accepted from consumers and does not include construction and demolition debris, municipal wastewater sludge, industrial debris, and other non-hazardous waste that typically makes its way to landfills. These figures are based on surveys, data estimates, and other means. U.S. EPA, Municipal Solid Waste Generation, Recycling, and Disposal in the United States: Facts and Figures (2014), https://www.epa.gov/sites/production/files/2018-03/documents/methodolgy_document_for_selected_municipal_solid_waste_products.pdf.
19. Ralph A. DeMeo et al., *More Flexible Cleanup in Florida: RCRA Corrective Action Reforms*, 77 Fla. B. J. 46-51 (2003).
20. Tracye Hockstad, *Conditional Innocence and the Myth of Consent: The Subtle Coercion of CERCLA's Contiguous Property Owner Protection*, 84 Mo. L. Rev. 93-120 (2019).
21. U.S. EPA, *Special Wastes*, https://www.epa.gov/hw/special-wastes (last updated July 6, 2021).
22. Diane M. Sicotte & Jessica L. Seamon, 2020, *Solving the Plastics Problem: Moving the U.S. from Recycling to Reduction*, 34 Soc'y & Nat. Resources 393-402 (Aug. 4, 2020)

companies have gotten involved in waste management early on and tend to make decisions based on economic motives, rather than the public good.[23]

When the Hooker Chemical Company started dumping industrial waste into an abandoned canal in upstate New York in the 1920s few companies thought about the legal liability of such actions and people were often unaware of the direct health effects of toxic exposures. When they sold the land to the city of Niagara Falls in 1953 for $1, the company was indemnified from legal liability in the transfer. By the end of that decade both a school and roughly 100 homes had been built on the site. By 1976, it was apparent that chemicals were leaching into homes, causing birth defects and abnormally high rates of miscarriage. By 1978, a state of emergency was declared.[24]

The Love Canal tragedy brought widespread attention to a national problem: there are millions of people living near industrial waste sites, which causes people to endure subsequent health effects, and government actions need to address the problem.[25] Congress passed CERCLA, also known as Superfund into law in 1980 to investigate, designate, and remediate sites contaminated with hazardous wastes throughout the United States.[26] CERCLA functions as a master fund that allows EPA to designate potentially responsible parties (PRPs) for cleaning up hazardous waste sites and to typically work with state environmental agencies or remedies for the site and monitoring and compliance issues related to long-term cleanup.[27] Sites that are considered priorities for further investigation are proposed for and potentially placed on the national priorities list (NPL). EPA currently lists 1,333 NPL sites, with 43 proposed and 448 deleted from the NPL.[28] CERCLA creates strict liability for property owners to cleanup or remediate contamination but

23. Sammy Zahran et al., *Rationality, Inequality, and Civic Vitality: The Distribution of Treatment, Storage, and Disposal Facilities in the Southeast*, 21 Soc'y & Nat. Resources 181 (2008).
24. Eckhart C. Beck, *The Love Canal Tragedy*, EPA Journal (Jan. 1979), https://archive.epa.gov/epa/aboutepa/love-canal-tragedy.html.
25. Emilee Scott Mooney, *Bona Fide Protection: Fulfilling CERCLA's Legislative Purpose by Applying Differing Definitions of "Disposal,"* 42 Conn. L. Rev. 958-59 (2010).
26. There were many other sites that made national headlines after Love Canal. One example is the Valley of the Drums outside of Louisville, Kentucky, which housed over 17,000 drums of chemical and other waste. State regulators had pursued legal action against the owner in 1975 and EPA placed it on the NPL in 1983. The site has still not been fully remediated. EPA, *A.L. Taylor, (Valley of Drums) Brooks, KY Cleanup Activities*, https://cumulis.epa.gov/supercpad/SiteProfiles/index.cfm?fuseaction=second.Cleanup&id=0402072#Status (last visited May 9, 2022).
27. Larry Schnapf, *How the CERCLA Notification Requirements Facilitate the Creation of Brownfields and What the EPA Can Do to Address This Problem*, 11 Sustainable Dev. L. & Pol'y 19-65 (2010).
28. U.S. EPA, *Superfund: National Priorities List (NPL)*, https://www.epa.gov/superfund/superfund-national-priorities-list-npl (last updated March 11, 2022).

does not typically focus on preventing the release of hazardous substances before an event occurs to release such materials.[29]

The Office of Superfund Remediation and Technology Innovation is responsible for administering Superfund. EPA is able to recover remediation costs from PRPs.[30] When they cannot they are able to utilize the Superfund Trust Fund to help pay for orphan sites where no PRP can be determined. If RCRA manages the generation, storage, transport, and disposal of waste, CERCLA functions as a companion Act.[31] It serves as a way to solve the problem of major chemical and toxic waste dumps, given the complexities of assigning responsibility, managing, and paying for cleanup, as well as acknowledging in many cases that no responsible party can be found or that the PRP lacks the ability to adequately fund the cleanup.[32] EPA has administered the Brownfields and Land Revitalization Program since 1995 to help stimulate cleanup and redevelopment of contaminated sites.[33]

Besides the difficulties of getting a site placed on the NPL and the time it takes to remediate, another major criticism of Superfund is that the tax assessed on businesses that generate hazardous waste was not renewed by Congress and it expired in 1995. This severely limits the Agency's ability to remediate orphan sites, particularly given that many sites can sit on the NPL for decades or require monitoring for the foreseeable future. It primarily funds the remediation of sites with PRPs via settlements that are kept in special accounts. For example, Love Canal was the first site placed on the NPL, but it was not considered fully remediated until 2004.[34] Many sites have

29. Desiree Gargano, *An Act of War: Finding a Meaning for What Congress Has Left Undefined*, 20 Touro L. Rev. 147-50 (2012).
30. Travis M. Trimble, *Environmental Law*, 64 Mercer L. Rev. 910-12 (2013).
31. Kiersten E. Holms, *This Land Is Your Land, This Land Is Mined Land: Expanding Governmental Ownership Liability Under CERCLA*, 76 Wash. & Lee L. Rev. 1013-71 (2019).
32. Paul Voosen, *Wasteland*, 226 Nat'l Geo. 128-37 (2014). Daniel E. Uyesato, *Superfund "Mega-Sites": How American Accounting Rules Exacerbate Difficult Challenges*, 48 Trends 10-13 (2017).
33. U.S. EPA, *Overview of EPA's Brownfields Program*, https://www.epa.gov/brownfields/overview-epas-brownfields-program (last updated May 4, 2022).
    Joel B. Eisen, *Brownfields at 20: A Critical Reevaluation*, 34 Fordham Urb. L.J. 721-56 (2007).
34. EPA reserves the Superfund Trust Fund for orphaned sites without PRPs. Since the fund has not been reauthorized it has Superfund special accounts. These accounts are funds set up when EPA locates PRPs and collects funds either via negotiated settlement or through litigation or other actions. The Agency has collected $7.9 billion in these special accounts, spent $4.5 billion on site cleanups, and has $3.4 billion reserved at the time of writing for future site cleanup. See: U.S. EPA, *Superfund Special Accounts*, https://www.epa.gov/enforcement/superfund-special-accounts (lats updated March 21, 2022).

been on the NPL for some time and sites can be removed without complete remediation.[35] Thus, the cleanup of Superfund sites remains backlogged.[36]

Love Canal today demonstrates the paradox of Superfund and the longer term strategy for managing current and past chemical and other hazardous wastes.[37] After evacuating and compensating about 900 families, $230 million was spent installing a plastic liner, capping the old neighborhood with clay, and covering it with topsoil.[38] In 1990 during this remediation process, about 260 homes were refurbished near the canal site in what was called Black Creek Village.[39] Current residents complain that chemicals have leached outside the 70-acre containment zone and caused health problems, but regulators maintain it is safe.[40] If Love Canal is a success story relative to the tens of thousands of other sites on the NPL and arguably at least that many sites that should be on it, it should give us pause.[41]

In 1986, Superfund was amended with the Superfund Authorization and Reorganization Act (SARA).[42] This both reauthorized Superfund and developed an equally important mechanism known as the Emergency Plan-

35. Being placed on the NPL means EPA has prioritized the site for investigation and cleanup. Making it to the NPL does not guarantee EPA has the funds or legal authority to require cleanup of some or all of the site. EPA proposes delisting sites in the Federal Register and solicits public comments, but this process does not guarantee the site has been deemed safe or has been remediated for all chemical hazards. In many cases remediation may involve removal or proper in situ disposal of the hazard through various means. *See, e.g.*, U.S. EPA, National Oil and Hazardous Substance Pollution Contingency Plan, 72 Fed. Reg. 45404 (Aug. 14, 2007), https://www.govinfo.gov/content/pkg/FR-2007-08-14/pdf/E7-15897.pdf.
36. Pam McFarland, *Superfund's Backlog Increases*, 284 ENR: Engineering-News Record, 16-19 (2020).
37. Gibbs can be credited in great part in popularizing the citizen activist role and the associated tactics for getting government to acknowledge the health effects of living near dump sites. She went on to found the Center for Health, Environment & Justice and the authors had the privilege of working with her on a few occasions. This helped spur other citizen movements and the development of tactics to make government pay attention to these problems. Another was activists, such as Denny Larson and Global Community Monitor that help citizens perform their own air monitoring and other methods to empower local communities to bring attention to their plights. Dr. Bob Bullard can be credited with bringing the study of environmental justice to academia and helping to popularize the struggle. Arguably, Superfund can be credited as a failure generally because the polluter pays principle is not significant enough to fund sites that many times cannot be adequately remediated. In terms of environmental justice, it would also fall flat. The United States likely has tens of thousands of sites that need to be on the NPL, but lack of funding and support for decades has left EPA few options to strengthen Superfund and deal with these issues. *See* Louis Gibbs, *Center for Health, Environment & Justice*, http://chej.org/lois/; Global Community Monitor, https://gcmonitor.org; Robert Bullard, Dumping in Dixie: Race, Class, and Environmental Quality (Routledge 2000).
38. Andrew J. Hoffman, *An Uneasy Rebirth at Love Canal*, 37 Environment 4-17 (1995).
39. Richard Clapp, *The Love Canal Story Is Not Finished*, 117 Envtl. Health Persp. A54 (2009). Ben Leitschuh, *Love Canal and the Rise of the Superfund*, 83 Planning 54 (2017).
40. Jennifer Thomson, *Toxic Residents: Heath and Citizenship at Love Canal*, 50 J. Soc. Hist. 204-23 (2016).
41. Associated Press, *"Love Canal" Still Oozing Poison 35 Years Later*, N.Y. Post, Nov. 2, 2013, https://nypost.com/2013/11/02/love-canal-still-oozing-poison-35-years-later/.
42. Eric G. Bachman, *Off-Site Emergency Response Plans: A Preparedness Tool*, 164 Fire Sci. 51-58 (2011).

ning and Community Right-To-Know Act (EPCRA).[43] Unlike abandoned chemical waste sites that slowly pollute communities or current sources of pollution that are allowed to legally pollute nearby communities, EPCRA addresses chemical hazards and emergencies stemming from the latter.[44] EPCRA directs states to create State Emergency Response Commissions and then divide the state into Local Emergency Planning Committees to develop plans to alert residents of chemical emergencies.[45]

Problems stemming from negligent or willful actions regarding the life cycle of hazardous and non-hazardous wastes can be managed through a criminal process when civil remedies fail to ensure compliance with the law. In Table 7, we list the criminal provisions of RCRA. The first set of criminal provisions focus on treatment, storage, or disposal without a permit and the second in violation of a permit.[46] These are treated as knowing violations under the law and carry a maximum penalty of two to five years plus a $50,000 per day violation. Transporting hazardous waste without a manifest or to an unpermitted facility may be treated as a knowing violation of the law and handled in a criminal manner. Making a false statement to investigators or on official reports or documents also can be categorized as a knowing violation of RCRA—as can altering, concealing, or destroying records.[47] Putting another person at risk of imminent danger or bodily harm is considered knowing endangerment and can be punished with a maximum of 15 years and a million-dollar fine. Illegally exporting hazardous waste can also be treated as a knowing violation.[48]

43. 2 U.S.C. §11001. The authors' own experience living near a petrochemical port and dealing with EPCRA and their local LEPCs has typically shown it to not be that active and generally encourage residents to shelter in place. Members are often local officials, an Emergency Management Coordinator, and representatives of local industry. City of Corpus Christi/Nueces County Local Emergency Planning Committee, http://www.cclepc.org.
44. Nimish Desai, American Chemistry Council v. Johnson: *Community Right-To-Know, But About What? D.C. Circuit Takes Restrictive View of EPCRA*, 33 Ecology L.Q. 583-612 (2006). Katherine Chekouras, *Balancing National Security With a Community's Right-To-Know: Maintaining Public Access to Environmental Information Through EPCRA's Non-Preemption Clause*, 34 B.C. Envtl. Aff. L. Rev. 107-42 (2007).
45. U.S. EPA, *Summary of the Emergency Planning & Community Right-To-Know Act*, https://www.epa.gov/laws-regulations/summary-emergency-planning-community-right-know-act (last visited Dec. 8, 2021).
46. Stephen J. Bottum, *Guilty Plea for RCRA Violations*, 32 Environment 22 (1990).
47. David T. Barton, *Corporate Officer Liability under RCRA: Stringent but Not…*, 4 Brigham Young U. L. Rev. 1547-72 (1991).
48. U.S. EPA, *Criminal Provisions of the Resource Conservation and Recovery Act*, https://www.epa.gov/enforcement/criminal-provisions-resource-conservation-and-recovery-act-rcra (last updated March 30, 2022). The data in Table 7 come directly from the information found in the link above.

Table 7. Criminal Provisions of RCRA

Violation	Statute	Knowing Penalty Max
Treatment, Storage, or Disposal Without a Permit	42 U.S.C. 6928(d)(2)(A)	5 years and/or up to $50,000 per day violation
Treatment, Storage, or Disposal in Violation of Permit	42 U.S.C. 6928(d)(2)(B) and (C)	2 years and/or up to $50,000 per day violation
Transportation Without a Manifest	42 U.S.C. 6928(d)(5)	2 years and/or up to $50,000 per day violation
Transportation to an Unpermitted Facility	42 U.S.C. 6928(d)(1)	5 years and/or up to $50,000 per day violation
False Statements	42 U.S.C. 6928(d)(3)	2 years and/or up to $50,000 per day violation
Alteration, Destruction, or Concealment of Records	42 U.S.C. 6928(d)(4)	5 years and/or up to $50,000 per day violation
Knowing Endangerment	42 U.S.C. 6928(e)	15 years and/or up to $250,000 or $1,000,000 if an organization
Illegal Export	42 U.S.C. 6928(d)(6)	5 years and/or up to $50,000 per day violation

In the following section we examine all cases investigated by EPA and subsequently criminally prosecuted since 1983 under RCRA and Superfund. This analysis will allow us, as in the previous two chapters, to explore how these criminal provisions have been used over time. It will also help us to explore the types of crimes investigated by EPA and ultimately be able to demonstrate the criminal focus government regulators and prosecutors have taken with the two laws over 37 years.

II. Themes in RCRA and CERCLA Prosecutions

Figure 14 tracks the evolution of RCRA prosecutions since. We see annual prosecutions rise and fall annually up to a high of 20 in 1993 during the Clinton era and then rise to a high of 22 in 1999 before G.W. Bush's election. Those numbers rise and fall again to a low of four in 2017 and then rising again to nine by 2019. There were 391 total RCRA prosecutions during this time period.

Figure 14. Total Annual RCRA Criminal Prosecutions Adjudicated Since 1983

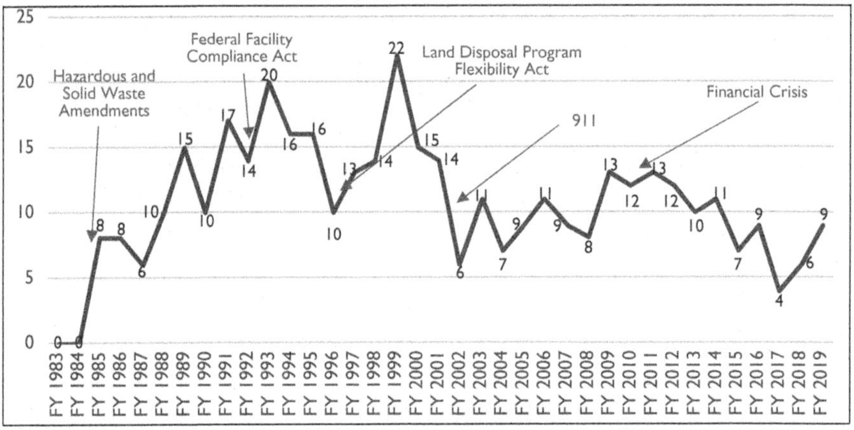

Superfund criminal prosecutions since 1983 are displayed in Figure 15. We find prosecutions reach a high point in 1991with eight annual prosecutions. This begins a rise and fall to a low of one in 1996. Then the trend line drops after never rising above three annual prosecutions.

Figure 15. Total Annual CERCLA Criminal Prosecutions Adjudicated Since 1983

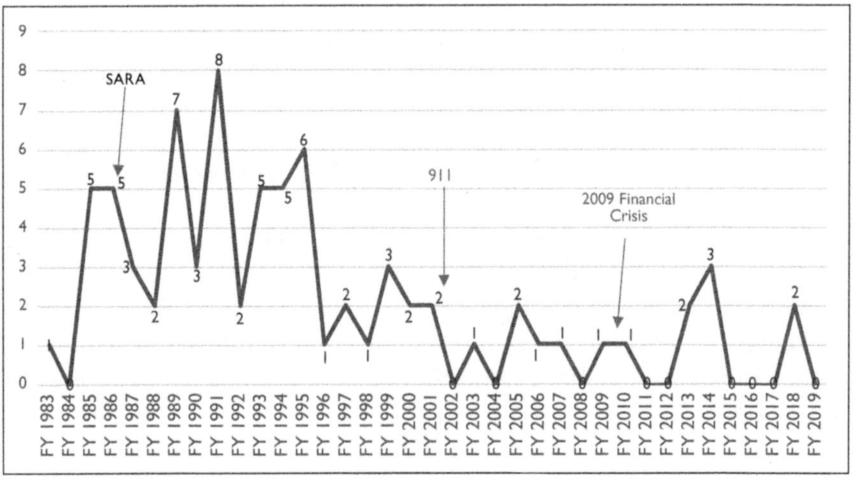

We break these prosecutions down in Figure 16 by U.S. state and territory for all annual RCRA prosecutions since 1983. Average prosecutions per state equal 7.8 over this time period. We find one prosecution in Washington, D.C., and two in Puerto Rico. States like South Dakota and Nevada have no prosecutions over the last 37 years, but California (30) and Texas (29) have the largest number of prosecutions.

Figure 16. Total RCRA Criminal Prosecutions by U.S. State and Territory Since 1983

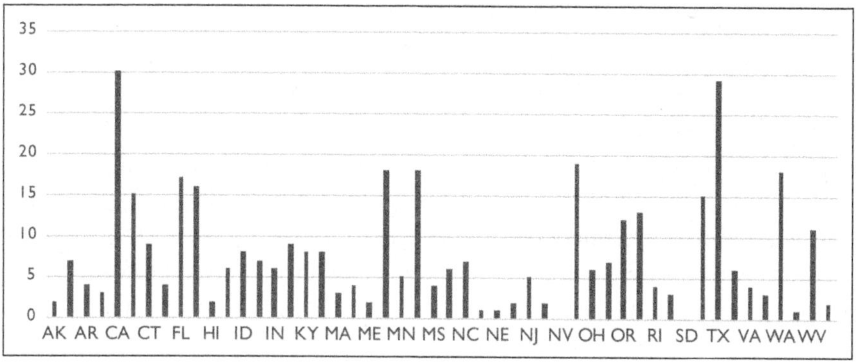

In Figure 17, we examine CERCLA prosecutions by state and territory since 1983. Twelve criminal prosecutions were settled in New York making it by far the state with the largest number of Superfund criminal prosecutions. Many states such as West Virginia or Nebraska contained no cases settled over the past 37 years.

Figure 17. Total CERCLA Criminal Prosecutions by U.S. State and Territory Since 1983

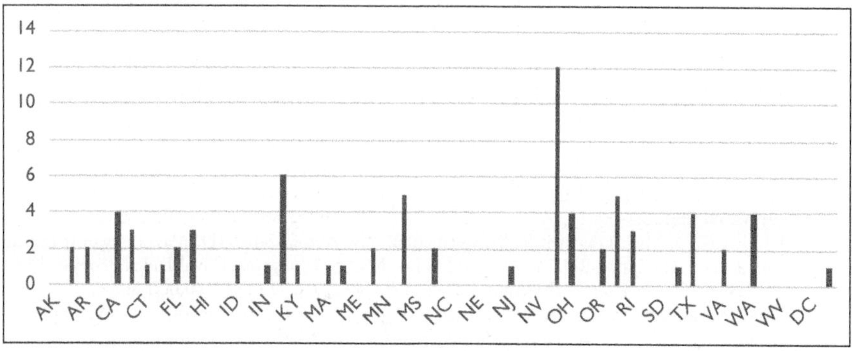

Figure 18. Major Themes in RCRA Criminal Prosecutions Since 1983

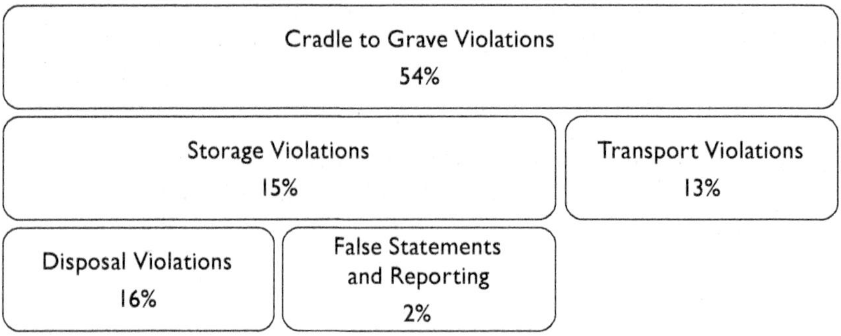

We now turn to Figure 18, which displays major themes we uncovered in RCRA prosecutions since 1983. We take the 391 prosecutions and organize them by theme, based in our judgment on the primary charge or crime that precipitated the investigation and prosecution in each case. RCRA charging patterns are relatively straightforward. Crimes involve illegal storage, treatment, transport, or disposal of hazardous wastes; a combination of these crimes; or giving false statements.[49]

The largest category (54% of total prosecutions) involved 212 prosecutions. We define these as prosecutions as individual actions related to a combination of illegal storage, transport, and/or disposal of regulated waste or company actions related to a combination of illegal storage, transport, and/or disposal of regulated waste. We label these cradle-to-grave violations, as they involve two or more of these crimes as the central nexus of the prosecution in our eyes. The prosecutions of Di Giorgio Corporation, Unichem International Inc., and American Ecology Recycle Center provide some case examples in this category.

Di Giorgio manufactured aluminum extrusion parts to produce window frames, doors, and other fixtures. The company pled guilty of knowing violations of RCRA in 1989 for the illegal storage and disposal of hazardous wastes.[50] Unichem International was in the business of blending chemicals

49. Total prosecutions since 1983 equal 395, but in four cases the information in the case narratives makes it too difficult to render proper judgment on the primary theme of the prosecution. This means these four prosecutions are excluded in Figure 18, but included in the following figures for penalties. These cases include the following: No. 4-89-CR-0281 (N.D. Ohio) (against Cuyahoga Wrecking Corp.); No. 90-80481 (E.D. Mich.) (against J&J Investments); No. A98-082-JKS (D. Alaska) (against Doyon Drilling, Inc.); and No. CR-7:14-MJ-174(TWD) (N.D.N.Y.) (against David Ladell Frisby).

50. No. 89-CR-364 (D. Colo.). The company was sentenced in 1990 to a $40,000 fine and to pay a $400 special assessment. The defendant also agreed to pay $452,670 on remediation and compliance measures ordered by the State of Colorado Department of Health.

for use in oil field operations and had a blending plant in Wyoming, New Mexico, and Louisiana. The company was charged with illegal storage, transport, and disposal of hazardous waste without a permit in violation of RCRA in 1990.[51] American Ecology Recycle Center in Tennessee was authorized to take recycling waste. The company had a chemline process to decontaminate metal that caught fire in July 1994 leaving behind 29,000 gallons of residue. In 1997, the company entered into a consent decree with EPA to manage the wastes, but investigators executed a search warrant in 1999 and still had 28 drums improperly stored on-site. The company paid a $100,000 civil penalty, but was charged with illegal storage, treatment, or disposal without a permit. Victor Lomnicki, the company's director of Regulatory Compliance, also gave false statements to investigators to obscure the fact the company had transported hazardous waste illegally.[52]

Fifteen percent of prosecutions centered on illegal storage of hazardous waste. A total of 59 prosecutions involved individual actions related to the illegal storage of regulated waste or negligent company actions related to the illegal storage of regulated waste. While many cases in the previous category involved illegal storage, we focus on these cases in this category, where the primary crime and focus of the prosecution as related to the storage of hazardous waste. Case examples of NIBCO Inc., Riddle Inc., and Robert Lewis illustrate illegal disposal prosecutions.

NIBCO manufactures valves, fittings, and pipping products. The company was charged with illegal storage of 1,1,1-trichloroethane without a permit. The hazardous chemical is often used as a solvent to clean metal parts or in cutting fluids for machining metal, which has been gradually phased out under the Montreal Protocol. The company was charged in 1989 and later pled guilty that year to the charge.[53] Riddle and owner Gene L. Riddle were charged for illegal storage under RCRA. The defendant admitted to investigators he did not have a permit to store hazardous waste in a warehouse in Monticello, Iowa. When nearby Kitty Creek flooded in 1993, 2002, and 2009, it sent floodwaters through the warehouse where the illegal wastes were stored. In addition to the illegal storage charge the defendants were charged under the CWA for illegal discharge of a pollutant into the waters of the

51. No. CR90-057 (D. Wyo.). The defendant was sentenced to 60 months of probation, fined $1.250 million on Count 1, fined $125,000 each on Counts 2 and 3 (suspended), and ordered to pay a $600 special assessment.
52. No. 3:02-CR-79-001 (E.D. Tenn.). AERC was sentenced to pay a $10,000 federal fine and a $400 special assessment. Lomnicki pled guilty and was sentenced to 60 months of probation, ordered to pay a $1,000 and a $25 special assessment.
53. No. 89-CR-164 (D. Colo.). The corporation was sentenced to pay a $10,000 fine.

United States without a permit.[54] Lewis owned Simple Solutions, a waste hauling business operating between May 2007 and April 2008. Lewis transported hazardous waste from a manufacturing plant to a licensed disposal facility during this time. On February 26, 2009, 40 55-gallon drums as well as 16 275-gallon totes (typically a heavy plastic surrounded with a metal grid that can be easily stored) of this hazardous waste material were discovered at a self-storage facility in Macon, Georgia. These wastes included flammable solvents and cyanide. Lewis was charged with illegal storage under RCRA in 2012.[55]

We find 62 prosecutions or 16% of total prosecutions center on illegal disposal. These include individual, as well as company actions related to the illegal disposal of regulated waste. Case examples of Steve Julius Kiss, Clinton Promise, and Norman Tetow illustrate the prosecution of illegal disposal cases under RCRA.

Kiss manufactured magnetic tape leader at a facility in Banning, California. He closed the business in 1992, but left behind hazardous waste. The ignitable waste was removed by EPA. Kiss was charged under RCRA for illegal disposal, as well as CERCLA for failure to notify.[56] In February 2007, EPA investigators were informed by the Texas Commission on Environmental Quality that H.O.T. Transport, a tanker truck cleaning business located in Lufkin, Texas, was illegally discharging hazardous wastes. Investigators found Promise and others routinely disposed of tanker trucks full of hazardous wastes at an unpermitted facility in this manner. Promise was charged under RCRA for illegal disposal without a permit in July 2011.[57] Tetow, owner of Gold Metal Paint Company, was operating an aircraft painting facility in a hanger near the Front Range Airport in Watkins, Colorado.[58] Investigators cited Tetow for illegally storing spent methyl chloride-based solvents in an underground tank. Tetow complied with investigators but decided to order his employees to later clean out the tank to save money and then had them leave the chemicals on the floor overnight to evaporate into

54. No. CR 10-118 (N.D. Iowa). The company was sentenced to 60 months of probation. Gene Riddle was sentenced to 60 months of probation and to pay restitution in the amount of $273,261 to EPA.
55. No. 5:12-CR-77-CAR-CHW (M.D. Ga.). Lewis was sentenced to 10 months of incarceration in March 2014.
56. No. CR-95-238 (Cal.). In July 1995, Kiss was sentenced to six months' incarceration, 36 months of probation, and a $5,000 fine.
57. No. 9:11-CR-00017-MAC-ZJH (E.D. Tex.). In November 2011, the defendant was sentenced to 36 months of probation and ordered to pay a $3,000 federal fine.
58. Press Release, U.S. DOJ, Owner of Colorado Aircraft Painting Company Pleads Guilty to Unlawfully Treating Hazardous Waste (March 13, 2013), https://www.justice.gov/opa/pr/owner-colorado-aircraft-painting-companypleads-guilty-unlawfully-treating-hazardous-waste.

the ambient air. The workers were not given safety gear. Tetow was prosecuted for the illegal disposal in 2013.[59]

Thirteen percent of cases, or 51 prosecutions, focus on illegal transport issues. These cases involve individual, as well as company actions related to the illegal transportation of regulated waste. Sbicca of California manufactured shoes in Los Angeles and Tijuana, Mexico. They attempted to transport hazardous waste illegally into Mexico but were refused entry. The defendants were caught in the United States when upon re-entry investigators found they were illegally transporting hazardous waste. They were charged under RCRA for illegal transport without a manifest.[60] Donald Hartung was the owner of Industrial Cleaning and Recyclers in Washington State. Hartung picked up drums of hazardous wastes from a variety of companies but was not licensed or permitted to do so. He illegally stored 55-gallon drums of waste at his home and at a storage locker facility in Auburn, Washington, and connected a bypass line to dispose of the hazardous waste into the municipal sewer near his home. He was charged under RCRA for the illegal transport of hazardous waste without a manifest and under the CWA for the illegal discharge into the sewer system.[61] Employees of U.S. Liquids in Michigan routinely dumped untreated waste into the sewer and bypassed sampling devices to conceal the illegal discharges. They sent hazardous waste with non-hazardous waste to a landfill only licensed to accept the latter and falsified treatment logs to conceal the crime. The company was charged under RCRA for illegal transport and the Refuse Act.[62]

In seven prosecutions, the primary thrust of the prosecution was to seek criminal punishment against defendants for false statements or reporting. These cases include individual actions related to false reporting, manifests, or statements to conceal regulated waste crimes and company actions related to false reporting, manifests, or statements to conceal regulated waste

59. No. 13-CR-00027-MSK (D. Colo.). Defendant was sentenced 24 months of probation and ordered to pay a $10,000 fine.

60. Sbicca of California and its president Dominic Sbicca were sentenced to 36 months of probation, 200 hours of community service, and fined $1,000. Edwardo Reyna was sentenced to 36 months of probation, 100 hours of community service, and a $500 fine. Juvenal Cabrear-Cruz was sentenced to 100 hours of community service.

61. No. CR96-89C (W.D. Wash.). In July 1996 the defendant was sentenced to 15 months' incarceration, 36 months of probation, and ordered to pay $75,000 in restitution to the EPA. In 1998, he violated the terms of his probation and was sentenced to 10 months' incarceration and 26 months of probation.

62. No. 02 CR 0967 (E.D. Mich.). The company was sentenced to 60 months of probation, ordered to pay a $925 special assessment fee, $1 million in restitution to the landfill for cleanup, and a federal fine in the amount of $4.5 million. Vice President Gazi George was sentenced to 27 months' incarceration and a $60,000 criminal fine. Plant manager Donald Roeser was sentenced to 12 months' incarceration and ordered to pay a $60,000 fine.

crimes. These cases represent 2% of the overall cases since 1983. In December 1995, Cleanmex prepared a false manifest claiming paint waste imported at Brownsville, Texas, was delivered to a certified facility in Texas, when it was actually delivered to a Mexican waste facility. The company was charged under RCRA with knowingly omitting material facts on the falsified manifest. Laidlaw Environmental Services was prosecuted for making false statements on a mislabeled manifest. Steven Ricci was employed by C&C Rhode Island, a company involved in metal plating and finishing. Ricci was sentenced for making false statements on hazardous waste inspection reports.[63]

We now look at the evolution of CERCLA prosecutions in Figure 19 since 1983. As with RCRA, we organize these prosecutions and produce a typology based on the central crime that led to prosecution. We find 77 prosecutions that are organized around failure to notify provisions. We break these down into five themes and show how CERCLA is then used as a companion to other major environmental statutes.[64]

Figure 19. Major Themes in CERCLA Criminal Prosecutions Since 1983

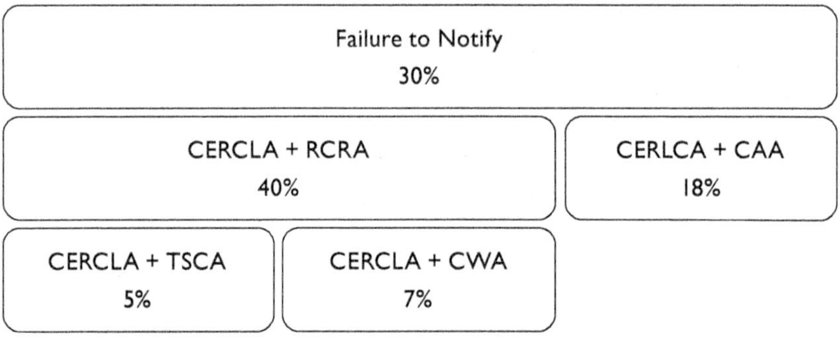

In the top quadrant, we show that 30% of prosecutions stem from failure to notify provisions in CERCLA. Both individual actions related to failure to properly notify officials of the release of a hazardous substance under and company actions related to failure to properly notify officials of the release of a hazardous substance under CERCLA were the focus of 23 prosecutions

63. No. B-00-519(S.D. Tex.). Cleanmex was sentenced to 12 months of probation and ordered to pay a $3,000 federal fine. No. 07-CR-000317-001 (N.D.N.Y.). The company was sentenced to pay a $400 special assessment fee and $250,000 in federal fines. No. CR08130S (D.R.I.). Ricci was sentenced to 12 months of probation and ordered to pay a $2,500 federal fine.

64. In two cases the exact focus of the CERCLA violation is too difficult to discern the primary charge in the case. One prosecution in Texas against Koch Industries was likely a failure to notify violation. The same happened with a Montana prosecution of Powell County Museum and Arts Foundation. No. CR-95-3-BU-PGH (D. Mont.).

since 1983. In 11 of these cases, individuals were the principal defendants and in 12 cases, companies were the principal defendants. Robert Clements Inc. was prosecuted in Virginia for failure to notify EPA of the release of a hazardous substance at a facility in Alexandria.[65] Alan Franko was prosecuted for removing asbestos pipe insulation under contract with the Naval Observatory in Washington, D.C. He was charged in 1985 with failure to notify provisions under CERCLA.[66] Owyhee Construction was prosecuted in Idaho for removing asbestos and failing to report it when undertaking a waterline renovation project.[67] The resulting asbestos cleanup cost EPA $4 million.[68]

In 40% of the CERCLA prosecutions, RCRA was used as the complementary charging statute. Individual actions related to the illegal storage, transport, and/or disposal of hazardous waste (RCRA) and failure to notify under CERCLA made up 10 of these 31 prosecutions. Company actions related to the illegal storage, transport, and/or disposal of hazardous waste (RCRA) and failure to notify under CERCLA made up 12 prosecutions. John Joseph Melle was prosecuted for removing labels on barrels of hazardous waste, transporting them without a manifest (both in violation of RCRA), and failure to notify government officials of the release of 100 pounds of an ignitable hazardous waste in violation of CERCLA.[69] Larry West was the owner of Cal Art Plastics in Cassopolis, Michigan. When the company moved to Niles, Michigan, he left behind 99 barrels of hazardous waste. He was charged under RCRA for illegal storage and under CERCLA for failure to notify.[70] Michael Raasch illegally disposed of a mercury-based pesticide on the Cape Cod National Seashore. He was charged under RCRA for illegal transport and under CERCLA for failure to notify.[71]

In 18% of prosecutions, defendants were charged with crimes related to CAA and CERCLA violations. These were all prosecutions related to asbestos. Individual actions related to the illegal abatement and disposal of asbes-

65. No. 85-00069 (E.D. Va.). The company was sentenced to pay a $4,000 fine.
66. No. 85-1146-M (E.D. Va.). Franko was sentenced to 30 days' suspended sentence plus 6 months of probation and ordered to pay a $150 fine.
67. For a related prosecution, see Associated Press, *Idaho Man Gets Prison for Mishandling Asbestos*, Deseret News, Aug. 14, 2013, https://www.deseret.com/2013/8/14/20455750/idaho-man-gets-prison-for-mishandling-asbestos.
68. Owyhee Construction Inc. was sentenced 36 months of probation, fined $100,000, told to implement a compliance and ethics program, and pay restitution.
69. No. G89-142CR (W.D. Mich.). Melle was sentenced to 12 months' incarceration (with work release privileges) and ordered to pay a special assessment of $50.
70. No. 1:93:CR:123 (W.D. Mich.). West was sentenced to 4 months' home confinement, 24 months of supervised release, a $10,000 fine and $40,000 in restitution to EPA.
71. No. 02-CR-10320 (D. Mass.). The defendant was sentenced to 36 months of probation and ordered to pay $10,000 in restitution to the U.S. National Park Service.

tos (CAA) and failure to notify under CERCLA made up the focus of nine prosecutions. Company actions related to the illegal abatement and disposal of asbestos (CAA) plus failure to notify under CERCLA were the center of 5 of the 14 prosecutions. G & Erie Associates owned buildings in Philadelphia and Walter Grzelak was contracted to remove and dispose of asbestos from various properties owned by the company. Both defendants were charged along with one of the company's partners, Daniel J. Lasdon Real Estate, for violation of NESHAP workplace standards under the CAA and failure to notify under CERCLA.[72] Charles Donahoo Jr. was in the business of demolishing buildings in Jefferson County, Kentucky, as Charlie Wrecking. He was contracted to demolish a building on the property of Tuscarora Plastics in Louisville, Kentucky. He was charged under the CAA for improper removable of asbestos, false statements, and failure to notify under CERCLA.[73]

Seven percent of prosecutions were the result of violations of the CAA and CERCLA. These involved company actions in five prosecutions related to the illegal discharge of regulated waste under the CWA and failure to notify under CERCLA. On January 2, 1985, a tank ruptured at the Pennwalt Corporation's Tacoma plant in Washington State.[74] The tank leaked sodium chlorate used as a bleaching agent in pulp and paper production into Hylebos Waterway that lead into Commencement Bay and then Puget Sound. Both the company and plant manager Orval High were prosecuted for negligent discharge under the CWA, false statements, and failure to notify under CERCLA.[75] Gary Products and Montgomery Tank Lines (MTL) were prosecuted for storing 102,000 gallons of hydrochloric acid owned by Montgomery in their facility in Gary, Indiana. On April 14, 1987, about 5,000 pounds of acid was discharged without a permit. The companies were charged along with co-defendants for failure to notify under CERCLA and with illegal discharge under the CWA.[76]

72. No. 92-192 (E.D. Pa.). Grzelak was sentenced to 90 days' home confinement, 36 months of probation, 400 hours of community service, and fined $5,000. Daniel J. Lasdon was sentenced to 90 days' home confinement, 36 months of probation, 400 hours of community service, and a $5,000 fine. G & Erie was fined $30,000. Charges were dropped against the other defendant.
73. No. CR89-00057-01-L(J) (W.D. Ky.). Donahoo was sentenced to 12 months' and 36 months' incarceration (to be served concurrently and all but 6 months suspended), 36 months of probation, and ordered to pay $75 to the Crime Victim's Fund.
74. Timothy Eagan, *The Law: Putting a Face on Corporate Crime*, N.Y. Times, July 14, 1989, https://www.nytimes.com/1989/07/14/us/the-law-putting-a-face-on-corporate-crime.html.
75. No. CR-88-55T (W.D. Wash.). The corporation was assessed a $500,000 fine and ordered to fund an environmental trust fund for the U.S. Coast Guard in the amount of $600,000. High was sentenced to pay a $5,000 fine and to serve 24 months of probation.
76. No. CR-92-17M (N.D. Ind.). William Keagle was sentenced to 12 months' incarceration (suspended) and ordered to pay a special assessment fee of $50 and was placed on 12 months' probation. MTL was sentenced to a $200 special assessment fee and fined $150,000. Ronald Zega was sentenced to a

Five percent of prosecutions involved failure to notify and violations of TSCA. Individual actions related to the illegal labeling, storage, or disposal under TSCA and failure to notify under CERCLA were the focus of two prosecutions. Company actions related to the illegal labeling, storage, or disposal under TSCA and failure to notify under CERCLA were also the focus of two prosecutions. Giacomo Catucci and David Dellinger were charged for illegally disposing of transformers containing PCBs. In January 1993, they were charged under TSCA for the illegal disposal of PCBs and under CERCLA for failure to notify.[77] William Kirkpatrick was indicted for illegally burying transformers containing PCBs at the landfill in the city of Stafford, Kansas. He was prosecuted under TSCA for improper disposal of PCBs and under CERCLA for failure to notify.[78]

III. Penalties in RCRA and CERCLA Prosecutions

In Figure 20 (next page) we examine criminal charging patterns in RCRA prosecutions since 1983. We examine each case to see if defendants were charged with non-environmental crimes as well. The most common non-environmental crime was false statements or reporting. In 12% of prosecutions at least one defendant gave false statements, falsified logs, records, reports, or other documents. We cataloged 47 cases where any of these charges were present in the case. The most common criminal charge we found was conspiracy. Typical conspiracy cases involved two or more defendants conspiring to hide a RCRA violation such as an illegal disposal crime or conspire to give false statements to investigators. In total we find that 16% of RCRA prosecutions involved conspiracy charges against one or more defendants. In 5% of cases or 18 prosecutions, at least 1 defendant was charged with fraud. This included mail, wire, tax, Social Security, and bank fraud. We find that obstruction and racketeering also occurred in 1% of cases.

$25 special assessment fee and fined $2,500. Gordon Babbitt was fined $125,000 and Merv Bridges was sentenced to a $25 special assessment fee and fined $2,500 as was Corey Niezgoda.

77. No. 93-009P (D.R.I.). A note on this case is that while both defendants were found guilty the narrative does not provide the punishment for either defendant. Instead, the EPA employee that completed the case made some personal comments and input a strange narrative from the wrong case.

78. No. 94-10094-01 (D. Kan.). The defendant was sentenced to 18 months' supervised probation with a special condition that 6 months of that be served as home confinement, was fined $3,000, charged a $50 special assessment fee, and ordered to attend mandatory substance abuse counseling.

Figure 20. Common Criminal Charges in RCRA Criminal Prosecutions Since 1983

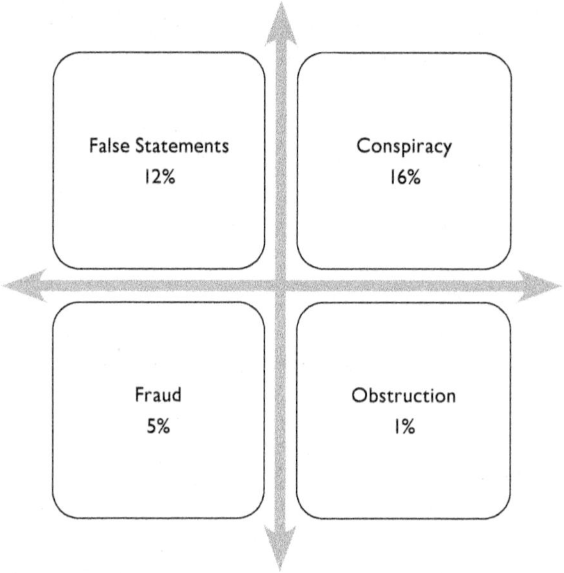

Figure 21. Total Penalties Assessed in RCRA Criminal Prosecutions Since 1983

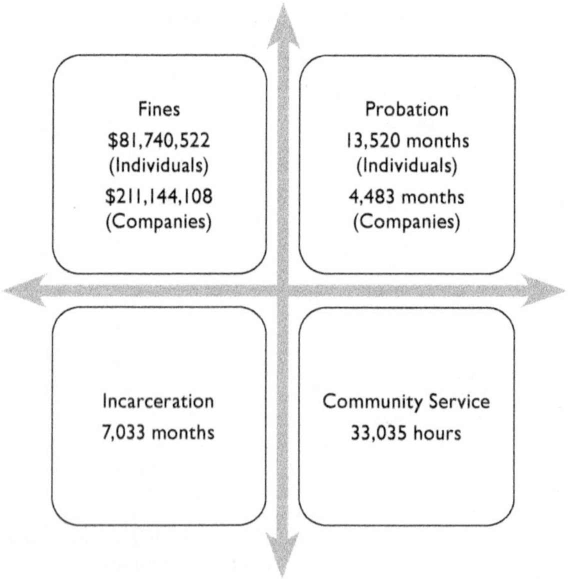

Figure 22. Common Criminal Charges in CERCLA Prosecutions Since 1983

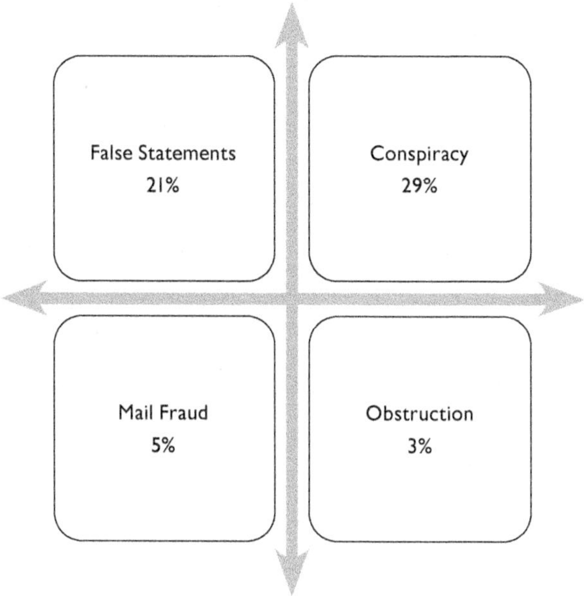

In Figure 21 we explore aggregate penalties assessed to all defendants in RCRA prosecutions since 1983. We find 269 prosecutions where individual defendants were fined. Total fines, restitution, and other monetary penalties assessed to all individual defendants equaled over $81 million. In 168 cases, companies were defendants and were cumulatively fined over $211 million in RCRA prosecutions since 1983. In 273 cases, individuals were assessed probation at sentencing. Total probation exceeded 13,000 months in RCRA cases since 1983. For company defendants, we catalog 105 cases totaling 4,483 months of probation. In 184 cases, individuals were assessed a cumulative total of 7,033 months of incarceration in RCRA prosecutions. We note that in 75 cases, defendants were sentenced to community service totaling 33,035 hours. Alternative punishments not included in the figure include 57 prosecutions where home confinement was assessed at sentencing totaling 383 months and in 18 cases, individuals received community corrections at sentencing totaling 496 months.

Figure 22 examines common criminal charges in CERCLA prosecutions since 1983. The most common charge was conspiracy. In 22 cases or almost one-third of the prosecutions, at least 1 defendant was charged with con-

Figure 23. Total Penalties Assessed in CERCLA Criminal Prosecutions Since 1983

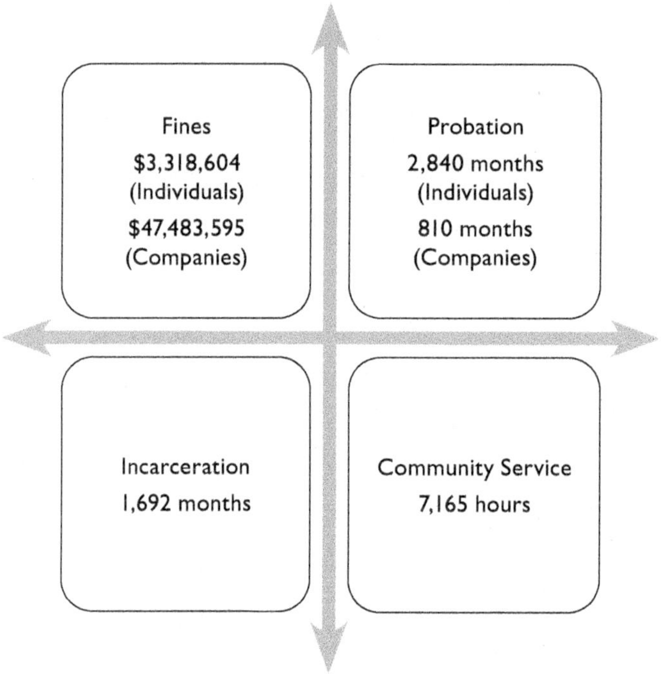

spiracy. In 16 cases or 21% of the prosecutions, at least 1 defendant was charged with false statements or false reporting. In 5% of cases, defendants were charged with mail fraud. And in two cases or 3% of cases, defendants were charged with obstruction or racketeering.

We look at total punishments assessed since 1983 to individual and company defendants in CERCLA prosecutions in Figure 23. In 54 cases, at least one individual defendant was charged with a fine, fee, restitution, or other monetary penalty. Total penalties exceeded $3.3 million. For companies they received monetary penalties in 37 cases exceeding $47 million. In 50 cases, at least 1 individual defendant was assessed probation at sentencing. Total probation assessed to individual defendants in CERCLA cases equaled 2,840 months. In 20 cases, companies were assessed probation at sentencing totaling 810 months. In 34 cases, individuals were assessed incarceration at sentencing totaling 1,692 months. We also find 17 cases where defendants were assessed community service totaling 7,165 hours. In 13 cases, defendants were assessed home confinement totaling 64 months, as well as in CERCLA prosecutions.

IV. Conclusion

This chapter uncovered patterns, themes, and penalties in RCRA and CERCA prosecution since 1983. We find that using these federal laws and their related criminal provisions to charge criminals is relatively straightforward in scope compared to the CAA and the CWA. RCRA is an effective tool for prosecutors when hazardous wastes are discovered. The cradle-to-grave provisions require permits and paper trails, which are used to prosecute offenders. We find comprehensive crimes involving storage, transport, and disposal to be fairly straightforward as best we can surmise across the case summaries. Illegal storage, disposal, and transport (without a permit and/or manifest) were the primary themes we found outside of comprehensive RCRA violations or false statements and reporting.

CERCLA was used almost universally alone or in companion with other major environmental statutes to prosecute offenders. Failure to notify officials of the release of a hazardous substance was a fairly uniform method to charge and prosecute defendants in the past 37 years. About 30% of prosecutions rely on failure to notify provisions alone. In the other cases, prosecutors sought companion charges under the CWA, the CAA, RCRA, and TSCA. Most common among these strategies was to charge under RCRA for illegal storage, transport, or disposal plus failure to notify under CERCLA (40% of prosecutions). The use of the CAA as a companion charging statute was typically done in asbestos cases and under the CWA for illegal discharge cases. TSCA cases typically involved the illegal disposal of PCBs, primarily from illegally discarded electrical transformers.

Chapter 5. Misapplication: The Criminal Enforcement of the Toxic Substances Control Act and the Federal Insecticide, Fungicide, and Rodenticide Act

I. Enforcing the Toxic Substances Control Act and the Federal Insecticide, Fungicide, and Rodenticide Act

By the 1970s, EPA had been empowered through the CAA, CWA, RCRA, and other statutes to address some of the country's worst environmental problems.[1] Hazardous substances could be studied, measured, risk assessments made, and rules put in place to protect humans, animals, and the natural environment.[2] As with all of these policy problems, EPA faced a few tremendous hurdles. The first was to quantify what substances posed threats and determine how to reduce those threats.[3] This approach typically resulted in a technology-forcing situation, where the Agency, unable to constantly monitor and regulate so many entities, looked to the private sector to develop technological solutions that were adaptable to current circumstances. This took time, but many innovations helped EPA meet its goals over time, such as stack scrubbers for coal plants, effective catalytic converters to control exhaust from passenger cars and commercial fleets, and chemical and mechanical processes to sanitize drinking water and manage solid waste.[4]

The second great hurdle they faced was that almost all of their decisions would have economic costs and thus they would encounter opposition from industrial interests that would increasingly organize to lobby against strin-

1. Richard J. Lazarus, The Making of Environmental Law 88-93 (Univ. of Chicago Press 2004).
2. Peter W. Preuss et al., *Risk Assessment at the USEPA: The Science Behind the Assessments*, 13 Human & Ecol. Risk Assessment 41-45 (2007).
3. Jack Lewis, *The Birth of EPA*, EPA J., Nov. 1985, https://archive.epa.gov/epa/aboutepa/birth-epa.html.
4. Emil Attanasi & David H. Root, *Coal-Fired Power Generation, New Air Quality Regulations, and the Future of U.S. Coal Production*, 6 Envtl. Geosci. 139-45 (1999).

gent regulation.[5] Countering this opposition would from the start mean that EPA would have to significantly compromise its efforts and focus on meeting broader goals for regional areas for air, water, and hazardous waste pollution, rather than developing broad protocols that reduced these sources from specific entities. That problem was and is addressed through a mix of incentives, i.e., the extensive grants to create municipal wastewater facilities that came with stipulations, regulatory flexibility in meeting air or water pollution standards, or punishments (consent decrees, civil and judicial measures or criminal sanctions to gain compliance for specific regulated entities). Because of the nature of their policy environment, EPA was much more successful regulating manufacturers or stationary sources of pollution than regulating at the individual level or with mobile sources of pollution.[6]

The third great challenge EPA faced is that by the time it was created and empowered as an agency in the 1970s, the genie had already escaped the bottle as weak national-level regulation of harmful substances had followed a massive boom in chemical production after World War II. At the consumer level, policymakers welcomed the chemical revolution to deal with the massive influx of consumption and the population boom that was going to follow the war. This revolution meant greater crop yields (chemical pesticides and fertilizers drastically increased crop yields when combined with industrial agriculture), cheaper food prices (pesticides and other food additives allowed food to be stored much longer and led to economies of scale that developed the corporate packaged food industry and corporatization of grocery stores), and cheaper building materials needed for sub-standard housing that would dot the country after the war. Various chemicals were created to develop siding, glues to create plywood and later oriented-strand board, fiberglass insulation, linoleum and vinyl tile, countertops, and other fixtures proliferated in the decades after the war, not to mention the proliferation of plastics that to this day remain ubiquitous in everyday American life.[7]

Most of the chemical substances that quickly made their way into all American lives faced little to no regulatory oversight. These innovations solved many problems for a rapidly expanding economy, but their effects on the health of our world could no longer be ignored by the 1960s. Scien-

---

5. Richard A. Harris & Sidney M. Milkis, The Politics of Regulatory Change: A Tale of Two Agencies (Oxford Univ. Press 1995).
6. Jocelyn B. Garovoy, *"A Breathtaking Assertion of Power?" Not Quite.* Pronsolino v. Nastri *and the Still Limited Role of Federal Regulation of Nonpoint Source Pollution*, 30 Ecol. L.Q. 543-45 (2003). Victor B. Flatt, *C(r)ap and Trade: The Brave New World of Non-Point Source Nutrient Trading and Using Lessons From Greenhouse Gas Markets to Make It Work*, 52 Hous. L. Rev. 301-05 (2014).
7. Jose Chamizo, *About Continuity and Rupture in the History of Chemistry: The Fourth Chemical Revolution (1945-1966)*, 21 Founds. Chem. 11-29 (2019).

tists worried that many chemicals would persist in the natural environment almost indefinitely and were finding their way into human and animal bodies with pernicious consequences.[8] The public was catching on to the downside of the government's "wild West" approach to regulating chemicals.[9] Americans woke up to a toxic reality, where chemicals were running wild and causing all manner of problems in our society.[10] Chlorofluorocarbons (CFCs) widely used as refrigerants were blowing a hole in the earth's ozone layer.[11] Asbestos used as an insulator and building material in about everything from pipe insulation to ceiling and floor tile, and as a cheap substitute for covering seams in ceiling sheetrock, was causing cancer.[12] PCBs used as a coolant was starting to show up in amphibians and waterways while polybrominated biphenyls (PBBs) were showing up in the food supply and breast milk. It was becoming hard to deny that the chemical revolution had consequences and that there was a need for consistent federal action.[13]

TSCA is the primary legislative vehicle that empowers EPA to regulate all manner of chemicals in the United States.[14] Through the Office of Pollution Prevention and Toxics (OPPT), EPA is given broad authority to regulate the importation, export, manufacturing, and use of chemical substances. TSCA defines "chemical substance" as, "organic or inorganic substance of a particular molecular identity, including any combination of these substances occurring in whole or in part as a result of a chemical reaction or occurring in nature, and any element or uncombined radical." These include organics, inorganics, polymers, and chemical substances of unknown or variable composition, complex reaction products, and biological materials. Other substances, such as pesticides, food additives, drugs, cosmetics, tobacco and tobacco products, nuclear materials, and munitions are not covered by the Act.[15]

8. Jama McMurtery Grove, *"Unjustified Expectations of Magic": Arkansas Agricultural Specialists, DDT, and 2,4-D*, 79 Ark. Hist. Q. 89-115 (2020). Simon Chang et al., *DDT Exposure in Early Childhood and Female Breast Cancer: Evidence From an Ecological Study in Taiwan*, 121 Envtl. Int'l 1106-12 (2018).
9. The Bioscience Resource Project, *The Poison Papers*, https://www.poisonpapers.org/.
10. Evaggelos Vallianatos, Poison Spring: The Secret History of Pollution and the EPA (Bloomsbury Press 2014).
11. Erica K. Jacobsen, *Landmark Lesson Plan: Chlorofluorocarbons and Ozone Depletion*, American Chemical Society, https://www.acs.org/content/acs/en/education/whatischemistry/landmarks/lesson-plans/cfcs-ozone-lesson-plan.html (last visited March 28, 2022).
12. John H. Lange, *Impact of Asbestos Concentrations in Floor Tiles on Exposure During Removal*, 12 J. Envtl. Health Res. 293-300 (2002).
13. EPA Alumni Ass'n, Toxic Substances a Half Century of Progress (April 2020), https://www.epaalumni.org/hcp/toxics.pdf.
14. Sheldon Krimsky, *The Unsteady State and Inertia of Chemical Regulation Under the Toxic Substances Control Act*, 15 PLos Biol. 1-10 (2017).
15. U.S. EPA, *How TSCA Defines "Chemical Substance"*, https://www.epa.gov/tsca-inventory/about-tsca-chemical-substance-inventory#chemicalsubstancedefined (last updated July 20, 2021).

While the CAA and the CWA focus on reducing air and water pollution more broadly, setting national or regional goals, the goal of TSCA is to regulate specific chemicals before they come to market, which it often fails to do.[16] This meant establishing protocols for determining which chemicals were potentially the most hazardous in terms of general public health problems, and later working to study specific chemicals.[17] The Toxic Substances Control Act Chemical Substance Inventory (TSCA Inventory) contains 86,405 chemicals and 41,484 of these are currently active.[18] This is the basis for reporting and recordkeeping and regulates all individuals or companies that import/export, manufacture, process, or distribute regulated chemical substances in commerce and sets requirements for notifying government officials if any of these substances they place on the market are known to pose risks to humans or the natural environment.[19] In addition to registration, recordkeeping, and notification provisions, the Act authorizes EPA to determine whether to require premanufacture notation for "new chemical substances" or determine if a chemical substance is a "significant new use" and be subjected to significant new use rules, which requires a responsible party to give notice to the Agency before a chemical substance meeting these guidelines is imported, manufactured, or processed for the intended new use. Industry must also engage in toxicity testing on substances and mixtures if required by EPA.[20]

Unlike identifying and managing air pollution regionally or water and waste, where goals are set more broadly on reducing harm within a particular region or industry, regulating chemicals must be done on an individual basis and the number of chemicals that come on the market is still proliferating rapidly. Managing this problem has been one of EPA's greatest challenges and failures, and this problem continues unabated today.[21] Over 41,000 known

---

16. Leonardo Trasande, *Updating the Toxic Substances Control Act to Protect Human Health*, 315 J. Am. Med. Ass'n 1565-66 (2016). Colin P. Eichenberger, *Improving the Toxic Substances Control Act: A Precautionary Approach to Toxic Chemical Regulation*, 72 Air Force L. Rev. 123-59 (2015).
17. Patrica D. Korman et al., *Population Susceptibility: A Vital Consideration in Chemical Risk Evaluation Under the Lautenberg Toxic Substances Control Act*, 17 PLos Biol. 1-11 (2019).
18. U.S. EPA, *How to Access the TSCA Inventory*, https://www.epa.gov/tsca-inventory/how-access-tsca-inventory#download (last updated March 7, 2022).
19. U.S. EPA, *Summary of the Toxic Substances Control Act*, https://www.epa.gov/laws-regulations/summary-toxic-substances-control-act (last updated Oct. 22, 2021).
20. Paul A. Locke & D. Bruce Myers Jr., *Implementing the National Academy's Vision and Strategy for Toxicity Testing: Opportunities and Challenges Under the U.S. Toxic Substances Control Act*, 13 J. Toxicology & Envtl. Health 376-84 (2010).
21. Sara A. Vogel & Jody A. Roberts, *Why the Toxic Substances Control Act Needs an Overhaul, and How to Strengthen Oversight of Chemicals in the Interim*, 30 Health Aff. 898-905 (2011).

chemical substances are listed in the inventory, which are currently in active use. Over 86,000 chemical substances have been listed to date and many harmful substances fall outside of the scope of TSCA leading to little control over the introduction of new chemicals.[22] Only 266 chemical substances that have historically been subject to testing rules and very few have been banned.[23] This number alone—given the known effects and potential of so many substances to injure animals, the environment, cause birth defects, cancer, and other maladies—shows the massive scope of the problem handed to the EPA and the diminutive historical response.[24]

What EPA did best under TSCA was not test or ban many specific chemical substances, but instead like the CAA and the CWA, it focused on examining broader national problems with certain chemicals and reducing their overall impact to society. The focus historically has been on six substances: (1) PCBs; (2) asbestos; (3) radon; (4) lead; (5) formaldehyde; and (6) mercury.[25] These broader goals can be seen in Table 8, which lays out the major statutory provisions of the Act. Subchapter I of TSCA delegates authority to EPA for the broader goal of defining and controlling toxic substances, including limits on the sale, distribution, or transfer of elemental mercury by federal agencies. PCBs were banned in 1979 from manufacture in the United States, but a few products, particularly electrical transformers, were still allowed to use them.[26] Subchapter II focuses on AHERA.[27] Overlapping with the CAA on authority to regulate asbestos, AHERA is an excellent example of EPA managing a chemical substance that causes broader public health problems than testing and regulating a particular chemical.

---

22. Andrew Hanan, *Pushing the Environmental Regulatory Focus a Step Back: Controlling the Introduction of New Chemicals Under the Toxic Substances Control Act*, 18 Am. J. L. & Med. 395-401 (1992).
23. U.S. EPA, *Sunset Dates of Chemicals Subject to Final TSCA Section 4*, https://www.epa.gov/assessing-and-managing-chemicals-under-tsca/sunset-dates-chemicals-subject-final-tsca-section-4-test (last updated March 24, 2022).
24. Christopher De Rosa, *The USEPA and the Toxic Substances Control Act (TSCA) of 1976: The Promise, the Reality, and the Reason(s) Why*, 16 Ecol. Risk Assess. 1227-33 (2010).
25. U.S. EPA, *Toxic Substances Control Act (TSCA) and Federal Facilities*, https://www.epa.gov/enforcement/toxic-substances-control-act-tsca-and-federal-facilities (last visited March 23, 2022). A mercury export ban was passed in 2008.
26. U.S. EPA, *Toxic Substances Control Act (TSCA) Compliance Monitoring*, https://www.epa.gov/compliance/toxic-substances-control-act-tsca-compliance-monitoring (last visited March 17, 2022).
27. Kevin Druley et al., *Asbestos Among First 10 Chemicals EPA to Analyze Under Updated TSCA*, 195 Safety & Health 13 (2010).

Table 8. Major Statutory Provisions of TSCA

Title	Description
Subchapter I	Authorizes EPA to control toxic substances
Subchapter II	AHERA
Subchapter III	Radon Abatement
Subchapter IV	Reduction of Lead Exposures
Subchapter V	Healthy Schools
Subchapter VI	Formaldehyde Standards for Composite Wood Products

AHERA requires school districts and most private schools to assess their asbestos risk in their facilities. They are required to inspect facilities every three years and create management plans as well as train relevant staff and provide notifications to parents. AHERA intersects with TSCA as it promulgates in-place guidelines for living with asbestos if it is not removed and does not present a health risk. If it is disturbed, the Act creates reporting requirements and mandates compliance with NESHAP standards for removing asbestos-containing materials. Criminal provisions are placed within the CAA and TSCA to manage compliance among willful offenders or knowing violations. In this, AHERA is a classic case of EPA responding to a broader public policy problem with a more ubiquitous harmful substance in a similar manner to how it has responded under their statutory authority with other acts of Congress.

Subchapter III contains provisions for radon reduction in indoor facilities. Radon, a naturally occurring radioactive gas, remains the second leading cause of lung cancer in the United States after smoking. Indoor radon exposure occurs more frequently in certain geographic areas of the United States and poses a significant health risk to occupants, particularly in basements, if proper technology to mitigate and vent the gas is not installed in homes. Congress set goals for radon in homes to be no worse than outdoor levels and states tend to have radiation or radon control divisions; EPA provides grant funding for indoor radon reduction.[28]

28. The most harmful radon gas seeps up through the bedrock into a home's foundation and beyond as a natural process. It also makes its way into home via showers and faucets when using well water. Measured in picocuries per liter (pCi/L) the United States is broken into three zones ranging from less than 2 pCi/L to over 4. The upper Midwest and parts of the Northeast tend to have the highest levels in the country on average. Radon mitigation systems tend to remove gas below a slab or before it enters the home with up to 90% efficiency for those whose home tests near the 4-liter mark. Kansas State Univ., *National Radon Program Services*, https://sosradon.org/mitigation (last visited May 11, 2022).

Subchapter IV focuses on lead-based paint hazards. Perhaps one of the more salient actions for homeowners, if you purchase a home built before 1978 you receive a lead-based paint disclosure. Sellers are required to disclose the presence of lead and certain precautions are needed to remediate or disturb lead-based paint. This became a growing health concern, particularly with the U.S. Department of Housing and Urban Development, as so many older homes contained lead and as it chips off with time, children are likely to become ill or even die after ingesting the chips.[29] These rules were promulgated after the passage of the Residential Lead-Based Paint Hazard Reduction Act in 1992 that allowed EPA to set standards for residential buildings or any buildings occupied by children for standards and certification requirements.[30] Subchapter V authorized an EPA state grant program to help develop environmental standards for schools, while Subchapter VI sets limits for formaldehyde in composite wood products.[31]

Another structural difference between the way EPA enforces the CAA or the CWA as opposed to TSCA is that it is not a state-delegated program. Enforcement and management of TSCA falls on the federal government and the EPA has fallen short of the original congressional goals of the Act. In 2016, Congress made significant changes to the way TSCA is implemented. Prior to 2016, EPA did not have a duty to review the hazards associated with any particular chemical and were told to assess the risk against the benefit of a chemical substance used in commerce. Rulemaking and testing requirements were lengthy and EPA did not test or rule on most substances.[32] The revisions to TSCA mandated EPA review existing chemicals, assess them against a public health-based or risk-based standard, and develop a faster review process.[33] EPA was required to identify 10 chemical substances by the end of 2016 to receive risk assessments, but determining real-world risks to make regulatory determinations is often wrought with as much politics as science.[34]

29. Emmanuel C. Gorospe & Shawn. L. Gerstenberger, *Atypical Sources of Childhood Lead Poisoning in the United States: A Systematic Review From 1966-2008*, 46 Clinical Toxicology 728-37 (2008).

30. Pub. L. No. 102-550.

31. Kay A. Dally et al., *Formaldehyde Exposure in Nonoccupational Environments*, 36 Archives Envtl. Health 277-80 (1981).

32. Charles W. Schmidt, *TSCA 2.0: A New Era in Chemical Risk Management*, 124 Envtl. Health Persp. 182-86 (2016).

33. Known as the Frank Lautenberg Chemical Safety for the 21st Century Act, Pub. L. No. 114-182.

34. Expert review panels and scientists that help with the risk assessment process bring validity to the process, but in practice such assessments are as political as they are scientific when it comes to taking

TSCA contains criminal provisions to punish knowing and willful violations. These are found in Table 9. Knowing or willfully violating the Act in a manner that places another individual in imminent danger of death or bodily injury can result in up to 15 years in prison and a $250,000 fine for individuals and up to $1 million if the perpetrator is a corporation. Failure to comply with a regulation order or inspection can result in up to one year and a $50,000 per day fine per violation. Knowingly or willfully refusing to comply with a PCB regulation, to submit notice to regulators that a chemical substance was a new chemical, failure to comply with recordkeeping requirements or denying EPA representatives access to a facility after appropriate notice was given can result in one year and up to a $50,000 fine per day violation.[35]

Table 9. Criminal Provisions of TSCA

Violation	Statute	Knowing Penalty Max
Knowing or Willful Violations	15 U.S.C. 2615(b)(2)(A)	$250,000 and 15 years in prison $1,000,000 if a corporation
Fails to Comply with a Regulation Order or Inspection	15 U.S.C. 2615(b)	1 year and/or up to $50,000 per day
PCB Violations	15 U.S.C. 2615(b)	1 year and/or up to $50,000 per day
Pre-Manufacture Notice Requirements	15 U.S.C. 2615(b)	1 year and/or up to $50,000 per day
Knowing or Willful Reporting Violations	15 U.S.C. 2615(b)	1 year and/or up to $50,000 per day
Knowing or Willful Denial of Entry	15 U.S.C. 2615(b)	1 year and/or up to $50,000 per day

FIFRA can be traced to the Federal Insecticide Act of 1910. The original Act regulated the quality of pesticides being brought on the market in the United States. FIFRA came into being in 1947 under the auspices of the U.S. Department of Agriculture. Key measures implemented at the time included the need for basic labeling requirements. As it became more obvious that pesticides were causing injury to wildlife, humans, and the natural

regulatory action. An industry tactic in these cases is simply to throw more lawyers and scientists at the problem to cast doubt on any strong regulatory decisions. This, alongside changing presidential regimes and declining funding relative to responsibilities, may continue to make TSCA much less effective than its potential. Environmental Defense Fund, *EPA's First Ten Chemicals Under Review*, https://www.edf.org/health/epas-first-10-chemicals-under-review (Sept. 21, 2018).

35. U.S. EPA, *Criminal Provisions of the Toxic Substances Control Act, TSCA*, https://www.epa.gov/enforcement/criminal-provisions-toxic-substances-control-act-tsca (last visited May 7, 2021). Data in this table comes directly from the above source.

environment, the Federal Environmental Pesticide Control Act was passed in 1972 to transfer regulatory authority to EPA. Another structural shift was to move away from solely truth-in-labeling requirements for pesticides to assessing health risks of their use on the market versus the economic benefits in commerce.[36] It was not until 1996, when Congress passed the Food Quality Protection Act, that EPA was further empowered to set tolerances for pesticides. The new standard was considered to be a reasonable certainty of no harm.[37] If the cost of removing a chemical from the market is too burdensome to industry, EPA may not be able to remove it if the adverse risks are deemed less than the economic costs, whether those effects cause harm to humans, animals, or the natural environment.[38] EPA's balancing act with FIFRA has caused many to see it as failing to protect vulnerable populations at the expense of revenue for companies.[39] The Pesticide Registration Improvement Act passed in 2013 modernized the Act and let EPA set fees for registering pesticides and provides remedies when administrative action is delayed on approvals.[40] An extension of the Act was passed in 2018 to revise EPA's ability to set fees, monitoring, and performance data for pesticides, as well as protections for agricultural workers and certification for applicators. The Federal Food, Drug, and Cosmetic Act passed in 2002 gives authority to EPA to set maximum residue limits for pesticides in food.[41]

FIFRA, as it stands today through these legislative amendments and additions over the past century, authorizes EPA to regulate all aspects of pesticides in the United States. This includes registration, production, distribution, sale, use, certification of commercial applicators, and disposal. A pesticide is legally defined as "any substance or mixture of substances intended for preventing, destroying, repelling, or mitigating any pest, or intended for use as a plant regulator, defoliant, or desiccant, or desiccant, or any nitrogen stabilizer."[42] Companies must register pesticides with EPA prior to selling

36. It has been argued that many pesticides are much more toxic than their labels let on and FIFRA only mandates that active ingredients be listed, not inert ingredients. *See* Bob Weihold, *Mystery in a Bottle*, 118 Envtl. Health Persp. A168-71 (2010).

37. Alex Trabolsi, Pollinator Stewardship Council v. EPA *and the Duty to Research FIFRA Applications*, 43 Ecol. L.Q. 503-10 (2016).

38. Danica Li, *Toxic Spring: The Capriciousness of Cost-Benefit Analysis Under FIFRA's Pesticide Registration Process and Its Effects on Farmworkers*, 103 Cal. L. Rev. 1405-10 (2015).

39. Anne, Rajotte, *Asthma and Pesticides in Public Schools: Does the ADA Provide a Remedy Where FIFRA Fails to Protect*, 31 B.C. Envtl. Aff. L. Rev. 31, 149-52 (2004).

40. The argument has been made for regulating certain pesticides as pollutants under the CWA instead of FIFRA. *See* John H. Minan & Tracy M. Frech, *Pesticides as "Pollutants" Under the CWA*, 47 San Diego L. Rev. 109-15 (2010).

41. 7 U.S.C. §136. Food Quality Protection Act, Pub. L. No. 104-170 (Aug. 3, 1996).

42. U.S. EPA, *FIFRA and Federal Facilities*, https://www.epa.gov/enforcement/federal-insecticide-fungicide-and-rodenticide-act-fifra-and-federal-facilities (last updated March 28, 2022).

or distributing them and those companies must show the pesticide does not cause unreasonable adverse effects defined as

> any unreasonable risk to man or the environment, taking into account the economic, social, and environmental costs and benefits of the use of any pesticide, or a human dietary risk from residues that result from a use of a pesticide in or on any food inconsistent with the standard under section 408 of the Federal Food, Drug, and Cosmetic Act.[43]

The Office of Pesticide Programs oversees the manufacture and use of registered pesticides. Most pesticides are used in commercial applications and only a small portion are available for sale to the public. There are different standards for pesticides, biopesticides, and antimicrobials. Applicants provide data that are used by the agency to determine risk based on where it will be used, the amount, frequency, and timing of use, and intended storage and disposal practices. Applicants pay fees to fund the registration process.

Compliance monitoring under FIFRA is heavily devolved to the states and in some cases tribal governments. EPA sets minimum standards, but certifies states to register pesticides, certify applicators, monitor, and enforce compliance.[44] Enforcement strategies under FIFRA tend to focus on improper use of registered pesticides, improper application of registered pesticides, and proper certification of commercial applicators. While FIFRA represents a more devolved enforcement strategy than TSCA, the greatest failure of both Acts lies in the sheer volume of chemical substances and registered pesticides on the market. While EPA has failed over the decades to properly test thousands of chemicals and rarely bans one, FIFRA relies on self-reported data to make generic risk assessments. While EPA could be criticized for this strategy and should be, scientific risk assessment is as political as it is scientific. Limited staff, the time it would take to truly examine pesticides in real-world applications, and the strong push against such a movement from the chemical industry has meant that most pesticides are approved,

43. U.S. EPA, *Summary of the Federal Insecticide, Fungicide, and Rodenticide Act*, https://www.epa.gov/laws-regulations/summary-federal-insecticide-fungicide-and-rodenticide-act (last updated Sept. 28, 2021). The Federal Food, Drug, and Cosmetic Act (Pub. L. No. 75-717 (1938)) gave the U.S. Food and Drug Administration (FDA) authority to regulate food, drugs, medical devices, and cosmetics. This came on the heels of a public scandal when Elixir sulfanilamide sold by the S.E. Massengill Company caused over 100 deaths. This event and other related poisonings empowered the FDA to require testing before certain drugs could come to market and the ability to legally define drugs, dietary supplements, and medical devices.
44. Tribal governments can enforce FIFRA but refer cases to appropriate EPA regional enforcement offices. Tribes can apply for pesticide enforcement grants. If EPA approves a State Certification Plan that meets EPA standards the state can develop programs for certifying commercial pesticide applicators.

based on self-reported data and very little of a precautionary approach.[45] The Agency admits just how vast the universe is for registered pesticides in terms of extant pesticides on the market, those coming on the market, and the size of the regulatory universe. EPA does not know for certain how many regulated entities exist in this universe of manufacturers, distributors, importers, exporters, and applicators. Their estimates in 2015 were 3.2 million.[46]

If FIFRA rules come down to packaging, labeling, worker protection standards, registration, applicators, experimental use permits, storage, disposal, transportation, and recall of pesticides. Criminal enforcement authority falls under §14(b)(1):

> Any registrant, applicant for a registration or producer who knowingly violates any provision of FIFRA is subject to a fine of not more than $50,000 and/or imprisonment not to exceed 1 year. Any commercial applicator of a restricted use pesticide; or any other person not described previously who distributes or sells pesticides, and who knowingly violates any provision of FIFRA is subject to a fine of not more than $25,000 and/or imprisonment not to exceed 1 year.

For §14(b)(2): "Any private applicator who knowingly violates any provision of FIFRA is subject to a fine of not more than $1,000 and/or imprisonment not to exceed 30 days."[47]

II. Themes in TSCA and FIFRA Prosecutions

We now turn to an analysis of the TSCA prosecutions undertaken since 1983. In Figure 24 (page 130), we show the annual prosecutions by fiscal year. Total prosecutions over the last 37 years total 72. In 1985, the first three cases are settled, and this rises to five by 1987 and five again by 1994. Annual prosecutions never rise above that number again, moving from zero in 2000 to four in 2018. A little less than two cases were settled on average per year. We do not see major spikes in different presidential regimes or during key developments in TSCA legislation over the years, such as the addition of AHERA, lead-based paint rules, the National Radon Action Plan,

45. U.S. EPA, *Overview of Risk Assessment in the Pesticide Program*, https://www.epa.gov/pesticide-science-and-assessing-pesticide-risks/overview-risk-assessment-pesticide-program (last visited March 31, 2022).
46. U.S. EPA, Compliance Monitoring Strategy for FIFRA (2015), https://www.epa.gov/sites/production/files/2015-09/documents/fifra-cms.pdf.
47. Information taken here comes from the following: U.S. EPA, *FIFRA and Federal Facilities*, https://www.epa.gov/enforcement/federal-insecticide-fungicide-and-rodenticide-act-fifra-and-federal-facilities (last updated March 28, 2022).

Figure 24. Total Annual TSCA Criminal Prosecutions Adjudicated Since 1983

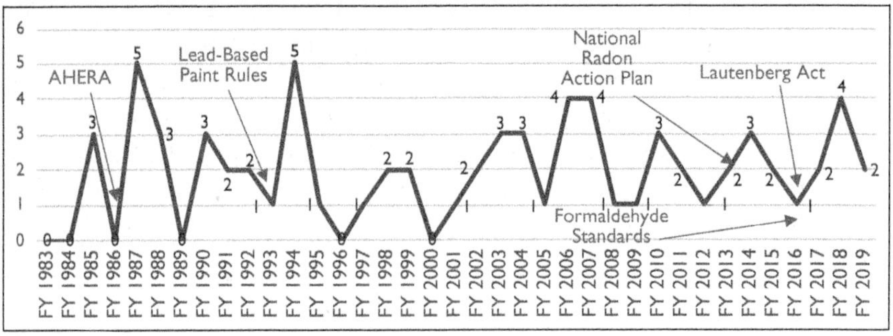

Figure 25. Total Annual TSCA Criminal Prosecutions by U.S. State and Territory Since 1983

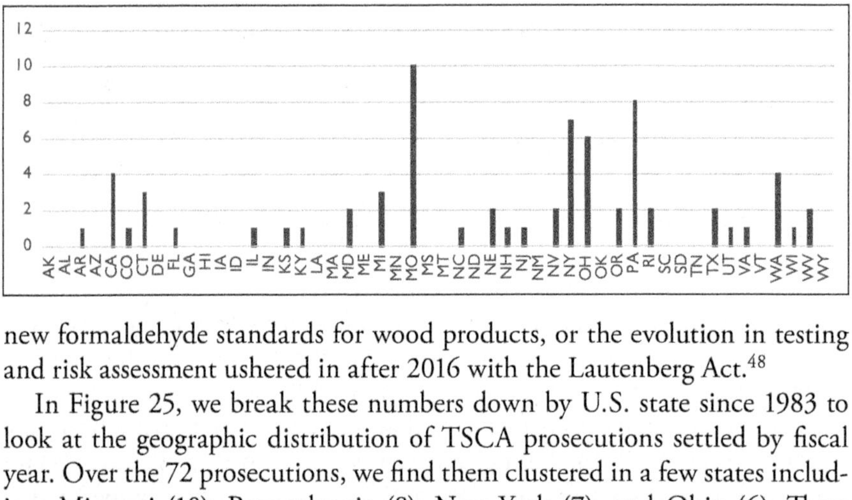

new formaldehyde standards for wood products, or the evolution in testing and risk assessment ushered in after 2016 with the Lautenberg Act.[48]

In Figure 25, we break these numbers down by U.S. state since 1983 to look at the geographic distribution of TSCA prosecutions settled by fiscal year. Over the 72 prosecutions, we find them clustered in a few states including: Missouri (10); Pennsylvania (8); New York (7); and Ohio (6). These four states make up 43% of total prosecutions since 1983. In many states no cases were settled including: Alaska; Alabama; Arizona; Delaware; Georgia; Hawaii; Iowa; Idaho; Indiana; Louisiana; Massachusetts; Maine; Mississippi; Montana; North Dakota; New Mexico; Oklahoma; South Carolina; South Dakota; Tennessee; Vermont; and Wyoming.[49]

48. In one prosecution against Aurelio Martinez the exact nature of TSCA is not possible to discern from the case summary. No. 14-938-M/14-CR-00564 (E.D. Pa.).

49. In one prosecution against Coast-to-Coast Inc., No. 3:03M330, it is not possible to identify the state in which it took place. The company and Manuel Cedeno were prosecuted under TSCA for illegal asbestos removal and charged in September 2003 with refusal to comply (likely with an inspection order). The company was sentenced in 2003 to pay a $10,000 fine. Cedeno pled guilty in January

Figure 26. Total Annual FIFRA Criminal Prosecutions Adjudicated Since 1983

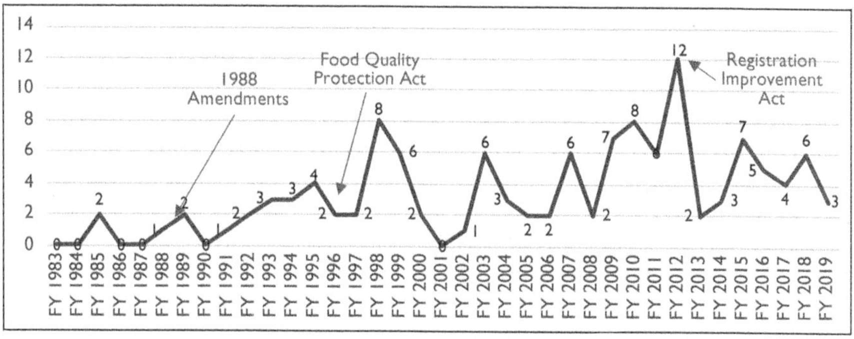

Figure 27. Total Annual FIFRA Criminal Prosecutions by U.S. State and Territory Since 1983

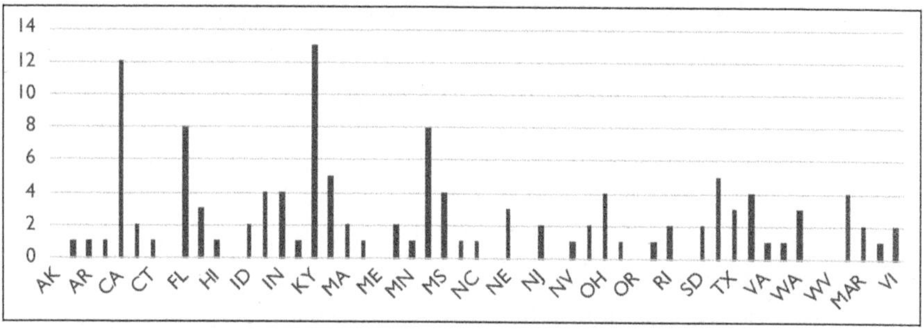

Figure 26 demonstrates the total number of FIFRA prosecutions adjudicated since 1983. Only five prosecutions are adjudicated in the 1980s. This number increases to 31 in the 1990s, followed by 31 additional prosecutions from 2000-2009, and 56 prosecutions from 2010-2019. We find that a total of 123 FIFRA prosecutions were adjudicated during this time period, with an average of 3.3 prosecutions per year.

In Figure 27, we examine FIFRA prosecutions by state and U.S. territory since 1983. Similar to TSCA trends, prosecutions are grouped in a handful of states. California (12), Kentucky (13), Florida (8), and Missouri (8) alone make up about one-third of total prosecutions. Many states, such as Alaska, Delaware, Iowa, Maine, North Dakota, New Hampshire, New Mexico, Oregon, South Carolina, Wisconsin, and West Virginia contained no pros-

2004 and was sentenced to 2 months incarceration, 12 months of probation, and ordered to pay a $25,000 federal fine.

Figure 28. Major Themes in TSCA Criminal Prosecutions Since 1983

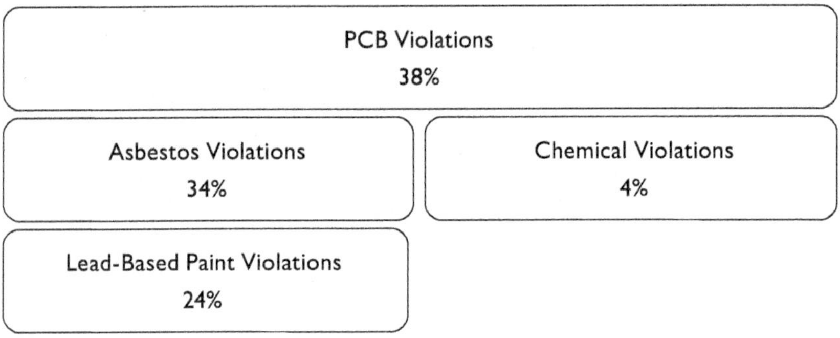

ecutions. The Northern Mariana Islands had two prosecutions, Puerto Rico had one, and the U.S. Virgin Islands had two, respectively.

We now examine the major themes that were uncovered in TSCA prosecutions since 1983. In Figure 28, we categorize prosecutions as in the previous chapter by what appears in our judgment to indicate the primary theme in the prosecution. We group these prosecutions according to these themes and uncover four themes in the data that explain what kinds of crimes EPA investigators have pursued and what kinds of charges have been brought by federal prosecutors over 37 years. These themes include what we term PCB violations, asbestos violations, chemical violations, and lead-based paint violations. All of these themes fit well within the context of which chemical substances EPA has sought to limit under TSCA historically and the criminal provisions of the Act under which prosecutors must work to charge and convict individual and company defendants.

The most prevalent theme we find in the data focuses on violations of the law related to PCBs. In 27 prosecutions or 38% of the cases we find the central nature of the crime to be related to violations of TSCA provisions regulating these harmful substances. Cases that fall into this category include illegal individual actions related to recordkeeping, storage, transportation, or disposal of PCBs. We find that 15 prosecutions meet this definition. The category also includes illegal company actions related to recordkeeping, storage, transportation, disposal, or distribution of PCBs. We find 12 prosecutions meet this definition.

Case examples of PCB violations illustrate how individual and company defendants broke the law, were charged, and convicted under the criminal provisions of TSCA. Patrick Perrin was the plant manager at the Martha C.

Rose Chemical Company in Holden, Missouri. The company transported and disposed of electrical transformers that used PCBs. Holden was charged in August 1987 with conspiracy, false statements, and violating TSCA.[50] Plymouth Utilities and James Carl Root were prosecuted for illegally disposing of electrical transformers owned by the city in a salvage yard in February 1991. Root was charged with the illegal disposal in violation of TSCA, because the transformers contained PCBs.[51] Hoskins Manufacturing was prosecuted in Michigan for violations of TSCA. A joint investigation by EPA and the Michigan Department of Environmental Quality revealed they had illegally disposed of transformers containing PCBs at their facilities.[52]

In 34% of cases the prosecution resulted from asbestos violations under TSCA. We find 24 prosecutions that fall under this theme. Illegal individual actions related to illegal certification, notification, removal, and disposal of asbestos-containing materials were at the center of 17 prosecutions. Illegal company actions related to illegal storage, removal, and disposal of asbestos-containing materials were the focus of seven prosecutions. Bernadette George was prosecuted in Pennsylvania and charged in 2004 under TSCA after asbestos floor tile was found to be illegally removed from Delcroft Elementary in Folcroft, Pennsylvania. Inspectors found the tiles and friable material in the dumpster.[53] John Bruce was prosecuted in Connecticut and charged with TSCA violations in 2009. Bruce owned Environmental Training and Consulting, which provided asbestos remedial clearance monitoring and asbestos mitigation training. Bruce's state license expired, but he continued to offer remediation certification courses.[54]

Twenty-four percent of prosecutions were related to lead-based paint violations. In 17 prosecutions, defendants violated lead-based paint rules. Illegal individual actions related to inspection, certification, or removal of lead-based paint were the basis for 14 prosecutions. Illegal company actions related to the notification and removal of lead-based paint were the basis for three prosecutions. David Dieu Nuyen was prosecuted in Maryland for failing to notify his tenants on the presence of lead-based paint. He lied to

50. United States v. Perrin, No. 87-00187-01-CR-W-9 (W.D. Mo. Aug. 6, 1987). Perrin was sentenced to 24 months incarceration, ordered to pay a $25 special assessment fee, and to pay a $50 fine.
51. No. 5:93MG3013 (N.D. Ohio). Root was sentenced to 12 months of probation, 80 hours of community service, and a special assessment fee of $25.
52. Hoskins was sentenced to 12 months of probation, ordered to publish an apology, and ordered to pay $1.7 million in restitution to offset emergency response costs. No docket number is given in the case.
53. No. 04-M-475 (E.D. Pa.).George pled guilty to the charge and was sentenced to 12 months of probation, ordered to pay a $25 special assessment fee, and to pay $3,600 in federal fines.
54. No. 309-CR00218-HBF (D. Conn.). Bruce was sentenced to 24 months of probation and ordered to pay an $800 federal fine.

federal investigators in order to conceal his crime. He was charged with false statements, obstruction, and failure to notify under TSCA.[55] Ira Eisenstein owned a home inspection business that provided lead inspections to homeowners in Princeton, New Jersey. He admitted to investigators that on at least three occasions he provided lead inspections without appropriate state licensure. He was charged with a knowing violation of TSCA in 2012.[56] Christopher Peterson was prosecuted in Ohio along with James Todt, Lee Orellana, and Modern Construction Group. Todt worked at the Cleveland Housing Network from 2005-2014, where he was in charge of supervising inspectors and awarding contracts. Todt accepted bribes from Peterson and Orellana in exchange for contracts.[57]

The final set of prosecutions was what we label chemical crimes that occurred in 4% or three prosecutions. We define these as illegal individual actions related to the importation, shipping, and disposal of chemicals. Merlyn Pollock, the owner of Posch Foundry, was prosecuted in Missouri for disposing of chemicals at a sanitary landfill and an open field.[58] He was indicted under TSCA and RCRA for the illegal disposal. Bryan Fabian was the owner of Americlean and was prosecuted in Nevada for wire fraud, false statements, and shipping a misbranded hazardous substance under TSCA. Fabian defrauded his clients by selling them used oil through his company without determining if the oil met appropriate regulatory standards.[59] Peiwen Zhou pled guilty in 2017 to charges under TSCA that he failed to properly declare the importation of toxic substances and engaged in the illegal transportation of hazardous substances.[60] Employees of his company, AK

55. United States v. Nuyen, No. DKC-01-0134; DKC-2001-0370; 01-0248 (D. Md.). Nuyen was sentenced to 24 months' incarceration, 36 months of probation, and ordered to pay a $50,000 federal fine.

56. Eisenstein was sentenced in 2013 to 24 months of probation and ordered to pay a $75 special assessment and a $1,500 federal fine (D.N.J.).

57. No. 116CR0186 (N.D. Ohio. Todt was sentenced to 30 months' incarceration, 36 months' supervised release, a $5,000 fine, and a $300 special assessment. Christopher Peterson was sentenced to 12 months incarceration and was fined $3,000. Lee Orellana was sentenced to 30 months incarceration and fined $1,000. Modern Construction Group was ordered to pay a $1,600 fine and serve 60 months of probation.

58. No. 87-00148-1-CR-W-8 (W.D. Mo.). Pollock was sentenced to 12 months of probation, on three counts to be served concurrently and incarceration, which was suspended. He was sentenced to pay a $25 administrative fine on each count and a $35,000 fine.

59. No. CRN-99-0163-HDM-RAM (D. Nev.). Fabian was sentenced to 72 months of probation, ordered to pay $2,000 in federal fines, and $1,800 in restitution to the Chemical Lime Company. Americlean was sentenced to pay a $2,000 fine and ordered to pay restitution in the amount of $1,800 the Chemical Lime Company.

60. American Shipper, *Owner of California Shipping Company Guilty of Hazardous Materials Violations*, FreightWaves.com, Jan. 9, 2018, at https://www.freightwaves.com/news/owner-of-california-shipping-company-guilty-of-hazardous-materials-violations.

Figure 29. Major Themes in FIFRA Criminal Prosecutions Since 1983

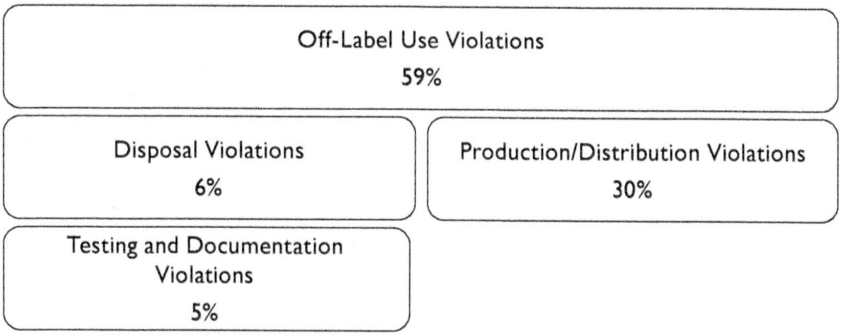

Scientific, failed to file TSCA import certifications on numerous occasions and Zhou admitted to failing to properly train his employees.[61]

In Figure 29, we examine major themes in FIFRA prosecutions since 1983. An analysis of all 123 prosecutions yields four primary themes that define the use of FIFRA as a charging statute in pesticide-related prosecutions. The most prevalent are what we term off-label use violations, which make up 59% of all FIFRA prosecutions. We define cases in this category as illegal individual actions related to using a registered pesticide in a manner inconsistent with its labeling. Such cases make up 60 of the 73 prosecutions in this category. Illegal company actions related to using a registered pesticide in a manner inconsistent with its labeling make up 13 prosecutions in this category.

Florida Waterway Management and owner Steve Weinsier were prosecuted in Florida for illegal application or off-label use of pesticides. Applicators for the company used Karmex and Direx (herbicides) in lakes and ponds, which were prohibited in aquatic areas.[62] Weinsier was indicated in 1993 under FIFRA for the unlawful use of a registered pesticide. Lee Poole was prosecuted in 1998. Poole was an unlicensed pesticide applicator that sprayed methyl parathion (an insecticide) in homes near Houma, Louisiana, which required an EPA emergency response cleanup response from Region VI costing the Agency $2.1 million. The insecticide is dangerous to humans

61. No. CR17-00091-JD (N.D. Cal.). Zhou was sentenced to serve five years' probation, during which he must perform 200 hours of community service, including 100 hours conducting presentations discussing the nature of his crimes at industry trade shows. He was also ordered to pay a criminal fine of $40,000, special assessment of $125, and resign his position as CEO and president of AK Scientific Inc.
62. No. 93-533-CR Highsmith (M.D. Fla.). Weinsier was sentenced to 36 months of probation, assessed a $50 special assessment fee, and a $20,000 fine.

and only approved in open areas.[63] Poole was prosecuted under FIFRA for using a pesticide in a manner inconsistent with its labeling. DLM Farms was prosecuted for spraying a tangerine orchard with the pesticide KOCIDE 20/20. The label forbids using it in areas where anyone other than protected handlers will be exposed. Instead of flagging cars near Sanger, California, an employee left his post and the pesticide entered a passing school bus exposing the driver and eight school children to a toxic substance via open windows. The company was prosecuted under FIFRA for using a pesticide inconsistent with its labeling.[64]

We categorize 30% of prosecutions as unlawful production/distribution violations. These are defined as illegal individual actions related to counterfeiting, production, distribution, and/or smuggling of registered pesticides, which make up 28 of the 37 cases in this category. Illegal company actions related to counterfeiting and/or distribution of registered pesticides make up nine prosecutions in this category. Guardian Protection was prosecuted in California for illegally adding MI-50, an unregistered pesticide, to its furniture fabric protection line. A total of 659 shipments occurred between 1993-1996, which contained the illegal pesticide and had to be recalled. The company was charged under FIFRA with the distribution and sale of an unregistered pesticide.[65] Oscar Miller was prosecuted in Louisiana for selling unregistered pesticides. Consumer complaints regarding roach spray purchased from Miller revealed upon testing that he sold methyl parathion to consumers. In doing so he illegally sold a registered pesticide and did so off-label. He was charged under FIFRA with illegally selling or distributing a registered use pesticide.[66] Scotts Miracle-Gro Company was prosecuted in Ohio for illegally applying Actellic 5E and Storcide II to its bird food products. The company knowingly sold the product for two years despite warnings of the danger from employees. Scotts sold more than 70 million units of the bird food before recalling the product. The company was charged under FIFRA with unlawful selling or distribution of an unregistered pesticide, one

63. No. 97-CR-50068-FL (E.D. Mich.). Poole was sentenced to 12 months' incarceration, 12 months of probation, ordered to pay a $200,000 federal fine, and restitution in the amount of $2,189,175.
64. No. MJ 00201 SKO (E.D. Cal.). DLM Farms was sentenced to pay a $2,500 federal fine. The company previously paid $7,516 in restitution to victims and $3,700 in fines to the Fresno County Department of Agriculture.
65. No. CRF-985315 (E.D. Cal.). The company was sentenced to 48 months of probation, a federal fine of $445,000, and a $375 special assessment fee.
66. No. 98-159 (E.D. La.). Miller was sentenced to 13 months' incarceration, 60 months of probation, and ordered to pay restitution in the amount of $61,000 to the Superfund and $1,500 to a victim of his crimes.

that is adulterated or misbranded, using a registered pesticide in a manner inconsistent with its labeling, and falsifying its registration application.[67]

Six percent of prosecutions focus on what we call disposal violations. These are defined as illegal individual actions related to the disposal of registered pesticides and make up three of the seven cases in this category. Illegal company actions related to the disposal of registered pesticides make up four cases in this category. Cenex Limited was prosecuted in Washington State for illegally disposing of a cement-lined containment pond. Employees sprayed the contents of the pond containing pesticides and hazardous wastes on a 100-acre farm. The company then collapsed the containment pond and filled it in with earth. The company was charged under FIFRA for producing, distributing, and using a registered pesticide in a manner inconsistent with its labeling, although the primary crime was the illegal disposal.[68] Employees of the Helena Chemical Company discharged unused pesticides on the ground, which then ran into Little Cabin Creek. The company was prosecuted in Oklahoma for unlawful disposal of unregistered pesticides.[69] Wal-Mart Missouri was prosecuted for failing to have in place a hazardous waste disposal and management plan at its facilities and to properly train its employees in such practices.[70] As a result, employees illegally disposed of pesticides in trash bins, in the sink, the local sewer system, or improperly transported to one of six product return centers throughout the United States. The company was charged with a knowing violation of FIFRA.[71]

The final theme we find in FIFRA prosecutions are cases centered on testing and documentation violations. These account for 5% of cases or a total of six prosecutions. We define these as illegal individual actions related to the testing and documentation of registered pesticides, which make up two prosecutions in this category. Illegal individual actions related to the testing and documentation of registered pesticides make up four prosecutions in this category. Craven Laboratories was prosecuted for conducting false pesti-

67. No. 2:12-CR-00024-JLG (S.D. Ohio). Scotts was sentenced to pay a $4 million federal fine and to contribute $500,000 to organizations that protect bird habitats. Co-defendant Sheila Kendrick was prosecuted for making a materially false statement and falsifying documents submitted to EPA and sentenced to three months' incarceration.

68. No. CR-95-025-JQL (E.D. Wash.). The company was sentenced to 12 months of probation and ordered to pay a $10,000 fine. The company was ordered to supply the city of Quincy with $3,000 worth of chemicals and to report to EPA any impoundments containing pesticides on company property.

69. No. 4:15-CR-00087-PJC (N.D. Okla.). The company was sentenced to a $150,000 fine and ordered to make a $75,000 community service payment, as well as serve four years of unsupervised probation.

70. Sandy Smith, *Wal-Mart Pleads Guilty to Federal Environmental Crimes, Will Pay More than $81 Million*, EHS Today, June 13, 2013, https://www.ehstoday.com/environment/article/21915759/walmart-pleads-guilty-to-federal-environmental-crimes-will-pay-more-than-81-million.

71. No. 4:13-CR-00135 (W.D. Mo.). The company was ordered to pay a $110 million fine.

Figure 30. Common Criminal Charges in TSCA Criminal Prosecutions Since 1983

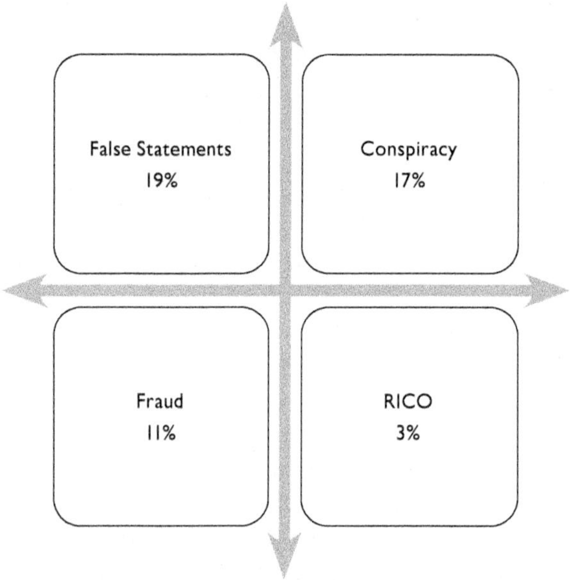

cide residue tests for companies in Austin, Texas.[72] The company and owner Don Craven were charged under FIFRA for a variety of offenses, including conspiracy to commit mail fraud, false statements, obstructing EPA proceedings, falsification under FIFRA, and misprision of a felony.[73] David Battigelli was a research director with Clancy Environmental Consultants. He was prosecuted in Vermont for falsifying research data to support an application to EPA for a water purification process.[74]

72. Keith Schneider, *U.S. Seeks to Learn If Tests on Pesticides Were Falsified*, N.Y. TIMES, Mar. 2, 1991, https://www.nytimes.com/1991/03/02/us/us-seeks-to-learn-if-tests-on-pesticides-were-falsified.html.
73. No. A-92-CR-152 (W.D. Tex.). The company was sentenced to pay restitution in the amount of $3,725,055 and was fined $15,499,279 and ordered to serve 60 months of probation. Don Craven was sentenced to 60 months' incarceration, 36 months' supervised release, and a $50,000 fine. The case summary mentioned additional defendants, but fails to name them in the summary as co-defendants in the data.
74. No. 1:06-CR-115-1 (D. Vt.). The defendant was sentenced to 12 months of probation, ordered to pay a federal fine of $500, and a special assessment fee of $50.

Figure 31. Total Penalties Assessed in TSCA Criminal Prosecutions Since 1983

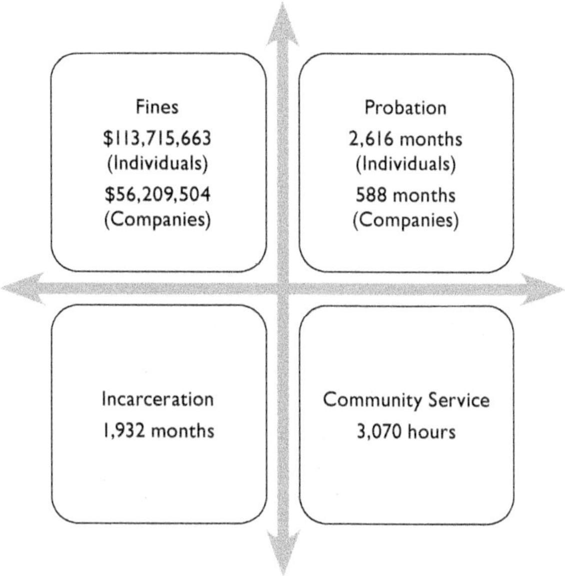

III. Penalties in TSCA and FIFRA Prosecutions

We now examine criminal charging patterns in TSCA prosecutions, as well as punishments since 1983. Figure 30 aggregates common criminal charges found in all TSCA prosecutions. Here we examine the number of cases that contain charges such as false statements, conspiracy, fraud, and the Racketeer Influenced and Corrupt Organizations Act (RICO), which we find to be the most prevalent in the prosecutions. In 19% of prosecutions, defendants were charged with false statements or falsification of records. This amounted to 14 total cases. In 17% of cases or 12 prosecutions, at least 1 defendant was charged with conspiracy. In 11% of cases or eight prosecutions, at least one defendant was charged with mail, wire, or tax fraud. We find two RICO cases in TSCA prosecutions amounting to 3% of prosecutions.

In Figure 31, we examine total penalties assessed to all individual and company defendants since 1983. In 56 cases, we find that at least 1 individual defendant was assessed a fine, fee, special assessment, or other monetary penalty. These totaled over $113 million in monetary penalties assessed to all individual defendants. In 23 cases, at least 1 company or corporation was

Figure 32. Common Criminal Charges in FIFRA Criminal Prosecutions Since 1983

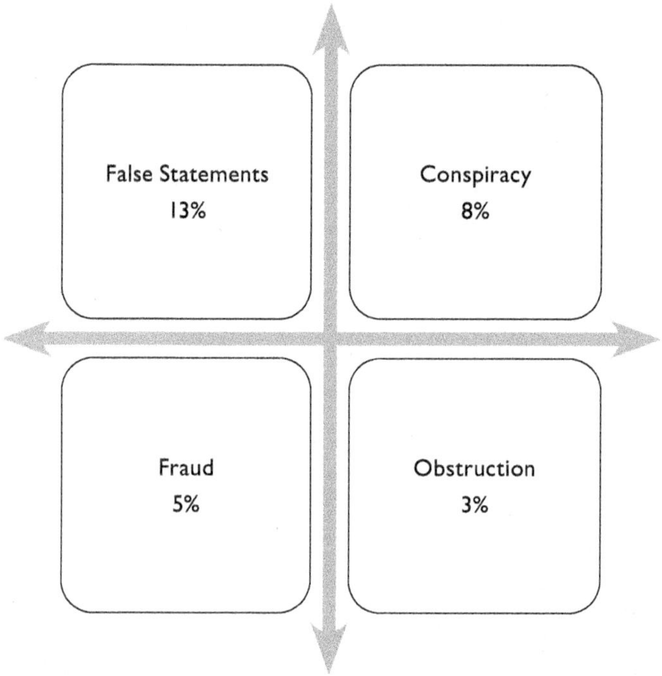

assessed a monetary penalty, with the aggregate total exceeding $56 million. In 50 cases, at least 1 individual was assessed probation at sentencing. We calculated that all individual defendants were cumulatively assessed 2,616 months of probation. In 15 cases, companies were assessed a grand total of 588 months of probation. In 25 cases, individuals were assessed incarceration at sentencing totaling 1,932 months. We also find 13 cases of community service assessed at sentencing totaling 3,070 hours, 11 cases of home confinement totaling 59 months, and 3 cases of community corrections totaling 50 months.

Figure 32 examines common criminal charges in FIFRA prosecutions since 1983. As with TSCA, the most common criminal charge we find is false statements. In 13% of FIFRA prosecutions or 16 total cases, defendants gave false statements to investigators or falsified records or other documents. In 8% of cases or 10 total cases, defendants were charged with conspiracy. In 5% of cases or six total cases, defendants were charged with mail or tax

Figure 33. Total Penalties Assessed in FIFRA Criminal Prosecutions Since 1983

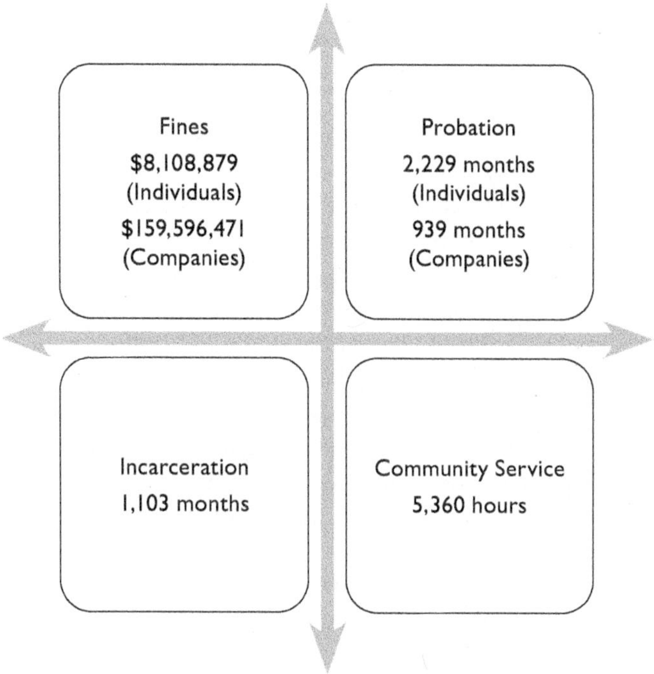

fraud. At least one defendant was charged with obstruction in four cases or 3% of the overall cases.

Total punishments assessed to individual and company defendants are found in Figure 33. In 95 cases or 77% of cases, at least 1 individual defendant was charged with a fine, fee, assessment, restitution, or other monetary penalty. These monetary assessments totaled over $8 million and averaged over $85,000 per prosecution. In 34 cases or about 28% of prosecutions, a company was assessed a monetary penalty. These penalties totaled almost $160 million and averaged about 4.7 million per prosecution. In 66 cases, at least 1 individual was assessed probation at sentencing. Total probation assessed to all individual defendants equaled 2,229 months. In 25 cases, companies were assessed probation totaling 939 months. In 38 cases, individual defendants were assessed 1,103 months' incarceration at sentencing, as well as 5,360 hours of community service, 267 months of community corrections, and 92 months of home confinement.

IV. Conclusion

Assessment of charging and sentencing patterns in TSCA prosecutions since 1983 reveals clear trends. The first is that they are much less frequent over time than the CWA, the CAA, or RCRA prosecutions, but better resemble CERCLA prosecutions in frequency, distribution, and the complexity of charging patterns. The chance of being prosecuted criminally under TSCA is very low and in many states it has yet to occur.

When defendants are charged and convicted for criminal violations of TSCA they tend to be charged in four basic ways. The first involves illegal use of PCBs, typically illegal disposal of electrical transformers that are difficult and expensive to dispose of properly. Of the 27 prosecutions of PCB crimes, EPA targeted most of these in the 1980s and 1990s; only 2 cases were prosecuted after 2000. Of the 24 asbestos crimes prosecuted under TSCA, most of these focus on illegal and disposal charges. Unlike criminal provisions of the CAA that were much more frequently used to target asbestos crimes, TSCA appears to be used somewhat randomly over time, commonly in conjunction with the CWA, with the exception of a series of cases prosecuted in New York State. Only about 14 prosecutions for asbestos crimes were TSCA-centric without additional charging statues.

The 24% of cases focused on lead-based paint crimes almost exclusively focused on failure to notify provisions in TSCA, where tenants were knowingly exposed to potential harm by landlords that did not provide proper disclosures. These cases can have serious consequences. In 5 of the 17 lead-based paint prosecutions, people were injured or killed after ingesting lead-based paint.[75] Other cases involved fraudulent testing, certification, failure to disclose by realtors, and grinding leaded paint that exposed individuals to harm.

75. Cases of identifiable victims resulting from criminal violations of TSCA's lead-based paint rules include the following: JTA Real Estate, No. 01-123-02-M (D.N.H.). Prosecuted for failure to notify and that a two-year-old boy died of lead poisoning. The company was sentenced to 36 months of probation and ordered to pay a $40,000 federal fine. United States v. Zauf, No. 4:05CR530 RWS (E.D. Mo. Oct. 1, 2006). Prosecuted for failing to notify in 11 rental properties and at least four children tested positive for lead exposure as a result. Zauf was sentenced to 36 months of probation, ordered to perform 100 hours of community service, pay a $25 special assessment fee, and pay a $500 federal fine. United States v. Patterson, No. 10CR20247 (E.D. Mich. Feb. 8, 2011). Prosecuted for falsely certifying homes were free of lead-based paint in exchanges for compensation. A child in one of these homes was hospitalized for lead poisoning and Patterson falsely certified the dwelling and threatened the occupants. Patterson was a city of Detroit Health Department lead inspector. Patterson was sentenced to 46 months' incarceration, 24 months of probation, and ordered to pay $662 in restitution to three victims in the amounts of $250, $212, and $200, respectively. United states v. Murrell, No. L-11-03330 (D. Md. June 6, 2012). Prosecuted for owning rental properties where children were found to have elevated lead levels. He was prosecuted for failure to notify and violations of workplace standards for abating lead. Murrell was sentenced to 12 months and a day of incarceration and 12 months' supervised release, including 6 months' home detention. United States

While TSCA focuses on managing risks from chemical substances, we did not find the criminal provisions of the Act used broadly to this effect. Outside of asbestos, lead-based paint, and PCBs, we only find three other crimes that involved illegal dumping of chemicals, fraudulently selling used oil, and failure to label and notify of the importation of regulated chemicals. Criminal prosecution to enforce TSCA thus focused historically on broader and publicly known health hazards stemming from asbestos, lead, and PCBs, which is in line with EPA's broader enforcement and rulemaking strategies. The Agency and federal prosecutors spent little time enforcing crimes involving specific chemical substances that are regulated under TSCA with the criminal provisions of the Act. With so few prosecutions over time, they again appear more opportunistic than intentional.

FIFRA prosecutions can also be aligned across four common themes, with about 89% of prosecutions falling into two primary themes. The most common form of prosecution was to pursue individuals for off-label use, which occurred in almost half of all prosecutions. These tended to be registered applicators that were applying pesticides improperly or unregistered applicators applying pesticides without proper certification. The second most common type of prosecution was against individuals engaged in unlawful production or distribution of registered pesticides, such as counterfeiting, smuggling, selling, or distributing pesticides improperly. Outside of these two primary themes, prosecutors pursued cases against individuals and companies for false statements and records, testing and documentation scams, and the illegal disposal of registered pesticides.

v. Walck, No. 17-MJ-1103 (W.D.N.Y. Jan. 10, 2018). Walck was a realtor in New York and had knowledge of lead-based paint in a home she was attempting to sell. Once the new owners purchased the home with the false disclosure their child became sick with lead poisoning. Walck was sentenced to time served, fined $1,000, and ordered to pay restitution to the victim in the amount of $53,326.07.

Chapter 6. A Framework for Understanding the Criminal Enforcement of Federal Environmental Laws

I. Synthesizing the History of Federal Criminal Enforcement Efforts

The goal of this chapter is to bring together the analysis from the previous chapters in an effort to develop a more holistic framework for understanding the history of the federal enforcement of environmental law. We have seen in the previous chapters how the federal government's efforts are concentrated toward a few key federal environmental statutes, such as the CWA, the CAA, and RCRA, and to a lesser degree CERCLA, FIFRA, and TSCA. We now take these specific findings from the chapters and provide an overview of federal efforts over the past 37 years, followed by a deeper analysis of the central themes in these efforts.

Figure 34 on the next page breaks down the percentage of cases prosecuted since 1983 by charging statute. In 828 cases or 32% of all cases prosecuted since 1983, prosecutors used the CWA to charge defendants. By far, the CWA is the most prevalent charging statute used over space and time in federal prosecutions making up almost one-third of all prosecutions. At 391 prosecutions or about 15% of total cases, RCRA was the second most commonly used federal statute in the 2,588 cases analyzed. The CAA is the third most commonly used federal statute, making up 15% or 377 total prosecutions. While important and substantively invoked, the CAA was used less than half as frequently as the CWA in federal prosecutions.

These three statutes alone were used in 62% of all prosecutions, allowing for the fact that defendants could be charged under multiple statutes in each case. Considering this fact, the CWA was used in conjunction with the CAA in nine prosecutions since 1983. In 57 cases it was used in conjunction with RCRA. The CAA was used in conjunction with RCRA 14 times since 1983. At 123 prosecutions, FIFRA makes up a modest 5% of all cases. At 72 prosecutions, TSCA cases and 77 CERCLA cases only took up a modest 3%

Figure 34. Percentage of Federal Prosecutions by Major Charging Statute Since 1983

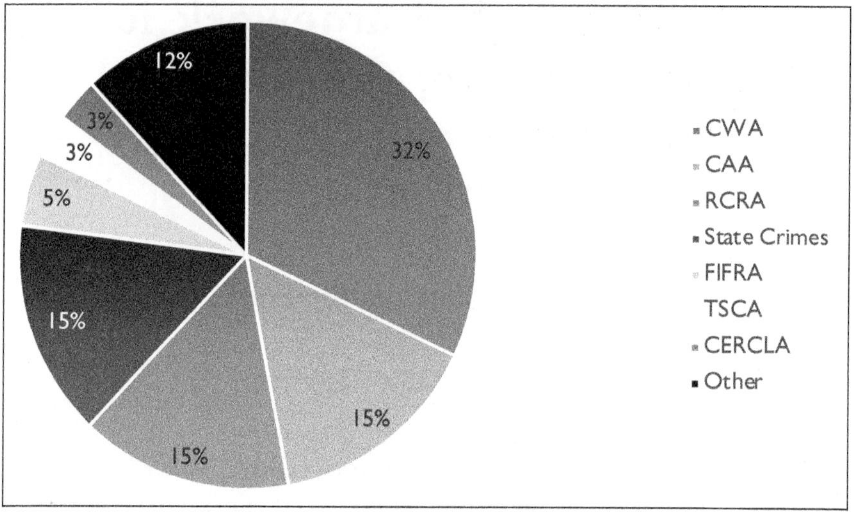

of cases each since 1983. CERCLA was often used in conjunction with other statutes, including: the CWA (13 prosecutions); the CAA (14 prosecutions); TSCA (8 prosecutions); and RCRA (31 prosecutions). At face value, these charging statutes would comprise 73% of all prosecutions, but less when considering overlap in cases that used more than one statute.

Another significant finding is that 15% of cases (396 prosecutions) end up charging defendants with a state crime and not a federal environmental crime. Taking this into consideration suggests that 15% of EPA investigations in the data are ultimately referred for state-level prosecution, reducing total cases to 2,192. We show in Figure 35 what the data from the previous figure would look like with this change. By this metric, CWA prosecutions would consist of roughly 38% of total cases prosecuted federally as opposed to 32% of total cases investigated and prosecuted in Figure 35. CAA cases would comprise 17% of prosecutions by this metric, RCRA 18%, FIFRA 6%, CERCLA 5%, and TSCA 3%. These statutes would cover 87% of total prosecutions bearing in mind, however, that some overlap between cases that use multiple charging statutes will reduce this number. Using either metric, the CWA, the CAA, and RCRA are ascendant when it comes to prosecuting federal environmental crimes.

We also find that in 342 cases, defendants are primarily charged criminally for false statements, conspiracy, obstruction, etc. without being charged

Figure 35. Percentage of Federal Prosecutions by Major Charging Statute Excluding State-Centric Prosecutions Since 1983

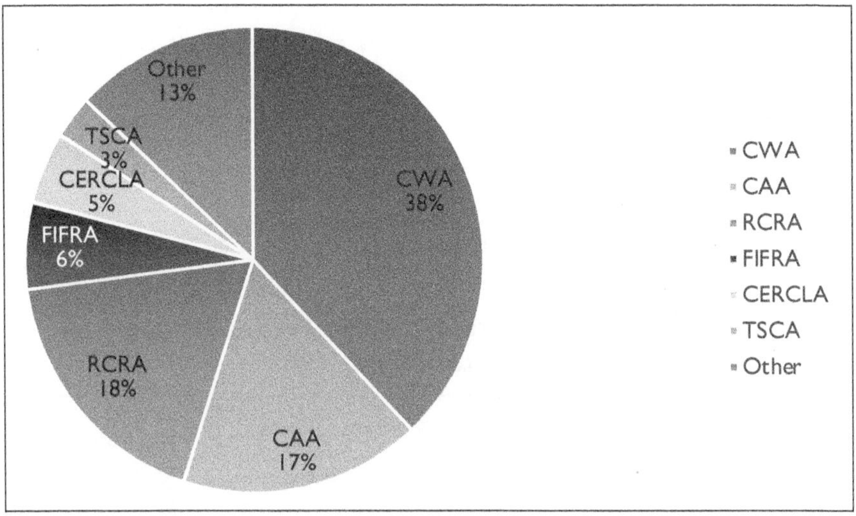

for a separate violation of a federal environmental statute, although in many of these cases the charges derive from the criminal provisions of the major statutes. The final themes in the cases we find are that 90 cases or about 4% of cases are charged for damaging waterways or the ocean, including charges under APPS, MARPOL, Rivers and Harbors Appropriations Act, and the Ocean Dumping Act. Forty cases focused on prosecuting wildlife crimes under the MBTA, and Gold Eagle Protection Act.

Figure 36 provides the total number of state-level prosecutions by fiscal year since 1983. We do not find any cases resulting from an EPA investigation that ultimately becomes a state-level prosecution until 1991, when four such cases emerge. We see only a few cases per fiscal year up until 2003, when the numbers increase to 32, and then a high of 42 in 2006, and declining again to 13 in 2017 and 2018, and 12 by 2019. This trend does not seem vastly different than the trends for overall cases prosecuted over time.

In Figure 37, we examine state-centric prosecutions by U.S. state since 1983. At 37, Ohio has the largest number of prosecutions. This is followed by Colorado (36), California (30), New York (30), Oregon (27), and Washington. In 13 cases, we cannot determine the state in which the case was settled. Arkansas, Maine, Minnesota, and North Dakota contain no cases.

Figure 36. State-Centric Prosecutions Since 1983

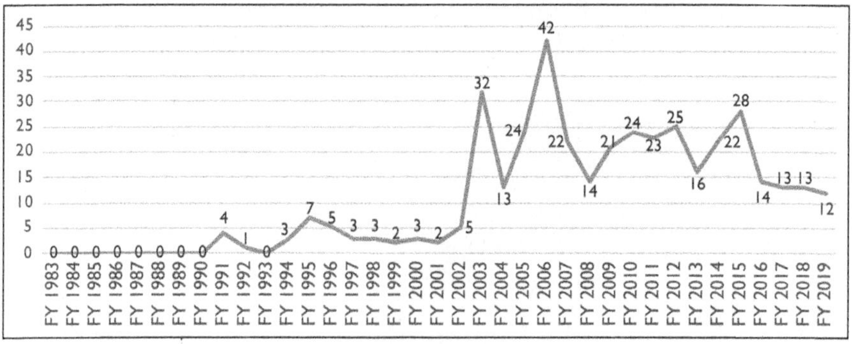

Figure 37. Total State-Centric Prosecutions by U.S. State Since 1983

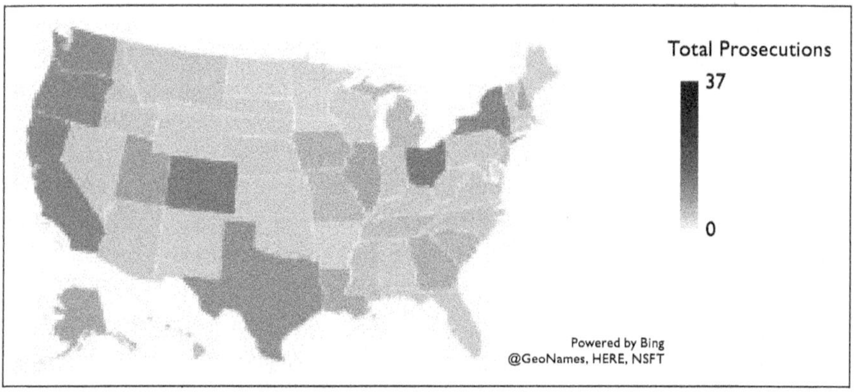

Our overall assessment here is that these numbers do not present a distinct pattern from the overall cases prosecuted over time.

In Figure 38, we explore penalties assessed to individuals and companies in state-centric prosecutions since 1983. In 301 cases individuals were assessed fines and other monetary penalties at sentencing totaling $17,878,274. In 107 cases companies were assessed such penalties totaling $42,940,365. The largest penalties here were against North Star Steel, prosecuted in Arizona for using fraudulent documents to obtain a less-restrictive air permit.[1] Green Compass Environmental and the Santa Clara Waste Water Company were

1. United States v. North Star Steel, No. STCTCR-2001-016528 (D. Ariz. June 23, 2001). The company was charged with violating state statutes and sentenced to pay $4 million in fines and restitution, as well as $7.5 million in civil penalties.

Figure 38. Total Penalties Assessed in State-Centric Prosecutions Since 1983

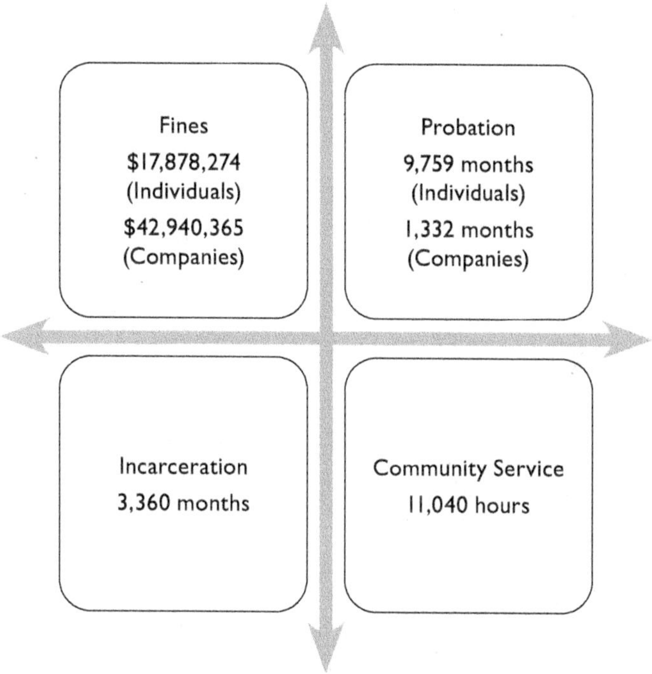

both charged in California for an explosion that occurred on November 18, 2014, at the corporate-owned wastewater treatment facility.[2]

In 248 cases, individual defendants were assessed probation at sentencing totaling 9,759 months.[3] In 41 cases, companies were assessed probation at sentencing totaling 1,332 months. In 157 cases individuals were assessed incarceration totaling 3,360 months.[4] Defendants were also assessed a total of 11,040 months of community service, approximately 19 months' home confinement, and 392 months' community corrections.

2. Ventura Cty & State of Cal. v. Santa Clara Waste Water, No. 2015023881 (Super. Ct. Cal. Dec. 1, 2015). Both companies were placed on three years' probation and each ordered to pay $2,647,621.35 in victim restitution.
3. United States v. Gray Container, No. CR-09-521249B (D. Ohio Oct. 26, 2009). Gray Container was prosecuted in Ohio after an EPA civil investigation in 2007 revealed 400 55-gallon drums containing illegally stored hazardous waste. The company, owner Kenneth Gray and L. Gray Barrel and Drum Company were charged with violating Ohio environmental laws. The sentence included 120 months' company probation, 60 months' individual probation, and fines.
4. The largest penalty case here is against Brent Bushau and nine co-defendants, charged with stealing $3 million in refrigerants for resale. No. 01CR0610. Total incarceration time assessed equaled 492 months. We cannot identify the state of which the crime occurred in the case based on the case summary.

Figure 39. Typology of Primary Themes in Criminal Enforcement Prosecutions Since 1983

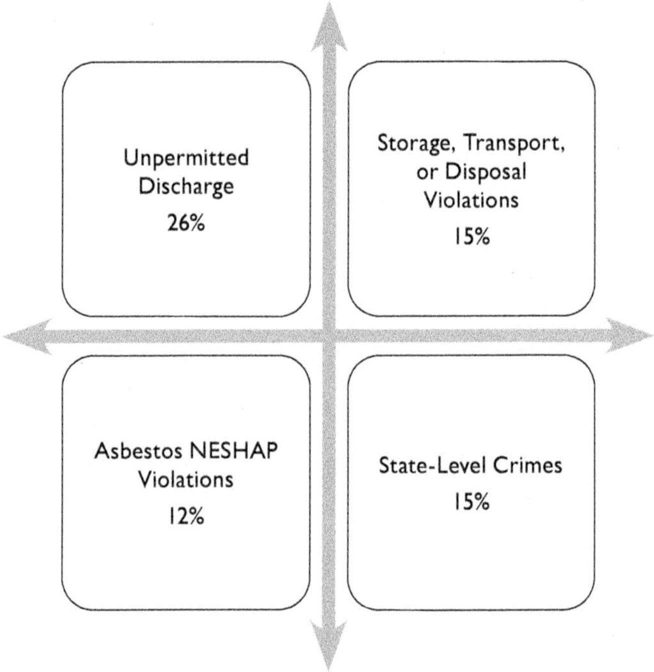

Figure 39 displays the primary themes we uncover that define the types of crimes most likely prosecuted by the federal government since 1983. By far the most common type of crime is prosecuting unpermitted discharges. In over one-quarter of cases (26% or 680 prosecutions), federal prosecutors focused their cases on unpermitted discharges charged under criminal provisions in the CWA. Put simply, if you were investigated by EPA and going to be prosecuted criminally for an environmental crime in the United States, there is about a one in four chance it would have been for an unpermitted discharge in the United States.

RCRA-related offenses of one or more crimes involving illegal storage, transport, or disposal of hazardous materials was the second most common environmental crime prosecuted by the federal government—384 cases or 15% of all prosecutions since 1983. Improperly handling hazardous waste, whether it meant a company or individual storing it without a permit, transporting materials without a manifest or proper manifest, or dumping it improperly, outside of unpermitted discharge prosecuted, the feds were more likely to come for you than in any other scenario.

The third major theme we find in the data is that 377 prosecutions of 9% of prosecutions focus on asbestos NESHAP violations. Of all the federal environmental crimes prosecuted by the government if you engaged in illegal disposal, abatement, violation of NESHAP workplace standards or related asbestos crimes, you would find yourself in the second most common club in the data. Outside of prosecuting POTWs, companies, and individuals for illegally discharging a range of materials into the waterways of the United States, asbestos-related malfeasance was the second most common type of prosecution undertaken since 1983.

The fourth most common theme uncovered in federal prosecutions is that the crimes ended up centering on state-level offenses. In 396 cases or about 15% of total prosecutions we find that thrust of the case focused on a state-level crime. It is quite interesting to find that crimes receiving attention from EPA criminal investigators, about 15% of the time, ended up going to the states to prosecute. This finding reduced federally focused criminal prosecutions stemming from EPA investigations to 2,152 cases since 1983 in all practical respects. Nevertheless, it is still important to catalog these cases as part of the universe of efforts to combat environmental crime and show the collaborative efforts between state and federal regulators to pursue these cases over the past four decades.

II. Explaining Federal Enforcement Efforts

Describing the history of the criminal prosecution of federal environmental crimes shows the narrowness of the approach to a small, but dominant subset of statutes and crimes. Charging statutes are driven by the CWA, the CAA, and RCRA, which constitute the majority of cases. When including cases where other criminal charges focus the prosecution or investigations that led to state-level offenses, these prosecutions dominate federal investigative and prosecutorial efforts since the institutionalization of the criminal enforcement process. FIFRA, TSCA, and CERCLA prosecutions round out these efforts.

When analyzing prosecutions by the type of offense instead of the statute the patterns are clear and narrow when analyzed thematically. About one-half of all total cases rest on crimes related to unpermitted discharges, asbestos crimes, or RCRA-related offenses involving unlawful storage, transport, or disposal of hazardous substances. Adding EPA investigations that led to state-centered prosecutions increases this number to 65% of prosecutions. What factors might help to explain these broader trends occurring since 1983? We offer three primary explanations including the nature of evidence in environmental prosecutions, the scope of each major environmental law in subsequent criminal enforcement provisions, and the context of Agency enforcement resources.

The criminal prosecution of an environmental crime does not require physical evidence of a crime. A critical factor in explaining the federal focus on unpermitted discharges, asbestos violations, and hazardous waste violations, however, is likely the presence of physical evidence. We find this evidence to be primarily present in two forms: (1) paperwork; and (2) hazardous substances.

The CWA contains many criminal provisions that provide opportunities to collect evidence of criminal acts that involve willful or severely negligent actions. One of the strongest tools these provisions provide is an ample paper trail. Any entity, public or private, that must maintain an active NPDES permit to operate must also keep a variety of logs and records subject to inspection by the government. Take the case of a POTW. If a company or individual illegally dumps a hazardous or restricted substance into a stormwater or municipal sewer system, this can be considered a crime. If the discharge violates local or pretreatment standards or causes harm to the facility, a crime has been committed. Failure to report the discharge is a crime. For stationary sources with monitoring devices, failing to have functional monitoring equipment as required by their permit or tampering with them is a crime. If an entity engages in illegal discharge of hazardous substances that places individuals in imminent danger (first responders, municipal workers, bystanders, employees of the treatment plant), they can be charged with knowing endangerment under the CWA. Regulated entities must keep logs of a variety of activities, such as testing and any discharges to a POTW or otherwise. If any responsible party including workers at the POTW falsify these records or give false statements to investigators to cover up an illegal discharge, they have potentially committed a knowing violation. By creating a system of monitoring and recordkeeping and the possibility of tracing physical evidence of an illegal discharge to a particular source, particularly when it is acute or chronic over time, the CWA has a powerful set of tools to prosecute criminal offenses.

RCRA creates a strong environment for enforcement by requiring cradle-to-grave regulations on hazardous waste. Treatment, storage, and disposal without a permit or in violation of a permit are all crimes. Transporting hazardous materials without a manifest or to an unpermitted facility are both crimes, as is illegal export, giving false statements, destruction or concealment of records, or actions leading to knowing endangerment of others. All of these recordkeeping requirements give investigators and prosecutors additional leverage to permit and record the life cycle of hazardous waste.

The CAA contains criminal provisions to permit facilities, record actions, and punish unpermitted emissions at stationary sources, as well as knowing endangerment clauses, prohibitions on false statements, violating state SIPSs, or NSPS, as well as violating an emergency order or tampering with a monitoring device. The number of emissions generated from permitted facilities is numerous and diverse, while also difficult to capture. States also provide variances for a variety of unpermitted emissions, such as maintenance, malfunctions, and upset events. Once emissions leave a facility it is much harder to trace them back to the source, as they would typically disperse into the ambient air, rather than a waterway, stormwater system, or end up in a POTW.

Criminally prosecuting asbestos violations does not engender the same limitations as other CAA violations dealing with ambient air emissions. The CAA has asbestos NESHAP criminal provisions that prohibit unlicensed workers from remediating or disposing of asbestos, as well as unpermitted removal or failure to notify provisions (CERCLA can be used in conjunction with failure to notify). Knowledge of residential, commercial, and asbestos hazards are widespread as has been the historical need to remove it as a pipe insulator, floor tiling, and ceiling texture. In so many of these cases individuals or companies chose to save money by violating one or more of these provisions of the CAA. Unlike other CAA crimes, asbestos violations, particularly for illegal removal or workplace violations, i.e., unpermitted removal, unlicensed companies or workers, or failure to notify or obtain necessary permits, typically leave evidence and are much easier to prosecute.

A second explanation for the prosecutorial focus over the years lies in the nature and scope of each of the major federal environmental statutes. The CWA, the CAA, and RCRA touch a vast number of individuals, companies, governments, and organizations. Water, air, and waste are necessarily broad and substantive goals EPA set out to manage early on. TSCA, FIFRA, and CERCLA are also broadly focused and extremely important acts from a perspective of public and environmental health. Yet the scope of what they regulate, how they do so, and the broader nature of the acts for criminal enforcement varies with the major three acts. TSCA criminal provisions prohibit a range of activities. These include failure to comply with a regulatory order or inspection, premanufacture notice violations, denial of entry to investigators seeking access to a facility, and restrictions on PCBs. FIFRA criminal provisions center on proper registration, application, and disposal of registered pesticides.

When we look at the overall trends in prosecutions and comparative trends for each federal statute, it becomes apparent that the scope of the prosecutions tends to reflect the Agency's historical and ongoing strengths and weaknesses. EPA was initially tasked with an almost impossible mission. Not only did the Agency have to clean up the air, water, hazardous waste, and chemical wastes, they had to determine which substances were dangerous and to what degree. The scope of environmental laws and their problems feeds into a third rationale for the outcomes: limited resources. The Agency simply had to choose a focus, to meet certain goals, and this would result in strengths in some areas and weaknesses in others.

EPA chose to focus on obtaining broader reductions in environmental threats and measure those reductions regionally, rather than at the level of a particular chemical, source, or firm. As a result, historical efforts focus on meeting broader obtainable goals for water, air, and waste often at the expense of other environmental problems. These weaknesses are most glaring when it comes to developing risk assessments for chemical substances or pesticides under TSCA or FIFRA.

Under the CWA, EPA sought to meet congressional goals in a country where control of waterways had always been a divisive issue and sanitizing wastewater represented a cost and learning curve few municipalities outside of large metropolitan areas were willing or able to take on. The POTW construction grant program was the lynchpin of federal efforts, as it provided significant funding to municipalities and via fiscal/cooperative federalism was able to create a set of federal standards alongside the construction of wastewater treatment plants. This gave EPA authority over a significant portion of this regulatory universe and it helped to tie in their program for developing permitting authority for point sources via NPDES in an effective manner. As these plants were built, the grants program morphed into the CWSRF, to further keep, albeit in a much more limited manner, fiscal incentives for compliance. Alongside wastewater, EPA was able to shore up the §404 permit program and the alteration of waterways and wetlands, as well as develop rules for biosolids and other methods to dispose of waste. While the CWA does not regulate drinking water, the Safe Drinking Water

Act gives it authority over about 170,000 public water systems in the United States.[5]

The CWA is thus emblematic of how Congress was able to appropriate funds and set broader goals for EPA to tackle pressing environmental problems via money and enhanced regulatory authority. As state enforcement regimes increased and regulations became more institutionalized over time, EPA has developed significant authority for compliance monitoring and permitting to the states in this area. It is unsurprising that when we look at the criminal enforcement regime's evolution over time, illegal discharges represent the vast number of cases investigated by the EPA that were successfully prosecuted by the federal government. Most of the infrastructure for the CWA's policy regime revolves around permitting facilities that discharge into wastewater, stormwater, or other waterways or treat these discharges and strict rules and recordkeeping requirements, i.e., such as DMRs and testing requirements, attached to these actions. Roughly one-half of the illegal discharge prosecutions (680 in total) were targeted at individuals and the other half companies and municipalities. The vast majority of the false reporting cases we recorded (99 prosecutions) were against individuals that falsified reports, gave false statements, or falsified data. Most of these willful acts were related to the permitting regime around the NPDES system and illegal discharges. Most of the tampering with monitoring devices we found revolve around this regulatory regime as well.

Illegal dredging, filling, and the altering of waterways regulated by the §404 permitting system involves cooperation with the Corps and is a much more diffuse permitting and compliance monitoring regime. These cases involve the illegal alteration of the course of a river in far off places in Wyoming, illegally filling in wetlands near the Gulf Coast to build neighborhoods, altering sandbars in the Pacific Ocean, and so many other crimes occurring on a case-by-case basis. It is not surprising we find 39 prosecutions alone focusing on these issues as opposed to cases of unpermitted discharges.

The CWA's emphasis on funding treatment plants, developing a permitting system for stationary sources, and nationwide minimum standards for treatment represent a successful early effort of what EPA does best to tackle a public problem and offer a broader regulatory solution for a country with a heavily devolved system of government and this strategy reflects its compliance monitoring strategy and criminal enforcement outcomes. This strategy has emphasized NPDES permits, rules for point sources and POTWs, illegal

5. U.S. EPA, Understanding the Safe Drinking Water Act (EPA 816-F-04-030) (June 2004), https://www.epa.gov/sites/production/files/2015-04/documents/epa816f04030.pdf.

dredging, filling, and altering of waterways and wetlands under §404, and illegal dumping in the ocean. We find the latter in the illegal discharge category, but it is not substantial compared to the stationary sources regulated and policed by the criminal division.

Other aspects of the problems addressed under the CWA have not been so successful and this is reflected in the absence of such cases generally in the criminal enforcement outcomes. EPA has historically done a poor job of regulating specific chemicals, toxic substances, or setting risk assessments and values for individual compounds and substances. It remains a laggard for non-point source pollution as well. While the CWA is effective at managing public wastewater systems and permitting certain flows, the act misses the mark on a host of chemical and non-organic substances that make their way into POTWs or stormwater systems. Many industrial chemicals routinely make their way into these systems and diffuse sources from households such as paint, solvents, or pharmaceuticals are extremely public health problems that go unaddressed. They remain so because EPA is simply not that effective at regulating specific toxic substances in such a manner, particularly when they come from nonpoint sources. We see this glaring regulatory gap reflected in their compliance monitoring strategy for the CWA, as well as the criminal enforcement outcomes over the last 37 years.

Our finding that CAA criminal enforcement leans heavily on asbestos related crimes is unsurprising in light of the above facts. Managing clean air has proven equally daunting over the last 50 years at EPA. Their regulatory strategy mirrors the CWA in part, as EPA focused on the idea of managing problems with ambient air regionally and focusing on specific and known harms rather than specific stationary sources or particular industries. EPA developed NAAQS and centered on regulating regions of the country to develop standards for attainment and non-attainment with these standards and worked to integrate states to develop SIPs to help with compliance. This was followed by NSPS for new stationary sources and NESHAP to supplement pollutants not covered by NAAQS. As with the CWA, the Agency had to focus on becoming a technology-forcing agency early on to combat the greatest contributions to air pollution either through best available or maximum control technologies.

Unlike the CWA, EPA was beset by the problem of mobile source pollution causing significant air pollution that could not be ignored. Fortunately, with technology it could set evolving standards at the level of the manufacturer to combat the problem. Major innovations came about, such as two-way catalytic converters to control carbon monoxide in 1975, followed by three-way converters in 1985 that helped EPA reduce air pollution from mobile sources in a significant way.[6] The invention of stack scrubbers to reduce SO_2 at coal-fired power plants was another major technological breakthrough that helped the Agency meet its clean air goals.[7] The 1990 CAA Amendments helped further define and broaden this regulatory regime for operating permits at stationary sources, the Acid Rain Program (ARP), and cap-and-trade system for SO_2.

EPA's CAA compliance monitoring strategy focuses on the ARP, point sources, nonpoint sources, asbestos, HAPs under NESHAP, BACT for point sources, accidental releases, ozone-depleting substances phaseouts, and NSPS for new stationary sources. We find the criminal enforcement outcomes to be quite diverse thematically for the act, which reflects the complexity of monitoring and enforcement the air regime. The strong focus on asbestos crimes reflects the reality of the regulatory regime for air. Unlike illegal discharges, illegal air emissions are harder to capture and police. The Agency has been successful regulating ambient air emissions on a regional level from point and nonpoint at least pertaining to mobile sources that can be managed at the level of the manufacturer through technology. Enforcing new standards on grandfathered facilities or even NSPS can prove difficult. Operational violations were often found at stationary sources, as were false statements and reporting. These represented 23% of prosecutions and reflect the compliance monitoring strategy. Mobile violations targeted at vehicles mostly focused on chronic clean scanning operations used to circumvent emissions standards for vehicles in non-attainment areas. Violating CFC restrictions comes under the banner of regulating ozone-depleting substances, but only makes up 5% of prosecutions, as does renewable fuel credit fraud at 2%. Asbestos crimes represent cases of physical evidence that focus on a nationally recognized and salient public policy problem. With the exception of some complex cases in New York State that involved RICO prosecutions, most of the 221 asbestos prosecutions involved individuals or small firms.[8] AHERA was often invoked when these illegal operations involved schools and other public

6. Tim Palucka, *Doing the Impossible*, INVENTION & TECH., Winter 2004, https://www.inventionandtech.com/content/doing-impossible-0.

7. David. B. Ryan, *What Do Scrubbers Do in Smoke Stacks?*, SCIENCING, Nov. 22, 2019, https://sciencing.com/do-scrubbers-do-smoke-stacks-5004709.html

8. United States v. AAR Contracting, No. 5:05-CR-49 (N.D.N.Y. Dec. 8, 2006). AAR Contracting represented one of the most complex cases here. United States v. Farbent, No. 02-CR-51 (N.D.N.Y. Feb. 21, 2000) The case against Farbent was tied into the prosecution of AAR Contracting, which provided fraudulent laboratory analysis and demolition of asbestos throughout New York State over the course of a 10-year conspiracy.

facilities. It is unsurprising criminal enforcement resources in 59% of cases went to prosecuting these cases over other compliance issues.

RCRA is another sufficiently broad environmental statute. The Act gave EPA broad authority to establish a national framework for hazardous waste. Another public health problem that had been present for decades, RCRA enabled EPA to establish a permitting regime for the life cycle of waste at 6,600 facilities and 20,000 processing units.[9] Permits could be issued for generators of waste, transporters, and disposal practices and companies. Strict recordkeeping rules help keep the regulatory regime for hazardous waste enforceable. EPA also acted through RCRA to ban open landfills and regulate nonhazardous waste disposal including household waste and sludge from wastewater treatment plants. Extant sites that involved significant dumping of hazardous wastes had to be handled by CERCLA. EPA's compliance monitoring strategy for RCRA encompasses the cradle-to-grave regulations for hazardous waste, used oil, universal and mixed wastes, import/export of hazardous waste, solid waste, and underground storage tanks.[10] We see this broad regime reflected in the criminal enforcement outcomes. Illegal storage, transport, and disposal or a combination of these crimes made up the outcomes since 1983.

CERCLA's more narrow regulatory focus on identifying and remediating contaminated sites rendered it less useful as a stand-alone tool to pursue criminal enforcement cases. We see it used only about two dozen times in the last 37 years. In those cases, it was used primarily for its failure to notify provisions to pursue criminal sanctions against individuals and companies that failed to notify officials of the release of a hazardous substance. In 14 prosecutions, CERCLA was used in asbestos cases in conjunction with the CAA, 5 with the CWA, 4 with TSCA, and 31 with RCRA.

CERCLA is a good example of EPA's failure to engage in significant actions against environmental criminals to remediate sites through a criminal process. This is not surprising as the Agency has done better historically when it sets broader goals to meet attainment for a problem and focuses on technological and permitting solutions to achieve those goals within an area, or industry, but rarely that successfully at the level of the individual firm. Placing a site on the NPL does not guarantee remediation, nor has it been as extensive as it should throughout the country. With 1,335 listed sites and 51

---

9. U.S. EPA, *Resource Conservation and Recovery Act, Overview* (RCRA), https://www.epa.gov/rcra/resource-conservation-and-recovery-act-rcra-overview (last visited July 14, 2021).

10. U.S. EPA, *Resource Conservation and Recovery Act (RCRA) Compliance Monitoring*, https://www.epa.gov/compliance/resource-conservation-and-recovery-act-rcra-compliance-monitoring (last updated July 13, 2021).

proposed it is naïve to assume there is not a significant known and unknown threat from these toxic dumps, but criminal enforcement action has not been nearly as robust as it has under the CWA, the CAA, or RCRA.[11] CERLA as a charging statute seems comparatively weak given the scale of the problem, but again the solution to the problem relies often on linking liability for a site to a particular responsible party and there is no simple technological fix, permitting mechanism, or automatic paperwork trail to help regulators. This, combined with the inability of EPA to clean up orphaned sites, makes CERCLA enforcement a troubling problem.

TSCA compliance monitoring demonstrates the Agency's desire to focus on larger public health problems, rather than focusing on determining health risks for specific chemicals. On the latter front one can argue TSCA has mostly failed. TSCA's inventory currently contains more than 41,000 active chemical substances.[12] The Agency has determined health risks or engaged in risk assessments for a very small percentage and banned even fewer historically (266 have been subjected to testing).[13] Even with significant changes under the Lautenberg Act in 2016, the agency has failed to act on specific chemical substances. Instead of managing the politics and science of risk, EPA focused on PCBs, asbestos, radon, lead, formaldehyde, and mercury in compliance and enforcement efforts.

We do not see the TSCA used to prosecute outside of four areas in this broader strategy including PCBs, asbestos, and lead. The importation, shipping, or disposal of chemical substances was only prosecuted in three cases. In 27 cases crimes mostly related to the illegal disposal of PCBs (primarily in electrical transformers) invoked criminal provisions of TSCA in the prosecution. Prosecuting asbestos-related cases happened two dozen times, and 17 prosecutions occurred for lead-based paint crimes. In all of these cases, physical evidence was likely present and the prosecutions fell within the broader compliance monitoring strategy for TSCA, as well as broader national problems focused on asbestos hazards in buildings particularly schools (AHERA), children ingesting lead-based paint, and the health and environmental effects of PCBs.

FIFRA suffers from the same politics of risk assessment as TSCA. As a consequence, mostly what EPA does under FIFRA is to focus on labeling

11. U.S. EPA, *Superfund: National Priorities List (NPL)*, https://www.epa.gov/superfund/superfund-national-priorities-list-npl (last updated March 11, 2022).

12. U.S. EPA, *How to Access the TSCA Inventory*, https://www.epa.gov/tsca-inventory/how-access-tsca-inventory#download (last updated March 7, 2022).

13. U.S. EPA, *Sunset Dates of Chemicals Subject to Final TSCA Section 4*, https://www.epa.gov/assessing-and-managing-chemicals-under-tsca/sunset-dates-chemicals-subject-final-tsca-section-4-test (last updated March 24, 2022).

and permitting of pesticides. We find most cases deal with physical evidence such as off-label use, unlawful production, or distribution, and to a much lesser extent illegal disposal or fraudulent testing cases. Like TSCA, and CERCLA, FIFRA is not used extensively in criminal prosecution. If physical evidence and the scope and nature of environmental statutes and their requisite public problems help to define criminal prosecution actions, another theme is simply resources. EPA has enormous responsibilities with declining congressional commitments to funding (adjusted for inflation) and enforcement-focused staff. The number of criminal enforcement agents has not matched statutory minimums for decades. Criminal enforcement cases represent resources. These resources must be spent in an environment where the big wins that were gained from more generous public spending, public attention, lack of rent seeking behavior, and before established lobbies and legal teams learned strategies to beat back regulations are no longer present. The EPA is now a mature regulatory agency entrenched in standard Washington politics. Its ability to move freely with discretion and the nature of upcoming problems and extant problems are vast. Its colossal mandates required being strategic and trying to make big wins before the doldrums of being enmeshed in divisive policy networks and the cost of fixing past mistakes competed with its ability to innovate and achieve specific goals. What can be done to ameliorate these problems on the margins and to utilize federal environmental statutes to improve the prosecution of environmental offenders is the focus of the final chapter.

Chapter 7. The Green Police: Criminal Enforcement and the Prospects for Deterrence in the Era of Climate Change

I. Resources for Deterrence

Perhaps the greatest problem facing the expansion of environmental enforcement is that of resources. The work of EPA's Criminal Investigation Division (EPA-CID) is a difficult one, which requires investigation, coordination, and follow through. Yet both EPA and CID face increasing responsibilities alongside dwindling resources.[1] At present there are less than 200 criminal investigators deployed across the country to investigate environmental crimes. In 2012, EPA employed only 175 agents, but this has diminished over time to 154 in 2015 and now it currently stands at 145 agents.[2] Strewn across some 40 locations in the United States and expected to investigate complex crimes in overlapping jurisdictions, this is simply well-short of what is needed to effectively police environmental crimes. Moreover, while numbers were high after 9/11, many enforcement staff were added and charged with taking on investigative responsibilities tangentially related to homeland security, rather than environmental crimes exclusively.[3]

For EPA-CID to be effective and for it to extend its reach, consider the investment in environmental law enforcement versus traditional law enforcement in the United States. In 2019, the U.S. Bureau of Census estimated the country's population at 328,239,523.[4] The Federal Bureau of Investigation's (FBI's) Uniform Crime Reporting Program notes that nationwide the rate of sworn law enforcement officers was 2.4 per 1,000 inhabitants and 3.4

1. U.S. EPA, Criminal Enforcement Program Overview 8-11 (EPA 310-K-11-001) (Oct. 2011), https://19january2017snapshot.epa.gov/sites/production/files/documents/oceft-overview-2011.pdf.
2. PEER, *EPA CID Agent Count*, https://www.peer.org/wp-content/uploads/2019/11/11_21_19-Federal_Pollution_EPA_CID_Agent_Count.pdf (Nov. 21, 2019).
3. *See* PEER, 2003 Survey of EPA Office of Criminal Enforcement, Forensics and Training Employees 2-3 (2003), https://www.peer.org/wp-content/uploads/attachments/EPA-OCEFT_Survey_Sample_Essay_Responses.pdf
4. Press Release, U.S. Census, 2019 U.S. Population Estimates Continue to Show the Nation's Growth is Slowing, Dec. 30, 2019, https://www.census.gov/newsroom/press-releases/2019/popest-nation.html.

per 1,000 inhabitants when considering sworn and civilian officers.[5] Raw numbers equate to more than 680,000 law enforcement officers and almost a million total law enforcement employees. This comparison would have to include the number of criminal enforcement agents across the states and in limited cases local government for comparison, which would be extremely tough to come by.

As another point of comparison, the Bureau of Justice Statistics (BJS) notes that in 2016 there were 100,000 full-time federal law enforcement officers in the United States and its territories with about two-thirds deployed to Customs and Border Protection, the Federal Bureau of Prisons, the FBI, and Immigration and Customs Enforcement; 47% worked in the U.S. Department of Homeland Security.[6] Looking at this as a trend between federal agencies, in 2008 EPA-CID employed 183 agents and that declined to 157 by 2016. Based on BJS data, numbers are slightly different—EPA-CID agents increased from 202 to 214.

During the same period, other federal agencies faced declines while some sectors saw sharp increases. The National Oceanic and Atmospheric Administration (NOAA) Office of Law Enforcement decreased 18.2% from 154 to 126 full-time officers, the U.S. Forest Service declined more than 20% from 648 to 514, and the National Nuclear Security Administration dropped almost 17% from 363 to 302. If we look at budgets and staff as statements of value, CID was lower than many other federal law enforcement priorities using 2016 data: Bureau of Land Management (253), National Park Police (560), Food and Drug Administration, Office of Criminal Investigation (231), U.S. Mint Police (292), Amtrak Police Department (427), and the Smithsonian Institution's Office of Protective Services (620).

Research suggests that companies and individuals would be deterred from committing environmental crimes if they were rational to the extent that the chance of them being caught was sufficiently high and the penalties associated with the crime sufficiently punitive.[7] Deterrence works on the principle that environmental law enforcement raises the costs of offending relative to the benefits to deter rational individuals and companies from offending (specific deterrence) and these actions set an example that deters other potential offenders indirectly (general deterrence).[8] Our data suggests that 2,588 envi-

5. FBI, *Crime in the United States (2018)*, https://ucr.fbi.gov/crime-in-the-u.s/2018/crime-in-the-u.s.-2018/topic-pages/police-employee-data (last visited May 11, 2022).
6. BJS, Federal Law Enforcement Officers, 2016-Statistical Tables (Oct. 2019), https://www.bjs.gov/content/pub/pdf/fleo16st.pdf.
7. Gary Becker, *Punishment: An Economic Approach*, 169 J. Pol. Econ.183-85 (1968).
8. Dietrich Earnhart & Lana Friesen, *Can Punishment Generate Specific Deterrence Without Updating? Analysis of a Stated Choice Scenario*, 56 Envtl. Res. Econ. 379-82 (2013). Carole M. Billiet & Sandra

ronmental crime prosecutions were undertaken as the result of EPA investigations over the last 37 years, which equates to an average of 70 per year and about 1.4 per state on average. This number is reduced further when we discount investigations that led to state-level prosecutions, which accounted for 396 or 15% of the prosecutions in our data. These numbers are very low to suggest specific deterrence in most cases or general deterrence. Cases such as *Deepwater Horizon* likely do set a specific deterrence example for the company and for the industry, but the media coverage and scope of the punishment for this case, as in Volkswagen's emissions rigging prosecution are significant outliers compared to run of the mill prosecutions.[9]

On first glance those numbers do not seem high enough to suggest a range of bad actors would be deterred from committing crimes. Winston Harrington noted that the low probability of corporate offenders being caught and the small fines suggest a paradox for why they do not simply disobey rather than comply with the law.[10] The nature of deterrence for generally law-abiding individuals and companies is beset by a series of problems to make this a true paradox, but there are inherent difficulties as well in measuring environmental crime rates or corporate crime rates generally.[11] Environmental regulation is often made in collaboration with the regulated community, which is very different than traditional law enforcement and offending.[12] Much of the data on offending per say is self-reported in an effort to overcome weaknesses in the oversight regime at the federal and state level that lack resources to police the regulated community.[13] These factors have lead many researchers to assert that environmental sanctions may do little to deter

Rousseau, *How Real Is the Threat of Imprisonment for Environmental Crime?*, 37 Eur. J. L. & Econ. 183-86 (2014) [hereinafter Billet & Rousseau]. Sarah L. Stafford, *The Effect of Punishment on Firm Compliance With Hazardous Waste Regulations*, 44 J. Envtl. Econ. & Mgmt. 290-93 (2002).

9. Michael J., Lynch et al., *Media Coverage of Chemical Crimes: Hillsborough County, Florida, 1987–1997*, 40 Brit. J. Criminology 112-14 (2000).

10. Winston Harrington, *Enforcement Leverage When Penalties Are Restricted*, 37 J. Pub. Econ. 29-53 (1988).

11. Carol Gibbs & Sally S. Simpson, *Measuring Corporate Environmental Crime Rates: Progress and Problems*, 51 Crime, L. & Soc. Change 87-92 (2009).

12. Harland Prechel & Alesha Istvan, *Disproportionality of Corporations' Environmental Pollution in the Electrical Energy Industry*, 59 Soc. Persp. 505-09 (2016).

13. Scott De Marchi & James T. Hamilton, *Assessing the Accuracy of Self-Reported Data: An Evaluation of the Toxics Release Inventory*, 32 J. Risk & Uncertainty 57-61 (2006). Lori S. Bennear, *What Do We Really Know?: The Effect of Reporting Thresholds on Inferences Using Environmental Right-To-Know Data*, 2 Reg. & Gov't 293-95 (2008). Kate Golden, *EPA's ECHO Database: Your Two-Faced Best Friend*, SEJ.Org, Sept. 15, 2012, at https://www.sej.org/publications/sejournal-su-fall12/epas-echo-database-your-two-faced-best-friend.

crimes, given the size of the regulatory community, nature of regulation, and limited resources and reach of the enforcement community.[14]

Criminal enforcement resources are limited and the probability of being sanctioned for a federal environmental crime in the United States is historically fairly low.[15] Research shows that while there are large penalties assessed in some environmental prosecutions, the historical probability of being punished in a significant way is not very high.[16] A related question addressed by previous research is whether sanctions are punitive enough to deter crime and if law enforcement agencies are motivated to seek such penalties. Matthew Crow and colleagues found that in Florida an analysis of FWS offenses demonstrated a focus on minor crimes.[17] The analysis of Florida by Joshua Cochran and others finds that relatively few felony prosecutions in the state courts stem from environmental crimes.[18] James Periconi notes that New York State has a long record of successful environmental crime prosecutions, but the number of prosecutions has become stagnant over time.[19] In one of the few studies on county-level environmental enforcement in Fulton, Georgia, Michael Lynch found the number of cases and mean fines to be fairly small.[20] Michael O'Hear finds that criminal sentencing for federal environmental offenders to be less punitive on the whole than other federal non-environmental offenders.[21]

Other studies show that federal environmental law enforcement agencies are motivated to seek more significant punishments for more serious crimes. Brickey's work on RCRA prosecutions finds that sanctioning outcomes are positively related to crime severity.[22] We find that the most consistent predic-

---

14. Raymond Paternoster, *How Much Do We Really Know About Criminal Deterrence?*, 100 J. CRIM. L. & CRIMINOLOGY 765-69 (2010). Harland Prechel & Lu Zheng, *Corporate Characteristics, Political Embeddedness, and Environmental Pollution by Large U.S. Corporations*, 90 SOC. FORCES 947-52 (2012). *See* Billet & Rousseau, *supra* note 8.
15. Michael J. Lynch et al., *Weak Probability of Punishment for Environmental Offenses and Deterrence of Environmental Offenders: A Discussion Based on USEPA Criminal Cases, 1983-2013*, 37 DEVIANT BEHAV. 1095 (2016).
16. Michael J. Lynch, *The Sentencing/Punishment of Federal Environmental/Green Offenders, 2000-2013*, 38 DEVIANT BEHAV. 991-95 (2017).
17. Matthew S. Crow et al., *Camouflage-Collar Crime: An Examination of Wildlife Crime and Characteristics in Florida*, 34 DEVIANT BEHAV. 635-37 (2013).
18. Joshua C. Cochran et al., *Court Sentencing Patterns for Environmental Crimes: Is There a "Green" Gap in Punishment?*, 34 J. QUANTITATIVE CRIMINOLOGY 37-40 (2018).
19. James, J. Periconi, *The State of Environmental Crime Prosecutions in New York*, 23 NAT. RESOURCES & ENV'T 15-19 (2009).
20. Michael J. Lynch, *County-Level Environmental Crime Enforcement: A Case Study of Environmental/ Green Crimes in Fulton County, Georgia, 1998-2014*, 40 DEVIANT BEHAV. 1090-92 (2019).
21. Michael M. O'Hear, *Sentencing the Green-Collar Offender: Punishment, Culpability, and Environmental Crime*, 95 J. CRIM. L. & CRIMINOLOGY 133-34 (2004).
22. Kathleen F. Brickey, *Charging Practices in Hazardous Waste Crime Prosecutions*, 62 OHIO ST. L.J. 1077-124 (2001).

tor of criminal penalties against environmental criminals was the severity of the crime in the case.[23] Greife et al. supports our finding that the strongest predictor of penalties against corporate environmental offenders is the severity of the crime committed.[24] David Uhlmann shows that federal prosecutors are motivated to pursue criminal charges when violations involve serious crimes measured through a series of aggregating factors, such as chronic offenses, significant harm, deceptive or misleading conduct, or operating outside the regulatory system.[25] Sarah Stafford shows that increases in statutory RCRA penalties in the early 1990s decreased violations, but it is hard to pin down exactly if the threat of stiffer punishments resulted in deterrence per say.[26]

Studies show there may be some deterrent effect of prosecution, finding some corporations prosecuted for environmental crimes suffer collateral financial damage.[27] Whether the federal environmental enforcement regime is effective at deterring crime is a complex phenomenon. While there is evidence that something straightforward such as the threat of inspections increases environmental performance, this idea of general deterrence rests on research about perceptual deterrence that may not be warranted.[28]

The existence of perceptual deterrence via the real potential of sanctioning through stiffer statutory maximum penalties, enforcement resources, and the motivation of prosecutors to pursue complex cases against big companies to seek maximum punishment is debated, but likely has already found an answer on the margins, i.e., in some cases and not others.[29] Prior to changes in environmental statutes in the 1980s and 1990s it was very difficult to suc-

23. Joshua Ozymy & Melissa L. Jarrell, *Why Do Regulatory Agencies Punish? The Impact of Political Principals, Agency Culture, and Transaction Costs in Predicting Environmental Criminal Prosecution Outcomes in the United States*, 33 Rev. Pol'y Res. 71-73 (2016)

24. Matthew J. Greife et al., *Corporate Environmental Crime and Environmental Justice*, 28 Crim. Just. Pol'y Rev. 327 (2017).

25. David M. Uhlmann, *Prosecutorial Discretion and Environmental Crime*, 38 Harv. Envtl. L. Rev. 159 (2014) [hereinafter Uhlmann].

26. Sarah L. Stafford, *The Effect of Punishment on Firm Compliance With Hazardous Waste Regulations*, 44 J. Envtl. Econ. & Mgmt. 290-93 (2002).

27. Matthew J. Greife & Michael O. Maume, *Do Companies Pay the Price for Environmental Crimes?: Consequences of Criminal Penalties on Corporate Offenders*, 73 Crime, L. & Soc. Change 337-56 (2020).

28. Paul B. Stretesky & Jackie Gabriel, *Self-Policing and the Environment: Predicting Self-Disclosure of Clean Air Act Violations Under the U.S. Environmental Protection Agency's Audit Policy*, 18 Soc'y & Nat. Resources 884 (2005).

29. See the debated positions by Lazarus and Brickey on these points, Richard J. Lazarus, *Assimilating Environmental Protection Into Legal Rules and the Problem With Environmental Crime*, 27 Loy. L. Rev. 867-70 (1994). *See* Kathleen F. Brickey, Environmental Crime: Law, Policy, Prosecution 9 (New York: Aspen Publishers 2008).

cessfully prosecute corporate officers for environmental offenses.[30] Penalties were often so low prior to this time that companies could simply in theory pay them rather than comply and many did.[31] While we do not find many corporate officers from large multinational companies charged in our analysis, we do find some cases for small- or mid-size companies and we certainly find that prosecutors are motivated to seek punishments, although their efforts tend to be tailored toward crimes that have physical evidence and are thus easier to punish, such as asbestos crimes and illegal discharge cases.[32]

Many companies may prefer regulation and engage in rent-seeking behaviors with government, such as protection from competition or developing preferential markets or solutions for dealing with hazardous byproducts of their operation such as for SO_2, coal ash, biosolids, or carbon dioxide. Weak regulations are often preferred to the open market by many companies for these reasons, as well as the potential for large companies to negotiate smaller fines, consent decrees, and other lesser penalties in court or know that the threat of litigation typically is enough to bring regulators to the bargaining table. In this sense, a weaker regulatory regime can be a positive outcome for the regulated community. They can show the semblance of regulation in place of a stronger regime and stave off public support for stronger regulation absent any government involvement.

Looking at this issue from the perspective of annual cases in Figure 40, one can see investigations by EPA-CID ended up as completed prosecutions only once in 1984. By 1989, this climbed to 22 prosecutions and further increased to 46 by 1998. The annual high point was 59 in 2006 and this decreased to 29 by 2008 and rose to 57 by 2012. By 2018, annual prosecutions dropped again to 20. Many prosecutions take multiple years to go from investigation to sentencing so each year itself has little meaning in most instances. The broader movement trends up over time with institutionalization of the crimi-

30. David T. Barton, *Corporate Officer Liability Under RCRA: Stringent But Not Strict*, 4 Brigham Young U. L. Rev. 1548-51 (1991).
31. David Wann, *Putting Offenders Behind Bars*, 29 Environment 5-7 (1987).
32. Increasing penalties for knowing violations not only raises the specter of punishment for offenders, but also works to encourage individuals and company employees to self-disclose violations to avoid such punishments. In the 1990s, the reinventing government era under President Clinton went further to encourage self-disclosures, as well as self-policing in the hopes that regulation would be less confrontational and deterrence-based and more innovative and conciliatory as companies would find more efficient ways to obey the law. Research casts some doubt on the efficacy of the latter. *See* Paul B. Stretesky & Jackie Gabriel, *Self-Policing and the Environment: Predicting Self-Disclosure of Clean Air Act Violations Under the U.S. Environmental Protection Agency's Audit Policy*, 18 Soc'y & Nat. Resources 871-87 (2005); Paul B. Stretesky & Michael J. Lynch, *Does Self-Policing Reduce Chemical Emissions?*, 46 Soc. Sci. J. 459-73 (2009); and Paul B. Stretesky et al., *Does the Modernization of Environmental Enforcement Reduce Toxic Emissions? An Examination of Self-Policing, Criminal Prosecutions, and Toxic Releases in the United States, 1988-2014*, 37 Sociological Spectrum 48-62 (2017).

Figure 40. Total Criminal Prosecutions by Fiscal Year Since 1983

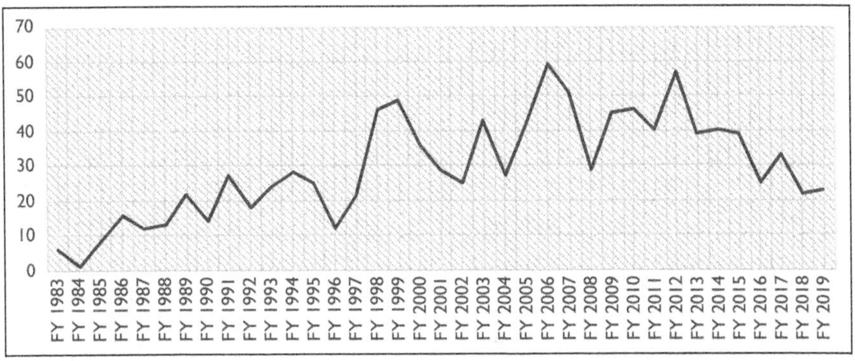

Figure 41. Total Cases Annually Involving at Least One Company Since 1983

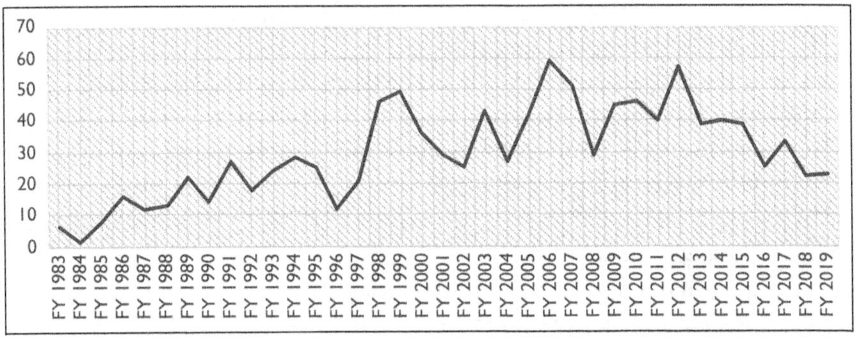

nal enforcement process in the 1980s and then increases significantly relative to past prosecutions by the 1990s, which does not become the apogee so much as the year more prosecutions happened to be settled. These numbers alone do not show a distinctly positive trend with time, but an ebb and flow. If annual settled prosecutions were the metric for deterrence, it would not seem as though EPA-CID creates much of a deterrent effect. Such a conclusion would again assume the typical relationship between offenders and law enforcement, which is simply not the case with environmental regulation and thus deterrence is a difficult concept to pin down.

In Figure 41, we break down the analysis to the total number of cases annually involving at least one company since 1983. We find a grand total of 1,092 cases prosecuted involving a company over the last 37 years. We find one case in 1984. This number rises to 27 in 1991, 49 by the end of the decade, and 59 by 2006. This trend falls and rises to 57 by 2012 and drops to 22 by 2018. The trajectory thus rises and falls over time, mostly increasing with professionalization, but starts to fall again in the last few years. Average prosecutions were about 30, which considering the number of criminal enforcement agents assigned to investigate environmental crimes, and the complex responsibilities of DOJ, the average number of prosecutions seems to generically come in line with expectations for resources, i.e. you would be alarmed with 10 annual prosecutions, but equally shocked if there were 200.

II. The Big Stick

Perhaps another method by which we can tackle the deterrent value of criminal enforcement is to look at the big penalty cases as the yardstick for perceptual deterrence. Large penalties represent the will of investigators and prosecutors to tackle large penalty cases and demonstrates their motivation to seek serious penalties for serious crimes.[33] Certainly, bad guys would look at the potential for punishment through the lens of highly salient prosecutions or at least their lawyers might advise them to pay attention.[34]

In Table 10, we give some examples of salient and expensive cases for corporate environmental crimes. Not unexpectedly, we do not see any relatively large penalty cases against corporations in the 1980s. The prosecution of A&A Land Development in 1991 prosecuted as a RICO case and illegal discharge represents a substantial $30 million fine. Adjusted for inflation in 2019 dollars, this equates to over $82 million today. The 1997 case against Refrigeration USA for an extensive and illegal freon importation scheme would be valued at over $59 million today. Besides the case against Louisiana Pacific in 1998, the next big penalty case comes against Evergreen International in 2005 with a $30 million CWA prosecution and Overseas Shipholding in 2007 for a MARPOL/conspiracy prosecution leading to a $37 million penalty.

Large penalty corporate cases then increase with the BP Texas City refinery explosion prosecuted under the CAA in 2009, the two cases against Wal-Mart Missouri and California in 2013 for violations relating to illegal discharges and lack of employee training for hazardous materials, and the Duke Energy coal ash spill settled for $102 million in 2015. The cases against Volkswagen AG and IAV Gmbh netted over $2.9 billion in penalties in 2019

33. *See* Uhlmann, *supra* note 25, at 159.
34. Richard A. Posner, *An Economic Theory of the Criminal Law*, 85 Colum. L. Rev. 1193-200 (1985).

Table 10. The Dirty Dozen:
Largest Corporate Monetary Penalties

Year	Company	Nominal Penalty	2019 Dollars
FY 1991	A&A Land Development	$44,002,800	$82,596,357.12
FY 1997	Refrigeration USA	$37,372,826	59,530,371.19
FY 1998	Louisiana Pacific	$37,235,000	$58,401,155.80
FY 2005	Evergreen International	$30,000,000	$39,271,428.57
FY 2007	Overseas Shipholding	$37,000,000	$45,621,769.83
FY 2009	BP Products	$50,000,000	$59,583,428.50
FY 2013	Wal-Mart MO/CA	$220,000,000	$241,437,432.66
FY 2013	BP, PLC	$4,000,000,000	$4,389,771,502.90
FY 2014	Transocean	$400,000,000	$431,969,789.13
FY 2015	Duke Energy	$102,000,000	$110,021,703.08
FY 2017	Volkswagen AG	$2,800,000,000	$2,920,363,903.39
FY 2019	IAV Gmbh	$35,000,000	$35,000,000

dollars, only eclipsed by the BP and Transocean prosecutions for Deepwater Horizon that resulted in over $4.8 billion in 2019 dollars.

To place these prosecutions in context, they demonstrate the ability and drive of federal prosecutors to pursue complex cases against multinational corporations. Certainly a $4 billion penalty for gross negligence and obstructing Congress sends a signal to potential offenders, as does almost $3 billion in inflation-adjusted penalties for a long-term emissions rigging scheme. Another way to contextualize these outcomes is that a dozen cases represent 76% of all corporate monetary penalties assessed in the data.[35] It would be very difficult to assess empirically the deterrent value of these large

35. *U.S. Inflation Calculator*, https://www.usinflationcalculator.com/. This measure uses the Consumer Price Index. Noting again here that the BP prosecution could not be found through normal search terms applied to the other cases during data collection and is thus not included in totals throughout the book. Legal citation for cases in the table follow: A & A Land Development (50% of the penalty was assessed to the related company, Vulpis Brothers, Ltd., S.D.N.Y. No. 89-446); Refrigeration USA (S.D. Fla No. CR:96-0267-CR-MORENO); Louisiana Pacific Corp. (D. Colo. No. 95-CR-215); Evergreen International SA (D. Or. No. CR 05-238-TJH); Overseas Shipholding Group (E.D.N.C. No. 7:06-CR-125-1F); Wal-Mart Missouri (W.D. Mo. No. 4:13-CR-00135); Wal-Mart California (C.D. Cal. Nos. 13-CR-033-JSC-1 & CR 13 334 MAG); BP Products North America (S.D. Tex. No. 4:07-CR-434); Transocean LTD (E.D. La. No. 2:13-CR-00001-JTM-SS); BP, PLC (E.D. La. No. 2:12-CR-00292-DEK); Duke Energy Progress, Inc. (E.D.N.C. No. 15-CR-00062,67,68); Volkswagen AG (E.D. Mich. No. 16-CR-20394); IAV GmbH (E.D. Mich. No. 16-CR-20394).]

Figure 42. Total Monetary Penalties Assessed to Companies by Fiscal Year in Current Dollars Since 1983

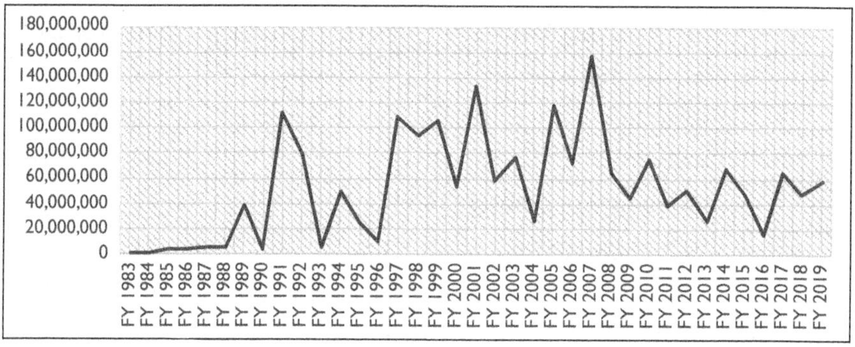

penalty cases, but they are certainly infrequent, if not substantial, particularly for potential violators of the CWA and the CAA.

If we exclude the Wal-Mart, BP, Transocean, Duke, and Volkswagen AG cases that are so substantial, we can graph these penalties over time with some semblance of order and perspective. In Figure 42, we adjust all nominal penalties against companies to 2019 dollars by fiscal year and graph them over time. We see these rising from almost $240,000 in 1983 to $111 million by 1991 if we adjust for inflation. By 2001, this rises again to over $133 million and then $156 by 2007. When you exclude these large penalty cases and adjust for inflation, the picture begins to change and overall company penalties start to drop after 2007 and decline to just over $16 million by 2016 and up to $58 million by 2019.

Most of these penalties were not against large multinational companies like BP or Transocean. Large penalties represented examples of prosecutions that put forth significant resources to punish willful and knowing violations of the law. Many cases involved smaller companies and such penalties would have been out of line with the nature of the crime and the need for punishment and deterrence. In this light, we can view the nature of punishing companies for committing environmental crimes as one of opportunity for prosecutors to have and to take. There are likely many examples of crimes settled through civil action to avoid the resources needed for prosecution, given the outcomes can be more flexible in civil cases and just as substantial. The cases in Figure 42 represent public prosecutions to both punish and make a point.

In Table 11 we explore 11 of the largest monetary penalties assessed to individual defendants in cases since 1983. In this table, we list the primary defendant and aggregate all monetary penalties assessed to individuals (not companies, although they are defendants in some cases), and the total months of incarceration and probation assess to all individual defendants in each case. If these are examples of salient cases against individuals there might be some argument for a general deterrent value. These cases also give some range of what types of crimes will receive such large penalties at sentencing.

Table 11.The Dirty Dozen II: Largest Individual Monetary Penalties

Year	State	Defendant	Crime	Nominal Penalty	Prison	Probation
2007	NY	Eric C. Farbent	Asbestos	$72,661,945	746	336
2013	TX	Jeffrey David Gunselman	Biofuel Fraud	$55,075,000	188	0
2013	MD	Rodney Rashawn Hailey	Biofuel Fraud	$51,300,000	150	0
2014	NC	Benjamin Franklin Pass	PCBs	$21,373,143	42	0
2015	WI	Randy Jones	Pipeline Spill	$19,337,785	0	120
2015	OH	William Bradley	Biofuel Fraud	$23,000,000	167	0
2015	OH	Richard Smith	Biofuel Fraud	$23,000,000	167	0
2015	TN	Newell Lynn Smith	Asbestos	$31,165,731	149	0
2016	TX	Philip Joseph Rivkin	Biofuel Fraud	$138,000,000	121	0
2017	IN	Brian Carmichael	Biofuel Fraud	$55,295,068	650	36
2018	OH	Gregory Schnabel	Biofuel Fraud	$26,244,437	63	0
2019	LA	Charles Ferris Callihan	Munitions Disposal	$35,397,347	225	0

The obvious trend in these cases is that seven are connected to biofuel fraud related to renewable fuel credit taxes discussed in the CAA chapter. Some, such as the case against Jeffrey David Gunselman and his co-defendants, involved false production of biofuels to fraudulently obtain tax credits. Rodney Rashawn Hailey sold renewable identification numbers to brokers and oil companies for biofuel that his company did not produce. William Bradley also engaged in the false production of biofuel to achieve renewable/tax credits. Brian Carmichael (primary defendant is E-Biofuels), Phillip Joseph Rivkin, and Gregory Schnabel, all engaged in a version of this fraud.

All but one was prosecuted under the CAA and all were prosecuted with concomitant criminal charges, such as false statements, conspiracy, and fraud.

The penalties tended to be so high, because the fraud, i.e. falsely claim to produce biofuels, take the tax credits, and/or then sell the renewable energy credits to unsuspecting buyers on the open market, generated substantial returns in the millions of dollars for the fraudulent behaviors. These cases were arguably easier than other crimes to prosecute, as you have a direct paper trail that can uncover the fraudulent tax filing, subsequently fraudulently sold renewable energy credits, and of course the fact that these companies and their owners either did not physically exist and produce biofuel or merely pretended to do so.[36]

In a way, the biofuel cases are an aberration in the individual penalty cases. The Farbent case is attached to the widescale fraudulent asbestos testing and demolition conspiracy prosecuted as a RICO case in New York. Newell Smith was also prosecuted for asbestos crimes. The only other outliers here are that of Benjamin Franklin Pass, owner of P&W Oil Company, who would transport and reprocess large amounts of oil to be resold. Pass became aware in October 2009 that testing showed the oil was severely contaminated with PCBs and he continued to instruct employees to illegally blend and mix the contaminated oil. Pass also falsely certified his employees, failed to pay income taxes, and was sentenced to 42 months in prison and ordered to pay over $22 million in restitution to Colonial Oil and International Paper that contaminated their facilities.

The Randy Jones case is a bit of an outlier. Jones was a corrosion coordinator for Shell Pipeline Company. He violated the Pipeline Safety Act and made false statements by failing to conduct corrosion tests from January to December 2011 for a pipeline that transported aviation fuel for Shell. A hole in the pipeline released some 9,000 gallons of fuel that melted asphalt and damaged other property at General Mitchell International Airport in Milwaukee, Wisconsin. The cleanup cost for the spill was $19.3 million. Jones was sentenced to 10 years of probation and ordered to pay $19,337,785 in restitution.

Charles Ferris Callihan is also somewhat of an outlier case. Callihan and his co-defendants, employees of Explo Systems a company whose primary

36. Case numbers for the table follow: Gregory Schnabel (S.D. Ohio No. 2:17-CR-169); Benjamin Franklin Pass (E.D. N.C. No. 7:12-CR-85-1-D); Eric Farbent (N.D.N.Y. No. 02-CR-51); Jeffrey Gunselman (N.D. Tex. No. 5:12-CR-00078-C-BG); Rodney Rashawn Hailey (D. Md. No. 1:11-CR-00540-WDQ); Randy Jones (E.D. Wis. No. 14-CR-220); William Bradley (S.D. Ohio No. 2:15CR44); Richard Smith (S.D. Ohio No. 2:15-CR-44); Newell Lynn Smith (E.D. Tenn. No. 2:11-CR-82); Philip Joseph Rivkin (S.D. Tex. No. H 14-603M/H14-250c); Brian Carmichael (S.D. Ind. No. 1:13-CR-0189SEB-TAB); Charles Ferris Callihan (W.D. La. No. 16-CR-00214-06).

business was to demilitarize military munitions, conspired to transport munitions to unpermitted facilities from January 2010 to November 2012 in an effort to defraud the U.S. Army. Callihan submitted false documents and gave false statements to landfills to dispose of the hazardous waste and to the government. On Octocer 15, 2012, an explosion occurred at Camp Minden at a facility leased by Explo that destroyed the bunker, trailer, derailed 11 rail cars, shattered windows in a four-mile radius, and caused an evacuation of the town of Doyline, Louisiana. In addition to the $35 million in restitution the defendants were ordered to pay, they also collectively were sentenced to 225 months in prison.[37]

Table 12. The Dirty Dozen III: Largest Prison Sentences

Year	State	Defendant	Crime	Prison
1986	NY	Charles Colbert	Importation Fraud and Conspiracy	312
1989	CT	Charles Arcangelo	RICO	564
1991	NY	Angelo Paccione	RICO	604
2001	MO	Mark Anthony Dorner	Methamphetamine production	953
2003	WV	Katie Dolinger	Chemical Production	232
2005	NY	Alexander Salvagno	RICO	619
2005	*	Brent Bushau	Conspiracy and Theft of Refrigerants	492
2006	MS	Robert J. Lucas, Jr.	Built a Subdivision on Wetlands	282
2007	FL	David Eugene Turner	Illegal Labor Camp	626
2014	MI	Kwame Kilpatrick	Public Corruption	603
2017	FL	Thomas Anthony Davanzo	Biofuel Fraud	256
2017	GA	Shamon Antwon Williams	Gang Activity	230

We can now examine the top-12 most punitive prison sentences handed down to all individual defendants in a single case since 1983. While both civil and criminal penalties can include probation or monetary penalties, Table 12 examines the biggest stick available to federal prosecutors when dealing with individual, rather than company defendants. We are leaving out the large incarceration prosecutions previously discussed for Eric Farbent and Brian Carmichael, although Farbent makes an appearance in the related

37. Vicki Welborn, *Update: Explo Officials Get Years Behind Bars, Ordered to Pay Millions in Restitution*, KTBS.com, Nov. 27, 2018, at https://www.ktbs.com/news/update-explo-officials-get-years-behind-bars-ordered-to-pay-millions-in-restitution/article_026d5874-f29b-11e8-a854-2b81dcfde752.html.

prosecution of AAR Contractors. Many of these cases were discussed in the previous chapters, but we will mention them briefly here as well.

The most common theme we see is the presence of serious criminal behaviors in these 12 cases. Four cases involve RICO or racketeering-focused cases. The previously discussed case against Charles Arcangelo was a RICO case centered on conspiracy and illegal disposal of hazardous materials under RCRA.[38] The RICO case against Angelo Paccione was tied into the previous case, which involved extensive operations to illegally dispose of asbestos and other hazardous materials through a series of company-owned landfills and recycling operations. Alexander Salvagno was a defendant in the illegal asbestos testing and demolition conspiracy case and it was tried as a RICO case and was tied to AAR Contractor.

The highest profile racketeering case we find is against the former mayor of Detroit, Michigan, Kwame Kilpatrick. The former mayor was indicted for his role in a high-profile public corruption scandal. Kilpatrick used his position as mayor, as well as a Michigan State House Representative, to engage in a racketeering conspiracy involving extortion, bribery, tax evasion, and mail fraud for which he was sentenced to 28 years in prison. The crux of this long-standing conspiracy was to extort public contractors to use Bobby Ferguson who obtained a portion of the $73 million in revenue obtained through the scheme of which he shared with Kwame and Bernard Kilpatrick. Mayor Kilpatrick also personally accepted payments and property totaling over $1 million from persons seeking business with the city. Thirty-two other individuals were convicted. Because Mayor Kilpatrick was investigated by EPA, the case is included in the data, although the focus of the case was the racketeering and conspiracy.

Brent Bushau was previously discussed as a case involving conspiracy to steal more than $3 million in refrigerants and resell them. The state of the crime is not listed in the case summaries. Robert Lucas Jr. was also discussed previously in the case against Bill Hill Acres, Inc. which illegally filled in a wetland and built a 2,600-acre subdivision in Vancleave, Mississippi. The project defrauded some 600 families as the septic and stormwater problems caused by the illegal action made the development uninhabitable for many home buyers. David Eugene Turner's case was also discussed prior. Turner

38. Case numbers for the table follow: Charles Arcangelo (D. Conn. No. N-88-43TFGD); Angelo Paccione (S.D.N.Y. No. 89-446); Alexander Salvagno (N.D.N.Y. No. 5:02-CR-51); Kwame Kilpatrick (E.D. Mich. No. 2:10-CR-20403-4TH SD); Brent Bushau (No. 01CR0610); Robert Lucas Jr. (S.D. Miss. No. 1:04CR60GuRo-001); David Eugene Turner (M.D. Fla. No. 3:05-CR-00159-TJC-MMH); Shamon Anton Williams (S.D. Ga. No. CR416-343-01); Thomas Anthony Davazo (M.D. Fla. No. 2:15-CR-00141-UA-MRM); Katie Dolinger (S.D. W. Va. No. CR:06-Nov-2002); Mark Anthony Dorner (E.D. Mo. No. 4:00CR396SNL); Charles Colbert (S.D.N.Y. No. 85-1134).

and his co-defendants operated an illegal migrant labor camp near Jacksonville, Florida, where they would round up homeless laborers, and pay them in untaxed cigarettes, alcohol, and crack cocaine. Besides conspiracy to distribute cocaine and illegal transport of laborers, they were charged under the CWA for pipping raw sewage into a creek. Shamon Anton Williams was prosecuted with seven other members of the Carver Village Thoroughbreds gang near Savannah, Georgia, for federal firearms and drug trafficking offenses. EPA-CID participated in the investigation.[39]

Thomas Anthony Davazo was involved in a previously discussed biofuel fraud case. Katie Dolinger was prosecuted with her co-defendants for manufacturing methamphetamines in West Virginia. Waste from the manufacturing process was dumped into a creek, bringing the attention of EPA-CID to the case, which was a similar scenario to the prosecution of Mark Anthony Dorner. Charles Colbert was president of a company prosecuted for fraudulently shipping a recycled chlorinated solvent mixture to a company in Zimbabwe.

Revisiting the central themes of the book shows us some of the obstacles to advancing the case for a greater push for enhanced criminal enforcement of federal environmental laws. We have found that enforcement of the CWA, the CAA, and RCRA disproportionately defines criminal enforcement in the United States. As we discussed in the previous chapter, much of this comes down to the way such criminal provisions are constructed, the scope of the act, and the regulatory reach. The CWA sets up a vast permitting system, beginning at POTWs and expands outward. Any person or entity discharging into the waters of the United States will run up against the Act with some important exemptions afforded to concentrated animal feeding operations, fracking, and a few other sectors of the economy. The regulated community includes public and private water treatment plants, sewers, stormwater, ships and vessels, residential subdivisions, and any development that involves altering a wetland or waterway. We would argue this permitting system, although flawed in what is allowed to be discharged or altered, was a great success, as was the significant investment that Congress made in constructing and updating POTWs in the 1970s and early 1980s. For mobile sources, the CWA has been much less effective.

Even though this permitting system has been devolved to the states, it sets up a paperwork trail and often physical evidence that aids in prosecu-

39. *"Drenched in Blood Itself": 8 Indicted in Savannah Violent Drugs/Guns*, Savannah Morning News, July 6, 2016, at https://www.savannahnow.com/crime-courts-news/2016-07-06/drenched-blood-itself-8-indicted-savannah-violent-drugsguns-gang-probe.

tion. With over 800 cases or 32% of prosecutions, the CWA reigns supreme in criminal enforcement. It is unsurprising that illegal discharges make up about one-quarter of all prosecutions stemming from EPA investigations over the last 37 years. The remainder of the prosecutions outside of unpermitted alteration of waterways, i.e., §404 permit and related violations, often had some relationship to prosecuted illegal or unpermitted discharges.

Excluding the BP *Deepwater Horizon* case, about $1.25 billion in monetary fines were levied against CWA offenders, alongside 34,000 months of probation, and over 5,000 months of incarceration. We see some of the largest penalty cases against corporate offenders levied under the CWA as well. Evergreen International, Overseas Shipholding, the Wal-Mart prosecutions, Duke Energy, and of course Transocean and BP for Deepwater Horizon all make for a significant portion of historical penalties. Including all cases moves the needle to over $5 billion, and that is important if you look at relative deterrence and specific deterrence for the particular companies that committed the offenses, this specific law, and the companies that are regulated by it and the corporate lawyers that proffer expensive advice on their behalf and talk about it at professional conferences and in closed conference rooms. Just removing the two against BP and Transocean drops penalties to about $866 million overall, which is not terribly significant given the size of the regulated community and related economic activity, but it is not insignificant either.

The criminal enforcement of the CAA reflects the difficulty of policing emissions from stationary sources. Asbestos-centric crimes became the focus of the criminal division and federal prosecutors early on. We find that 12% of total prosecutions focus on asbestos and about 59% of CAA prosecutions are asbestos-centric. With over $3.6 billion in monetary penalties assessed to defendants over the last 37 years that criminally violated the CAA the number is substantial. Like the CWA prosecutorial universe, this number is greatly skewed by the $2.8 billion Volkswagen AG prosecution and as we have seen previously the biofuel tax credit fraud cases greatly skew this number as well. Still some 16,000 months of probation, 7,600 months of incarceration, and over 17,000 hours of community service was metered out.

RCRA violators were subjected to a grand total of about $293 million in monetary penalties, 18,000 months of probation, 7,000 months of incarceration, and 33,000 hours of community service. Their crimes were generally straightforward, and a combination of illegal transport, storage, disposal, and other issues related to the improper handling of hazardous wastes. Fifty-four percent of these prosecutions involved one or more of these cradle-to-grave crimes. RCRA crimes made up 15% of total prosecutions since 1983 and was second only to illegal discharge cases in the major themes we uncovered in Chapter 6.

III. Politics and the Future of Criminal Enforcement

Our own summary judgment on what many scholars, practitioners, and the career staff at EPA itself would mostly agree with is that criminal enforcement had its heyday long ago. As with any established regulatory agency, the initial years are beset by greater freedoms, public involvement, and mission-driven work.[40] New employees have fewer rules, more professional discretion, and the opportunities to work with the regulated community seem greater.[41] EPA-CID was always designed to make hard choices with limited resources and from the very beginning the unit realized, as will all federal environmental law enforcement, it would have to be selective in its enforcement decisions.[42] As the director of the Office of Enforcement Earl Devaney noted to staff over two decades ago, it is unlikely it will ever be large enough in size to fully defeat the ever-expanding universe of environmental crime and it must maximize its presence and impact through discerning case selection, and then proceed with investigations that advance EPA's overall goal of regulatory compliance and punishing criminal wrongdoing.[43] DOJ-ECS falls roughly into the same category.[44]

As any scholar of bureaucracy may note, this rosy picture declines over time.[45] The regulated community starts to understand how to manipulate the regulatory agency. They often engage in rent-seeking behaviors, or find ways to cope with regulation and use it as a tool for relative stasis, rather than substantive change.[46] Any organization of relative size will realize the

40. Joel A. Mintz, Enforcement at the EPA: High Stakes and Hard Choices 10 (Univ. of Texas Press 2012).
41. Joel A. Mintz, *Some Thoughts on the Interdisciplinary Aspects of Environmental Enforcement*, 36 ELR 10495-96 (July 2006).
42. U.S. DOJ-ECS, *Historical Development of Environmental Criminal Law*, https://www.justice.gov/enrd/about-division/historical-development-environmental-criminal-law (last updated May 13, 2015).
43. Earl E. Devaney, The Exercise of Investigative Discretion 2-3 (1994), https://www.epa.gov/sites/production/files/documents/exercise.pdf.
44. Judson W. Starr, *Turbulent Times at Justice and EPA: The Origins of Environmental Criminal Prosecutions and the Work That Remains*, 59 Geo. Wash. L. Rev. 900-02 (1991).
45. *See* Joel A. Mintz, *Treading Water: A Preliminary Assessment of EPA Enforcement During the Bush II Administration*, 34 ELR 10912 (Oct. 2004)
46. Daniel J. Fiorino, The New Environmental Regulation (MIT Press 2006). Theodore Lowi, The End of Liberalism: The Second Republic of the United States (Norton 1997). Dan Wood & Richard Waterman, *The Dynamics of Political Control of the Bureaucracy*, 85 Am. Pol. Sci. Rev. 801-28 (1991). Dan Wood, *Modeling Federal Implementation as a System: The Clean Air Case*, 36 Am. J. Pol. Sci. 40-67 (1992).

statistical odds of getting caught with your pants down for an environmental regulation are rare. EPA and state regulators do not police private businesses and when they investigate, they often give advanced notice. There are no environmental police on the beat—you know when they are coming, and it is not often. As the regulated community has grown and disinvestment has occurred, much of what EPA has accomplished in the regulator scheme works in substance, but much of it does not because of weak enforcement. The corollary to a few cops on the beat is that while important federal statutes such as the CAA, the CWA, and RCRA do cover a lot of regulatory territory, they also cede significant ground to the regulated community.[47]

At the half-century mark, EPA has become an established federal regulatory agency. In this environment there will be few big wins, the foundations have been laid, and resources are limited.[48] Politicians also disagree on the scope of criminal enforcement and have historically fought over the reach of EPA-CID.[49] Even in the best of times, EPA's political and financial support has been mixed.[50] EPA-CID has come of age and big-time wins or major changes seem unlikely. The unit still maintains a strong culture of professionalism and focus on deterrence and willingness to do its job, despite significant obstacles.[51]

In February 2020, a national poll of registered voters asked participants to pick their top-three issues that will affect their presidential vote choice in November. Republicans noted the economy, immigration, and healthcare as the top-three issues, with none noting environmental policy generally, and only 6% noting climate change was a top issue. While Democrats and Independents did not mention environmental policy, they did note climate change as a top issue at 29% and 19%, respectively.[52] In a country facing

47. Joshua Ozymy & Melissa L. Jarrell, *Wielding the Green Stick: An Examination of Criminal Enforcement at the EPA Under the Bush and Obama Administrations*, 24 ENVTL. POL. 40-42 (2015).
48. Joel A. Mintz, *Running on Fumes: The Development of New EPA Regulations in an Era of Scarcity*, 46 ELR 10510-12 (June 2016).
49. Theodora Galactos, *The United States Department of Justice Environmental Crimes Section: A Case Study of Inter- and Intra-Branch Conflict Over Congressional Oversight and the Exercise of Prosecutorial Discretion*, 64 FORDHAM L. REV. 590-95 (1995).
50. *See* Joel. A. Mintz, *Neither the Best of Times Nor the Worst of Times: EPA Enforcement During the Clinton Administration*, 35 ELR 10390-93 (June 2005).
51. Memorandum From John Peter Suarez, Assistant Administrator, U.S. EPA Office of Enforcement & Compliance Assurance, on Management Review of the Office of Criminal Enforcement, Forensics and Training, at 5 (Dec. 15, 2003), *available at* https://www.epa.gov/sites/production/files/documents/oceft-review03.pdf.
52. Top Issues for Voters, PROCON.ORG, https://2020election.procon.org/view.resource.php?resourceID=007111#climatenexus (Feb. 2020). Even after the onslaught of Covid-19 and the subsequent economic collapse, a poll of likely voters asking their top issue responded as follows: 54% preventing Social Security cuts; 29% universal healthcare; 26% raising the minimum wage; 25% reducing the wealth gap; and 24% fighting climate change. This was followed by deporting illegal aliens (18%),

Figure 43. EPA Budget in Nominal and Inflation-Adjusted Dollars Since 1980

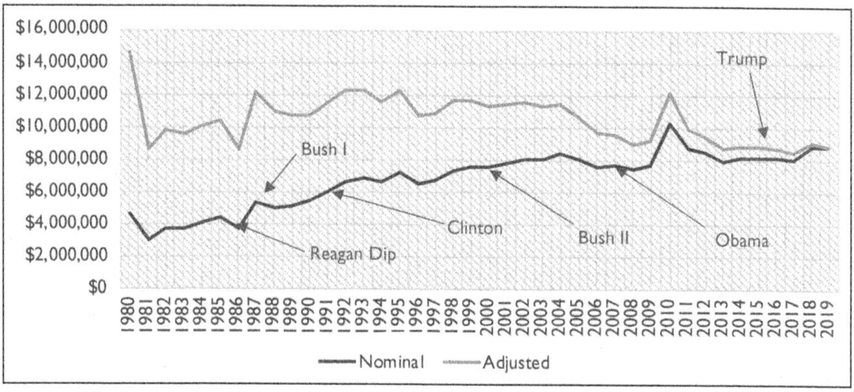

intense competition from globalization, the financialization of the economy that amplifies boom/bust cycles, decades of governmental policies that have allowed severe inequality to blossom, disinvestment in infrastructure, and an escalating debt load at all levels of government that faces financial catastrophe from current demographic shifts, if voters across the spectrum care more about healthcare, jobs, and immigration, can climate change bring resources and attention back to EPA to help it accomplish an even more difficult mission in the future?

With a renewed focus on its mission, EPA would still face a few serious problems—the somber reality of discretionary federal spending and the mixed support between political parties in Congress for stronger environmental policy. EPA funding over time, when adjusted for inflation, is not increasing. Inspections have been decreasing in recent years in face of the inertia of neglect and inconsistency levied at the Agency.[53] Figure 43 graphs the trends in EPA's budget from 1980-2019 in nominal and inflation-adjusted dollars in $1,000 units. In nominal dollars it appears that EPA's budget has been on an upward trajectory since 1980, with a larger dip in the Reagan Administration and a rise in the Obama Administration. The Agency's nominal budget in 1980 was about $4.6 billion but adjusted for inflation it was actually over

protecting the Second Amendment (17%), and building a U.S.-Mexican border wall (16%). Lorie Konish, *Preventing Social Security Benefit Cuts Is a Top Priority for Americans in 2020 Election, Survey Finds*, CNBC, Aug. 19, 2020, at https://www.cnbc.com/2020/08/19/preventing-social-security-benefit-cuts-is-a-top-priority-in-2020-election.html.

53. U.S. EPA, Fiscal Year 2019 EPA Enforcement and Compliance Results 10 (Feb. 13, 2020), https://www.epa.gov/sites/production/files/2020-02/documents/fy19-enforcement-annual-results-data-graphs.pdf.

$14 billion in current dollars. In nominal dollars, we see a dip in 1986 and 1996, but mostly an upward trajectory through FY 2005. Spending reached a high point by exceeding $10 billion in 2010 and then slowly declined to $8.8 billion by 2019.

Adjusted for inflation we see that the budget has been declining for the past 39 years.[54] This decline certainly reflects politics, but not to the severe degree one might assume. Republican and Democratic presidents and Congresses are often at loggerheads over environmental regulation and funding strong policies and enforcement.[55] Whether particular presidents can greatly impact the shorter term trends in support is not disputable, but one can argue the point over the longer trends.[56]

In a principal-agent game there are multiple institutional and non-institutional actors trying to influence the policies and outcomes of regulatory agencies.[57] The president, Congress, the courts, interest groups, and even social movements attempt to have their say in what government does.[58] EPA is beset by high-salience activities paired with complex policy mandates, which gives it both attention and discretion (see the Social Security Administration for a federal agency that has little discretion or attention to its day-to-day activities).[59] This makes their decisions political, but affords them greater professional autonomy to do their job because Congress can empower them with funds or legislation, yet often does not have the time or knowledge to construct complex policies or enforce them. These information asymmetries between principals that seek control and agents that seek growth and autonomy benefit the Agency.[60]

---

54. U.S. EPA, *EPA's Budget and Spending*, https://www.epa.gov/planandbudget/budget (last updated May 2, 2022).
55. Joshua Ozymy & Melissa Jarrell, *Why Do Regulatory Agencies Punish? The Impact of Political Principals, Agency Culture, and Transaction Costs in Predicting Environmental Criminal Prosecution Outcomes in the United States*, 33 Rev. Pol'y Res. 71-73 (2016).
56. Joshua Ozymy & Melissa Jarrell, *Administrative Persistence in the Face of a Hostile Regime: How the EPA Can Survive the Trump Administration*, 10 Envtl. Just. 1-3 (2017).
57. Matthew A. Auer, *Presidential Environmental Appointees in Comparative Perspective*, 68 Pub. Admin. Rev. 68-71 (2008). Ronald H. Rosenberg, *Doing More or Doing Less for the Environment: Shedding Light on EPA's "Stealth" Method of Environmental Enforcement*, 35 B.C. Envtl. Aff. L. Rev. 175-80 (2008).
58. Jeb Barnes, *Courts and the Puzzle of Institutional Stability and Change: Administrative Drift and Judicial Innovation in the Case of Asbestos*, 61 Pol. Res. Q. 636-48 (2008).
59. James Q. Wilson, Bureaucracy: What Government Agencies Do and Why They Do It (Basic Books 1991).
60. Mark Atlas, *Enforcement Principals and Environmental Agencies: Principal-Agent Relationships in a Delegated Environmental Program*, 41 L. & Soc'y Rev. 939-80 (2007). James A. Barnes, *Implementing Presidential Policy Agendas Administratively: A View From the Inside*, 69 Pub. Admin. Rev. 586-94 (2009).

Principals must also compete and over the past four decades the federal government has been defined by divided, rather than unified government. Rare is the opportunity to strongly empower EPA or destroy it. What we find is more of a pattern with enforcement outcomes in the book mirroring "neither the best of times nor worst of times."[61] Democratic presidents never seem to have enough time, will, or opportunity with Congress to truly empower the Agency and Republicans chip away at it, but have failed to render its criminal enforcement efforts mute over the years. Unfortunately, this means CID and EPA often plod along playing catch up in more sympathetic political environments and trying to survive hostile ones.

Ronald Reagan is probably the best example of a Republican president trying to deal a death blow to an agency only a decade in its development. The Reagan Administration was fairly hostile to environmental regulations and he used the bully pulpit and appointment of Anne Gorsuch as chief both as a cudgel to reduce spending, reach, and scope of enforcement. Gorsuch did all of the things President Reagan promised she would do in speech and practice-reducing enforcement, lowering budgets, not filling key positions, and trying to change the culture of the Agency. Many of these efforts succeeded in the short term and we see the dip in funding by 1986 that actually follows Gorsuch being cited for contempt of Congress for withholding records, infighting in the Agency and with congressional supporters of EPA, the demoralization and exit of staff, but ultimately her resignation in less than two years on the job. We then see William Ruckelshaus being reappointed to fill the gap as head administrator and these efforts to weaken enforcement and demoralize staff dissipate.[62]

George H.W. Bush's Administration saw key additions to the CAA, a rising budget, and staff. President Clinton did not end up supporting the Agency as much as thought and disappointed many in the environmental community. Beset by a hostile U.S. House of Representatives, better political organization by the Republican party, and more conservative attitudes developing in the American public against welfare and big government, President Clinton failed to truly advance the Agency's mission in a systematic manner.[63] His contributions were not negative, but certainly not as positive as environmentalists would have hoped to reverse the negative trends of the Reagan era. This trend may have changed if Vice President Al Gore had been

61. *See* Mintz, *Neither the Best of Times Nor the Worst of Times*, *supra* note 50.
62. Joel. A. Mintz, *EPA Enforcement of CERCLA: Historical Overview and Recent Trends*, 41 Sw. L. Rev. 645-59 (2012)
63. Mintz, *Some Thoughts*, *supra* note 41. Evan. J. Ringquist, *Political Control and Policy Impact in EPA's Office of Water Quality*, 39 Am. J. Pol. Sci. 336-63 (1995).

elected in 2000, given his public support and importance set on the environment in his campaign and overall environmental record in Congress. He, however, like President George W. Bush, may have just as easily been beset by the 9/11 attack that would have rerouted his ambitions.

President Bush employed tactics similar to President Reagan's. He was not supportive of environmental policy, focused on a traditional Republican ploy of returning authority to the states in order to reduce the federal enforcement presence, and focused on the appointment of loyalists rather than careerists in key positions in the Agency.[64] President Barack Obama made many strides toward enhancing environmental policy, particular in light of growing public concern over climate change. The Agency's budget increased, as did staffing, and the emphasis of stronger regulation for coal plants that occurred alongside the developing of fracking that made natural gas reserves abundant, and consistent federal tax credits to develop wind power and solar power, the country saw a shift away from building new coal plants in Bush II toward such plants shutting down for the first time in generations.[65] These increases in funding for staff and enforcement were not strong enough to counter long-term neglect of the Agency.[66]

EPA's workforce numbers are also stagnant and declining over time. We show total workforce in Figure 44. Total workforce in 1980 was 13,078. This started to drop in President Reagan's first term, but began to rise in George H.W. Bush's Administration up to a high point of 18,110 in 1999. With a few exceptions, workforce numbers begin a slow decline by 2000 falling to 14,172 today. As discussed previously, CID enforcement agents have been declining as well. Outside of the initial Reagan drop, we generally see an increase through Clinton, but then mostly stasis. While there was some investment in the Obama Administration, it was not enough. The line starts to trend down again by his second term and continues to this day.

Political principals compete with an Agency culture born out of the need to deter criminal action. Like law enforcement in general, EPA-CID must operate with much fewer officers than it needs to deter specific and general crimes. That culture of valuing deterrence has persisted throughout various presidential and congressional regimes that have been hostile or supportive. The long-term effects on Agency morale and goal achievement have been more permanent.

---

64. Mintz, *"Treading Water,"* *supra* note 45.
65. *See* Mintz, *EPA Enforcement of CERCLA*, *supra* note 62.
66. Public Employees for Environmental Responsibility (PEER), *EPA CID Agent Count*, https://www.peer.org/wp-content/uploads/2019/11/11_21_19-Federal_Pollution_EPA_CID_Agent_Count.pdf (Nov. 21, 2019).

Figure 44. EPA Workforce by Fiscal Year Since 1980

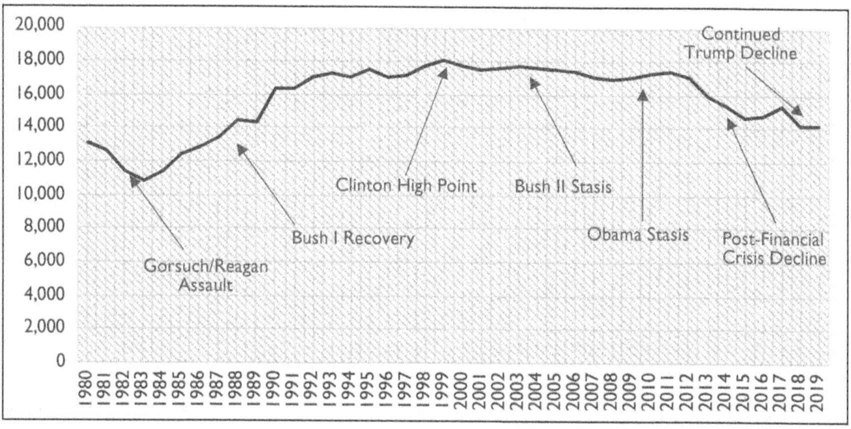

Opponents of EPA realized there was too much public and political support to simply end a large federal regulatory agency. Reagan's hard-charging attitude certainly affected the Agency in many negative ways, as did Bush II, and certainly President Donald Trump. Trump actively sought to impugn most government agencies, staff the highest positions with arguably unqualified people, sow dissent, reduce budgets and scope, and lower morale. The Agency and its enforcement efforts as we have seen through this book have persisted in this environment for 37 years, but the aggregate effects on the Agency and its staff over so many years and setbacks, as well as disappointments from supporters, have taken a permanent toll. The Agency's criminal enforcement efforts will persist, but it will likely have to do more with less because of a lack of political agreement in Washington, D.C., over its value and general existence, as well as longer term structural forces in the federal budget of which it has little control.[67]

EPA's budget was, like many regulatory programs, a victim of the 2008-2009 financial crisis. Funding did not return to many agencies and non-discretionary spending and entitlements have increasingly eaten up the lion's share of the federal budget. The Congressional Budget Office (CBO) provides a stark outlook on U.S. debt and spending as current long-term demographic trends continue. Prior to the Covid-19 pandemic, which will no doubt escalate the financial problems of the federal government, the CBO estimates the number of Americans over aged 65 will skyrocket as will concomitant

67. *Running on Fumes*, *supra* note 48. Joshua Ozymy & Melissa L. Jarrell, *Wielding the Green Stick: An Examination of Criminal Enforcement at the EPA Under the Bush and Obama Administrations*, 24 Envtl. Pol. 38-56 (2015).

entitlement spending in Social Security, Medicare (particularly Medicare), and debt to fund it. By 2049, healthcare spending, Social Security, and interest on the debt will dominate federal spending and push out other programs as debt reaches close to 150% of the gross domestic product.

This trend was already happening prior to 2008, which escalated the problem more quietly in the form of reduced spending for everything else, and it will continue to increase exponentially. As the CBO noted in their 2019 report, this debt is directly affected by investor confidence and the desire to purchase U.S. Treasury securities. Now that the government has taken on arguably much more debt in 2022 than in response to 2008's crisis, the U.S. Federal Reserve was forced to keep interest rates ultra-low or federal debt would reach astronomical proportions if interest rates had to be increased even modestly to attract investors to buy such securities.[68]

How EPA can muscle for additional funding in this environment will prove difficult. The federal government has been moving for years to increase spending for the elderly at the cost of the young. The latter pays for this shift in personal debt and declining long-term prospectus for social services themselves when they reach advanced age. Without changes in healthcare policy in the United States in particular, efforts to shore up Social Security, and increased revenues to lower debt, the outlook for federal spending on environmental policy and enforcement looks bleak over the next three decades, even with a more sympathetic administration.

Even a renewed emphasis on the environment in the public's mind via the specter of climate change will have to compete with non-discretionary spending, past promises made, a constituency that always votes, and the growing acknowledgment that the interests of the elderly and working age populations are incongruent. Unless the former are willing to accept cuts in benefits now, the latter will have to accept that those cuts will likely come to them later, if they have not already. Regardless of how different groups see their interests, cuts will likely come regardless of their entrenchment. Hopefully, investment in the environment will not come because the effects of climate change are seen much more rapidly than anticipated.

68. *Budget and Economic Data*, Congressional Budget Office, https://www.cbo.gov/about/products/budget-economic-data#4 (last visited March 12, 2022).

Notes

Notes

Notes

Notes

Notes

Notes

Notes